Adoption of Children

Adoption of Children

J F Josling
Solicitor

Ninth Edition

Oyez Publishing Limited

© 1981 Oyez Publishing Limited,
Norwich House, 11/13 Norwich Street,
London EC4 1AB

ISBN 0 85120 541 0

First edition 1947
Second edition 1950
Third edition 1953
Fourth edition 1956
Fifth edition 1959
Reprinted 1960
Sixth edition 1965
Seventh edition 1972
Eighth edition 1977
Ninth edition 1980

Set in Baskerville by Typescan (Systems) Limited, Renfrew
and printed in Great Britain by
Robert MacLehose and Co Ltd, Renfrew

Contents

Table of Cases

Abbreviations

'AA' followed by the number of a year = the Adoption Act of that year;

'CA' or 'CYPA' = the Children Act, or the Children and Young Persons Act of the year mentioned;

'the 1958 Act' or 'the Act of 1958' = AA 1958;

'the 1975 Act' or 'the Act of 1975' = CA 1975;

'the Acts' or 'the Adoption Acts' = AA 1958, 1960, 1964, 1968 and CA 1975, or any two or more of these as the context requires;

'DPMCA' = the Domestic Proceedings and Magistrates' Courts Act 1978;

'MCA' = the Magistrates' Courts Act 1980;

'H Ct R' = the Adoption (High Court) Rules as specified on p 62;

'Co Ct R' = the Adoption (County Court) Rules (see p 62);

'Mag Ct R' = the Magistrates' Courts (Adoption) Rules (see p 62).

Note on the Adoption Legislation

At the date when this edition goes to press, the process of implementing the reforms effected by the Children Act 1975 has been carried further in two main respects. First the provisions, refined from the Adoption Act 1968, enabling the High Court and the Court of Session in Scotland to make Convention adoption orders were brought into effect on 23 October 1978 (SI 1978 No 1430). This has meant that in some places where, in previous editions, the future tense was used, propositions can now be stated as current law, with such augmentations as new rules of court have made necessary. But while so few countries have ratified the relevant treaty (see p 6) these provisions are likely to be but rarely used.

Then adoption proceedings before magistrates are no longer a concern of the juvenile court, for the enlargement of the scope of domestic proceedings so as to include, among other subjects, the adoption jurisdiction has been effected through the medium of Pt IV of the Domestic Proceedings and Magistrates' Courts Act 1978, in force from 1 November 1979 by virtue of SI 1979 No 731.

Nearly all of the Adoption Act 1968 is also now in force, either in its original form, or as amended by the Children Act 1975.

Other parts of the 1975 Act continue to wait in the wings. Some of these are heralded in the text by way of giving the reader notice of the points at which the changes will affect the law and practice. A fuller account of these as yet unimplemented provisions is given in Appendix II, though at various points this will need to be rounded out when regulations or fresh rules are made so as to bring the relevant portions of the

Act to life. Attention may be drawn to s 108 (8), under which the Secretary of State may by order adapt the statute for transitional purposes.

The Adoption Act 1976 is a consolidating measure which received the Royal Assent on 22 July of that year but no part of which is yet in force. Read in the light of the Domestic Proceedings and Magistrates' Courts Act 1978, it forms a valuable, if convoluted, compendium of the law of adoption as it will stand when all the proposed reforms are in operation. For the present it remains in the guise of an escrow. Tables translating section numbers from the present Acts are to be found in Halsbury's Statutes, Continuation Volume for 1976, and in Current Law Statutes 1976, Vol 1.

The Domestic Proceedings and Magistrates' Courts Act 1978 has been treated as fully in force, a very few quite minor passages in the text of the booklet (eg at p 4) thereby being rendered anticipatory. The Magistrates' Court Act 1980 (purely a consolidation so far as adoption is concerned) is expected to be in force early in the life of this edition, and is accordingly referred to to the exclusion of the provisions it replaces.

A list of abbreviations used is at p xvi.

Chapter I

Introductory

1 Historical

It was not until a little over fifty years ago that our law recognised the legal possibility of adoption, though Roman law was familiar with it, Indian civilisations have long admitted it, and some continental and American systems have followed the ancients in acknowledging the transfer from one person to another of parental rights and obligations. In the English common law such rights and liabilities were not transferable by voluntary act (*Humphreys* v *Polak* [1901] 2 KB 385 per Stirling LJ at p 390); and indeed s 85 (2) of the 1975 Act has now codified this proposition by declaring that (except pursuant to a separation agreement between spouses within s 1 (2) of the Guardianship Act 1973) a person cannot surrender or transfer any parental right or duty that he has as respects a child.

Nevertheless, it has always been possible, in given circumstances, for a man, whether relative or stranger, to put himself *in loco parentis* towards another person, ie to perform the office and duty of a father in making provision for that person; and from this kind of assumption of responsibility society inferred at least a moral duty of maintenance during infancy or disability, the law allowed the same rights of reasonable chastisement (for instance) as a father possessed, and equity equated the person who was *in loco parentis* with a true father for the purposes of some of its doctrines, eg advancement, satisfaction or ademption, and undue influence. Although adoption is now regularised (and closely regulated) by statute, a person may still, without the necessity for any judicial process, stand *in loco parentis* to another, with all the old consequences. And in particular, a father may *de facto* adopt his illegitimate child so as to become bound legally to provide for it, according to Somervell LJ in *Perry* v *Dembowski* [1951] 2 KB 420 at p 423 (a Rent Act case on the phrase 'member of the tenant's family').

It may be observed, too, that spouses may treat *any* child as being a 'child of the family' for the purposes of the Matrimonial Causes Act 1973 and the Domestic Proceedings and Magistrates' Courts Act 1978.* Such treatment of a child, if there be also failure to provide for or contribute to its maintenance to a reasonable extent, may ground an application under s 1(*b*) of DPMCA or s 27 of the 1973 Act. Moreover, the child may become the subject of an order for its support if the statute in question is invoked for other reasons.

Some books still contain precedents of adoption agreements, but the enforceability of any such arrangement (even where it does not positively infringe CA 1975, s 85 (2), cited above) would certainly be subject to the question whether it was for the child's benefit; and in many such cases the requirements for the protection of foster children contained in CA 1958 and Pt II of CYPA 1969, or alternatively those arising under Pt IV of AA 1958 (see pp 163–167) will fall to be carefully observed. The statutory provisions mentioned are in course of piecemeal amendment by CA 1975.

The Adoption of Children Act 1926 made general provision for the statutory adoption of children by means of a court order vesting in the adopter the natural parents' rights and liabilities *in respect of the future custody, maintenance and education* of the child. Rights and interests in property were expressly left undisturbed by the order. By subsequent statutes, usually applying only to adoptions effected after their enactment, more incidents (notably rights of inheritance) were by degrees carved out of the natural relationship and added to the adopted one, and provisions were introduced for translating dispositions of property so as to treat the adopted person as the child of the adopter and not of his natural parents.

---

*The expression 'child of the family' had a slightly different meaning in the Matrimonial Proceedings (Magistrates' Courts) Act 1960, which DPMCA superseded.

In AA 1958 a peak was reached in this process of insinuating (legally speaking) the adopted person into his new family and shutting him off from the old, notwithstanding which CA 1975 has scaled a higher one. At present, this appears to be the summit of the range, but only unpredictable eventualities can penetrate the mists of such a generalisation. The 1975 Act gives a new structure to the status conferred by adoption as from 1 January 1976. On and after that date, or from the date of the adoption if later, it places the adopted person for all purposes of law (not just the few which have come to Parliament's mind as the most important) squarely into his adoptive family, at the same time divorcing him from the old, by a provision which treats him, not simply as the child of the adopter, but as if he *had been born* the child of the adopter or adopters in lawful wedlock, thus giving him a place in the new family's history. Priorities *vis-à-vis* other children are, of course, dealt with by the Act. But it needs emphasising that the 1975 scheme is not designed to affect events which had already occurred, so that dates can still be material to the nature and incidents of a particular pre-1976 adoption. The situation is further examined at pp 133–155, where also some qualifications of the general position are noted.

Subject to this question of date, the 1975 Act even-handedly gives the same effect to an adoption whether or not it results from an order of our own courts, so long as the law of England and Wales recognises it. Such recognition may arise in several ways (Sched 1, para 1 (2): see p 135), one of which is the automatic acceptance of an overseas adoption within the meaning of s 4 (3) of AA 1968 and the designation order made thereunder (see p 111). This Act of 1968 also prospectively broke new ground in that, by way of implementing the Hague Convention, it paved the way for the conferment on the superior courts in Great Britain of jurisdiction to authorise adoptions in cases in which the ordinary conditions as to domicile and parental agreement are not satisfied, though certain alternative qualifications must be. Such adoptions in Great Britain are effected by Convention adoption orders, regulated by s 24 of CA 1975, operative as from 23 October 1978 and superseding s 1 of AA 1968, which never came into force (see pp 12, 24, 27).

The full title of the Convention is the Convention on Jurisdiction, Applicable Law and Recognition of Decrees relating to Adoptions, concluded at The Hague on 15th November 1965 (Cmnd 2613). Only Austria, Switzerland and the United Kingdom have so far ratified the Convention.

2   The Nature of Adoption

In England and Wales a legal adoption is effected by an 'adoption order' made by an authorised court on an application by a person or persons wishing to adopt a child. An adoption order vests in the adopter the parental rights and duties relating to the child. In its modern form (see p 195) it orders that the adopter *do* adopt the child, which seems designedly to go further—certainly to be more decisive—than the mere authority to adopt conferred by orders made before 26 November 1976.

The making of such an order is in all cases discretionary. While the court must see to the fulfilment of specified conditions, the applicant is not entitled to the order merely because the conditions are satisfied. The procedure for the making and hearing of an application is governed by rules of court (pp 62–63).

A successful applicant for an adoption order is commonly called the 'adopter' of the adopted child, but CA 1975, Sched 1, para 4, encourages the use of the adjective 'adoptive' to describe a relationship existing as a result of an adoption. Thus 'adoptive parent' is the same as 'adopter', and 'parent' or 'natural parent' are to be distinguished in the terminology. The legislature continues to vacillate in the description of a person under age: he is now a 'minor' in most contexts (see s 12 of the Family Law Reform Act 1969), but in modern adoption law (as in the matrimonial statutes) the word used is 'child'. Not only does CA 1975 employ this word throughout; it also substitutes it for 'infant' wherever that description is used in the unrepealed sections of AA 1958 (1975 Act, Sched 3, para 21 (2)). 'Child' does not invariably in law imply minority (and indeed it was for a limited time after 1926 possible for certain adults to be adopted: Adoption of Children Act 1926, s 10); but in both the 1958 and 1975 Acts (s 57 (1) as amended, and s 107 (1) respectively) it is defined, except where used to express a relationship, as a person who has not attained eighteen.

The solemnity and importance of adoption were emphasised by Lord Greene MR in *Skinner v Carter* [1948] Ch 387 at p 391, and again by Lord Goddard CJ in *Hitchcock v WB* [1952] 2 QB 561 at p 569. The tendency of the courts is not to approve mere accommodation adoptions. Thus where, in a Scottish case, the sheriff thought the purpose of the application to be to make it easier for a parent to remarry, he gave this as a ground for not making an order (*EO Petitioner* [1951] SLT (Sh Ct) 11). And there have in recent years been several judicial statements decrying the adoption process when it seemed to be regarded by those concerned as a mere means of changing the child's name to that of a step-parent (eg *Re D (Minors)* [1973] Fam 209). See also *Re A (an Infant)* [1963] 1 WLR 231, and other cases cited on pp 9–10. In *Mr and Mrs L, Petitioners* [1965] SLT (Sh Ct) 66, adoption was allowed of a fourth child, said to be 'unwanted', of married parents, the applicants being a childless relative and her husband.

Nothing in the 1975 Act appears to have diminished the seriousness with which the climacteric of adoption is to be regarded. Indeed, the wider effect now given to adopted status, as mentioned above; the prospective provision of a 'midway' possibility of custodianship (see p 18); and the preferential consideration which courts are directed to give in divorced-parent-and-step-parent cases to the alternative of a divorce court custody order (p 20); all these tend to stress the gravity of irrevocably transplanting a child from one legally related group of persons into another. For adoption normally 'presupposes a complete and final separation between the child and its natural parents. The child looks thenceforth to the adopters as its parents, and the natural parents, relinquishing all their parental rights and duties, step, as it were, for ever out of the picture of the child's life' (per Vaisey J in *Re DX (an Infant)* [1949] Ch 320; *sub nom A B (an Infant)* [1949] 1 All ER 709). The likelihood of the natural parents being brought back into the picture after an adopted person has reached adulthood has been, perhaps, a little increased by the enactment of CA 1975, s 26 (p 130) and its attendant publicity, but Vaisey J's words 'for ever' will stand for the vast majority of cases.

3   The Duty to Promote the Child's Welfare

Though an adoption order affects the rights of parents, the welfare of the minor has always important, and has become more so under CA 1975, s 3. Whilst it is not the case, as it is in some other contexts, that the child's welfare is to be regarded as the first and *paramount* consideration, the legislature has by this section required that welfare to be given *first* consideration. The section is to be observed not only by all courts but also by all adoption agencies. It provides that, in reaching any decision relating to the adoption of a child, the court or agency shall have regard to all the circumstances, first consideration being given to the need to safeguard and promote the child's welfare throughout his childhood; and that the court or agency shall so far as practicable ascertain the child's wishes and feelings regarding the decision and give due consideration to them, having regard to his age and understanding.

In *Re L A (a minor)* (1978) 122 SJ 417, Baker P said that a boy aged nine would not appreciate the legal implications of adoption.

As compared with the former welfare provision (AA 1958, s 7 (1) (*b*), repealed) merely requiring the court to be satisfied, before it sanctioned adoption, that to do so would be for the child's welfare, s 3 of CA 1975 is clearly wider in its application. It comes into placement arrangements, as well as into the court's general view of the adoption proposed. But after early doubts it is now established at Court of Appeal level that the words 'any decision relating to the adoption of a child' in s 3 of CA 1975 do not include a decision as to the reasonableness or otherwise of a parent's attitude in withholding agreement to an adoption (see *Re S* (1976) 120 SJ 819, following *Re P (an Infant)* [1976] 3 WLR 924, and p 45).

Moreover, the open-ended nature of s 3 may be observed. 'First consideration' in a weighing of all the circumstances, and 'due consideration' according to a child's age and understanding, are not degrees which can easily be evaluated either by those reaching decisions or by those enquiring subsequently into their soundness. The result may be to render nearly all issues discretionary, and thus to leave them almost entirely in the hands of those to whom it falls to make the first decision (cf p 118, where the function of an appellate court is discussed). However, the phrase 'first consideration' seems to have been given a temporal meaning by the Divisional Court in *Re W (a minor)* (1976) 120 SJ 857. It was there said that the court of first instance should consider its decision in two stages. First it should consider whether an adoption order should be made in all the circumstances of the case in accordance with s 3 and, when applicable, s 10 (3) [or s 11 (4)] (see pp 20–22). If the conclusion is in favour of adoption, the court must then consider whether it is satisfied that the requirements of s 12 are fulfilled, including, in this second stage, where a protesting parent is involved, whether agreement is being withheld unreasonably (see pp 43–47). This two-stage consideration when dealing with a single adoption application may be contrasted with the 'balancing test' enjoined on a court faced with simultaneous applications for adoption and access respectively (see p 37).

Welfare can be translated as 'benefit' (*Re D (an infant)* [1959] 1 QB 229; *Re A (an infant)* [1963] 1 WLR 231), but it is not to be confined to material benefit. The statement of Wilberforce J in *Re Adoption Application* 41/61 (*No 2*) [1964] Ch 48 at p 53 was approved by Lord MacDermott in *J v C* [1970] AC 668. According to this the court must take into account 'all the merits and demerits of the alternative proposals as they seem likely to bear upon the child's welfare; not limiting itself to purely material factors, but considering, as they may bear upon the welfare of the infant, such matters as the natural ties of blood and family relationship. The tie (if such is shown to exist) between the child and his natural father (or any other relative) may properly be regarded in this connection, not on the basis that the person concerned has a claim which he has a right to have satisfied, but, if at all, and to the extent that, the conclusion can be drawn that the child will benefit from the recognition of this tie.'

The effect of the status of an adopted person on proprietary rights (see p 145) might be sufficient benefit, as might the acquisition of British nationality (see p 143), provided that it was combined with the benefits of belonging to a family (*Re R* [1967] 1 WLR 34, distinguishing *Re A*, above, where Cross J pointed out that the child's citizenship did not depend on adoption by the particular applicants before him, who had not satisfied his lordship that they were *in loco parentis* to the child). The court may have to consider whether an adoption order would be recognised in the country of the child's previous nationality (*Re B (S) (an Infant)* [1968] Ch 204).

In *CD, Petitioners* [1963] SLT (Sh Ct) 7 the court declined to treat an attempt to avoid the stigma of illegitimacy as *alone* justifying an adoption order, but *Re D* [1959] 1 QB 229 shows that this may validly be taken into account as a factor. See also the judgment of Harman LJ in *Re E (an Infant)* [1968] 1 WLR 1913.

The fact that the applicants proposed also to adopt another child (of the opposite sex) was treated *Re Adoption Application* 41/61 (*No* 2), above, as a consideration tending to the child's welfare.

It is not necessarily fatal to an adoption application by a child's father jointly with his wife that he has been once convicted, many years before, of an indecent assault on a child (*Re G (DM) (an Infant)* [1962] 1 WLR 730).

4   The Appropriateness of Adoption

Before an application is made in England or Wales for an adoption order, it is necessary to consider the statutory provisions as to capacity to adopt and to be adopted together with some other conditions precedent. And as will appear (p 24) there are special provisions as to capacity with other conditions in Convention applications.

It will be well now to emphasise that adoption is not necessarily the only, or the most suitable, course open to those wishing to assume responsibilities towards a child. The law as to guardianship, for instance, provides for the appointment by the court of any person as guardian of a minor who has lost both parents, without the restrictions on capacity which apply to adoption applications (Guardianship of Minors Act 1971, s 5). See also *Re E (An Infant)* [1964] 1 WLR 51 (ward of court: care and control); *Re F (T) (an Infant)* [1970] 1 WLR 192, in which the Court of Appeal thought adoption by other than close relatives the better course in the special circumstances; and *Re*

B (Adoption by Parent) [1975] Fam 127, where Bagnall J said that the advantages which adoption might bring to a child could almost always be secured by other means.

In a case where a child had already become integrated, after the death of his father, into the family of his mother and her second husband, the High Court thought adoption by them to be inappropriate, since it would sever ties with his late father's family (*Re L A (a minor)* (1978) 122 SJ 417).

Then Pt II of CA 1975 will in due course introduce 'custodianship' (see Appendix II, para 9), a status which has been described compendiously as 'midway between that of adopter and fosterparent' (Hansard HL, 21 January 1975, col 17). The legislature plainly regards this as preferable to adoption in certain cases, particularly some where the adult concerned is a relative of the child or is the spouse of the natural parent (see s 37 of the 1975 Act).

Moreover the occasion for an adoption application has often been associated with the breakdown of a marriage followed by divorce proceedings. In those proceedings the divorce court has power, by virtue of s 42 of the Matrimonial Causes Act 1973, either before or after decree absolute, to make orders for the custody and education of any children of the family, and 'custody' includes 'access' (s 52 (1)). The provisions of CA 1975 as to capacity to adopt (ss 10, 11: see pp 16–23) append subsections by which the court hearing a post-divorce adoption application in which a step-parent joins is bound to leave the divorce court to exercise its powers under s 42 of the 1973 Act if the adoption court thinks that the matter would be better so dealt with (ss 10 (3), 11 (4)). The likelihood or otherwise, on the detailed facts of the particular case, of the adoption application being dismissed on this score should be weighed by the applicant and his advisers before making that application.

The incidents and effects of adoption and custody or guardianship are, of course, quite different. In *J v C* [1970] AC 668, a case concerning a ward of court, the House of Lords pointed out that an order for custody of the ward (or, it could be added, for someone other than a parent to have care and control of him) is subject to review, and does not sever the minor's ties with his natural parents. The same may be said of custodian-ship, when it becomes available. Adoption is an altogether more indelible matter.

Again, the marriage of a child's parents may legitimate him or her, and, under the Legitimacy Acts, since 1959 this may be so though one of them was married to a third person when the child was born. Legitimation may be more beneficial to the child than adoption, as appears to be recognised in the legisla-tion (see p 108). In *Re CSC (an infant)* [1960] 1 WLR 304 at p 308, justices were criticised on appeal for not considering whether, in a case where there was a likelihood of the natural parents marrying, that course would not be preferable to adoption; and see per Harman LJ in *Re O (an Infant)* [1965] Ch 23 at p 29.

Those interested in the (declining) statistics of adoption in England and Wales in recent years should refer to the First Report to Parliament of the Secretaries of State on the working of the Children Act 1975 (HMSO).*

5   The Scope of the Subject

(a) *Two Types of Application*

The special qualifying provisions for a Convention applica-tion which apply in place of those normally laid down and to which reference is made above should not be read as importing any significant difference in the quality or the effect of the resulting adoption order. There is in truth only one kind of adoption, full or in appropriate circumstances (see p 55) provisional, obtainable in our courts; though, in regard to jurisdiction, conditions as to capacity, consents and procedure, Convention *applications* differ in important respects from other applications and so demand separate treatment at several points in this book, rare as they necessarily are while so few countries are ratified signatories to the Convention (see p 6).

Cases other than Convention cases may usually be dealt with in the High Court, in a county court or by magistrates in a domestic court at the option of the applicant. The choice between the courts may be dictated by considerations of

---

*It appears from other sources that there are still about four times as many adoptions in England and Wales as in France, for instance.

expense. But the jurisdiction of the inferior courts is strictly localised (see p 60), so that the much greater cost of High Court proceedings probably buys a more effective guarantee of privacy than the strict observance of the confidentiality precautions (p 75) can possibly secure in, for instance, a remote locality. The High Court may, on application, take into its own cognisance an adoption matter begun in a county court (see p 62); and some difficult cases may be declined by a magistrates' court (p 61), which also cannot make a provisional order (p 55).

Convention applications, on the other hand, are cognisable only by the High Court. The conditions on which they are entertained are designed to harmonise with those agreed by countries signatory to the Hague Convention (see p 6) and are now represented by s 24 of CA 1975.

(b) Agencies

The Adoption of Children (Regulation) Act 1939, supplementing the Act of 1926, regulated, *inter alia*, the making of arrangements by adoption societies and other persons in connection with the adoption of children and provided for the supervision of certain children by local authorities (see pp 152–167). An adoption society is defined as a body of persons whose functions consist of or include the making of arrangements for the adoption of children; but such a society cannot make any such arrangements unless it is registered with the local authority. (See Appendix II, para 1, as to the eventual centralisation of registration and the establishment, under CA 1975, ss 1, 2 and 4–7 when in force, of co-ordinated adoption services embracing local authorities and approved adoption societies.) Local authorities for the purposes both of the 1958 and the 1975 Acts are, in England and Wales, the councils of non-metropolitan counties, of metropolitan districts and of the London boroughs, the Common Council acting for the City of London (AA 1958, s 28 (1); Local Government Act 1972, Sched 23; 1975 Act, s 107 (1)).

To be eligible for registration with a local authority under the existing scheme (which is in Pt II of AA 1958), a society must be a charitable association, ie it must exist only for the purpose of promoting a charitable, benevolent or philanthropic object, though 'charitable' need not bear its normal meaning in law, and it must apply the whole of its profits or other income in promoting such object. Matters relating to the registration and control of adoption societies are not further dealt with in this booklet. A list of registered adoption societies (which number just over fifty in England and Wales) may be obtained from the Department of Health and Social Security. The Department's head office dealing with adoption and other matters relating to children is at Alexander Fleming House, Elephant and Castle, London SE1 6BY. Apart from a local authority the only body of persons (whether or not incorporated) which may lawfully make any arrangements for the adoption of an infant is a registered adoption society (1958 Act, s 29 (1)). When in CA 1975, or in AA 1958 as amended by the 1975 Act, the term 'adoption agency' is used, it is at present to be interpreted as meaning a local authority or an adoption society registered under the 1958 Act (CA 1975, s 108 (5)).

Solicitors asked to advise those who are seeking a child to adopt, and are proposing to apply to a local authority or an adoption society, may wish to bring to their clients' notice in advance the particulars which such societies have to obtain about their applicants (Appendix I D, p 220) and the purport of the Adoption Agencies Regulations 1976, summarised on pp 158–161.

For assistance in selecting a society suitable in the circumstances, clients may be advised to approach the Association of British Adoption Agencies, 11 Southwark Street, London, SE1 1RQ; the services of the Adoption Resource Exchange, of the same address (not itself an adoption agency) may be found helpful in linking up adopters and children in special categories. It has been officially observed (First Report: see p 12) that agencies, both statutory and voluntary, are increasingly concentrating on finding suitable homes for children with special needs.

(c) Other Parts of the United Kingdom

The law and procedure described in the present booklet is the English law of adoption, applicable in the courts of England, Wales and Berwick-on-Tweed. Since the subject is at present divided between the 1958 and 1975 Acts, it may be well to remind readers that Wales is included in the term 'England' in statutes passed before 22 July 1967, but requires separate mention in those passed subsequently (Wales and Berwick Act 1746, s 3; Welsh Language Act 1967, s 4). The present statutes embrace the Scottish law, pending the operation of the consolidating Adoption (Scotland) Act 1978, and many cases usefully illustrative of principle may be found in the reports of judgments in Scotland, where cases in the courts of first instance have been more freely reported than in England. Legal adoption was introduced in Northern Ireland in 1929, and is there regulated by the Adoption Act (Northern Ireland) 1967.

In dealing with the *effects* of an adoption it is not for the future usually necessary to distinguish according to the part of the United Kingdom in which it was made (see p 133).

Chapter II

Capacity to Adopt

1 In Cases Other than Convention Cases

The Acts have always laid down qualifications and restrictions concerning the competency of a person* or persons to apply for an adoption order. These have related to the applicant's age and domicile and his or her relationship to the child; and his place of residence, or ordinary residence, formerly influenced venue and may still modify some of the conditions precedent to a successful application. Different qualifications (discussed at p 24) will be required in Convention cases. The provisions as to the capacity of persons to make ordinary applications for an adoption order on and after 26 November 1976 are set out in CA 1975, s 10, for married couples, and in s 11 for sole adopters. They fall to be interpreted in relation to the condition of the applicant at the date when the case comes before the court for consideration, whether at first instance or (at any rate where the court below has refused an order) on appeal (cf p 118).

(a) Age

Each applicant for an order must have attained the age of twenty-one, three years more than the modern legal majority.

---

*Notwithstanding the wide definition of 'person' contained in Sched 1 to the Interpretation Act 1978, and the use of that word to describe a sole applicant for adoption (s 11 of CA 1975), it seems clear that a corporation cannot be an adopter. But when ss 14 and 23 of CA 1975 come into force, there may be or become vested in an adoption agency, which may be a local authority or other body of persons incorporated or otherwise, certain parental rights and duties (as defined) relating to a child, usually for a potentially temporary purpose (see Appendix II, para 3).

16

The former requirement that any applicant who was not the child's parent or related to it had to be at least twenty-five has been dropped. On the other hand a parent could, until November 1976, apply to adopt her or his child whatever the parent's age. There is now no such exception from the general age minimum.

(b) Number and Status of Applicants

An adoption order may not be made on the application of more than one person unless the applicants are a married couple (s 10 (1)). A sole applicant must not be married; or if he or she is married, the court must be satisfied:

(*a*) that his or her spouse cannot be found; or

(*b*) that the applicant and the spouse have separated and are living apart, and that the separation is likely to be permanent; or

(*c*) that the spouse is, by reason of ill health, whether physical or mental, incapable of making an application for an adoption order (s 11 (1)).

Quite apart from this express restriction, adoption by only one of two spouses living together in normal circumstances might easily give rise to anomalous relationships, both juridical and practical. Condition (*c*) seems capable of a reflex effect: it should be borne in mind, as several writers have pointed out, that ill health of the incapacitated spouse might be such as to militate against the child's welfare. If the court thought that there was a probability of this, the ill health escape clause in s 11 (1) might prove illusory.

In 1978 some publicity was given to the fact that the present legislation permits, or at least does not prohibit, the adoption of a child by an unmarried man not related to it (see *The Times*, 5 July 1978 p 2, 'Bachelors' adoption applications').

(c) Domicile

The applicant, or at least one of two applicants who are a married couple, must be domiciled in a part of the United Kingdom, or in the Channel Islands or the Isle of Man (ss 10 (2) (*a*), 11 (2) (*a*)). But for the present it is still possible for persons domiciled outside Great Britain to apply for a *provisional*

B

adoption order under s 53 of the 1958 Act (see p 55; and cf Appendix II, para 7, as to the eventual replacement of provisional adoption by CA 1975, s 25). As to domicile, the practitioner should note the provisions of the Domicile and Matrimonial Proceedings Act 1973, particularly in so far as they affect the traditional doctrine of a dependent domicile.

All residence requirements, in the technical sense, have been repealed. But the local authority within whose area an applicant has his home has in some cases to be notified (see p 30) and a corresponding expression governs local jurisdiction in the case of certain ancillary applications (p 62), though not applications for an adoption order.

(d) Relationship to Child

Before November 1976 adoption by the child's mother or father (ie the natural or putative father in the case of an illegitimate child), either alone or jointly with the parent's spouse, was not uncommon. There have also been many cases of adoption by grandparents, aunts or other relatives.

But a body of social opinion set itself against adoption by relatives and by step-parents, arguing that the probable continuity of old relationships along with new tends to confuse the child, and in any case contradicts the concept of 'transplanting' him from one family into a new one. The 1975 Act accordingly introduced conditions which discourage such adoptions and, indeed, may eventually render adoption virtually impossible in many circumstances in which it was formerly commonplace. 'Eventually' is apposite because cases that survive the new restrictions introduced in November 1976 are likely to be just those in which, under s 37 of CA 1975 (Appendix II, para 9) when it comes into force, the court will have to give preference to custodianship over adoption (or may do so), even when the application is for adoption. For the present adoption by relatives* is not in terms restricted by that part of the 1975 Act

---

*'Relative' is here used in the sense defined, for both the 1958 and 1975 Acts (ss 57 (1) and 107 (1) respectively), as a grandparent, brother, sister, uncle or aunt of the child, whether of the full blood or the half-blood, or by affinity (ie relationship by marriage) and includes the father of an illegitimate

which is operative; but the following provisions apply in the particular circumstances mentioned.

(i) Own children

Section 11 (3) forbids the making of an adoption order on the application of the mother or father of the child alone unless the court is satisfied that the other natural parent is dead or cannot be found, or that there is some other reason justifying his or her exclusion. The reason for making the order in these excepted circumstances must be recorded by the court (see p 101).

Ex hypothesi the child in a s 11 (3) case will be illegitimate (there would be no need for sole adoption by a parent otherwise), and that is no doubt why the Act makes no mention of adoption by *both* natural parents. They would not be eligible to apply unless they had married each other (s 10 (1)), and after 1959 that would, in all but the most exceptional cases, legitimate the child.

The Act does not say what reason other than death or disappearance would justify the exclusion of the other natural parent. If the father were applying to adopt, or if the mother were applying and the father had become a guardian as defined by s 107 (1) (see p 35*n*) by obtaining a custody order under the Guardianship of Minors Act 1971, then their interests and their conduct would be looked into by the court during the ordinary adoption process requiring their agreement to be obtained or dispensed with (see s 12 (1), p 35). In that kind of case the latter part of s 11 (3) may be tautologous. But if the mother were the applicant and the father not a person whose agreement was necessary, then it is suggested that he could be excluded on

---

child and persons who would stand in one of those relationships to an illegitimate child if he were the legitimate child of his mother and natural father. 'Adoptive relatives' (ie persons who would be relatives within this definition if the adopted child or any other adopted person were the lawful child of his adopter) were formerly expressly included, but the paragraph referring to them in the original s 57 (1) was removed from the 1958 Act by CA 1975, Sched 4, Pt I. However, the effect of ibid, Sched 1, para 3 (p 134) is to restore the position by treating any adopted person as related in law to his adoptive relatives, for he would be related to them in fact if born to his adopter or adopters as para 3 hypothesises.

grounds similar to those which would be adequate under s 12 (2) for dispensing with his agreement, and also (since those grounds are not specifically mentioned in s 11 (3)) on exceptional grounds falling short of the grounds for dispensation.

As an instance of a situation in which adoption by a natural mother was resorted to in the past, the Houghton Committee recalled that this had been sometimes done so that the mother might protect herself from the anxiety caused by repeated and vexatious applications for guardianship made by the putative father. But Parliament has not particularised this state of affairs, and whether the circumstances described amounted in a given case to a sufficient reason justifying the father's exclusion from the adoption application would depend on the factual context. It may be that in a s 11 (3) decision the child's welfare is not the first consideration, if the analogy with s 12 (2) (suggested above) is apposite (cf *Re S*, referred to at p 8). If the child's welfare *is* the first consideration, Houghton's instance may not be an automatic justification for an application by the mother alone.

(ii)   By step-parents, following divorce
   (1) Where one parent and a step-parent of the child apply (as a married couple) for an adoption order, the court is bound to dismiss the application if it considers that the matter would be better dealt with by an order for custody (which by definition includes access and in practice, allows for 'care and control' orders) and education of the child under s 42 of the Matrimonial Causes Act 1973 (s 10 (3)). This might be so in a case where, eg, the mother's marriage has been dissolved or annulled and she has subsequently remarried, she and her new husband being the applicants for adoption. It cannot apply, on its terms, where the mother has not previously been married, or where her only previous marriage (whether to the child's father or not) ended not in divorce but in her husband's death (but see *(iii)* below).

In the case which s 10 (3) envisages, the step-parent may not have been a party to the divorce proceedings, but the divorce court could nevertheless on his application award him the custody or the care and control of the child, possibly with access to the divorced father (Matrimonial Causes Rules 1977, r 92 (3)). The step-father could usually by his will put the child into the same material position as if it stood to inherit as an adopted person: if for some special reason he could not, that might be a reason for preferring adoption to a custody application. The child to whom this head of s 10 relates is likely to be a legitimate one, though it is possible to conceive a case in which the first husband had treated his wife's illegitimate child as a child of the family, so as to bring it within the scope of s 42 of the Matrimonial Causes Act 1973 (see ibid s 52 (1) and cf pp 3–4), and thereby give rise to a s 10 (3) problem.

The Court of Appeal has considered s 10 (3) in a contrasted pair of cases both reported as *Re S*. In the earlier of these (*Re S (Infants)* [1977] Fam 173), it was said that the subsection required the court to consider three courses: (*a*) adoption; (*b*) a joint custody order in favour of the applicants (but see *(iii)* below), and (*c*) the arrangements which already existed, usually custody to the parent-applicant, with perhaps access to the other (divorced) parent.

Only if adoption would, in the court's opinion, safeguard and promote the child's welfare better than either of the other courses would an adoption order be appropriate under the subsection. The children in this 1977 case had grown up with their father, and the mother's remarriage had taken place comparatively late in the children's lives. They knew the proposed adopter was their stepfather, and in those circumstances the court thought that adoption would be an artificial step. Custody was to be preferred as recognising the reality of the situation.

The distinction between this case and *Re S* (1978) 9 Fam Law 88 lies in differences in their respective facts. In the later *S* case, the boy's natural father had had only a few moments' contact with him about three weeks after the boy's birth. Mother and father had then already separated and their marriage was dissolved when the boy was two-and-a-half years old. From the time when the boy was six months old his future stepfather (whom the mother married immediately after the divorce and by whom she later had a child) was 'on the scene'. These circumstances constituted the step-father the real father-figure in the boy's life. The element of artificiality was at a minimum and the court answered the s 10 (3) question by making an adoption order in favour of the mother and the stepfather. Section 10 (3), Ormrod LJ observed, was clearly not intended virtually to prohibit adoption by a step-parent and a parent.

These two precedents may be regarded as lying at the two extremes of the post-divorce situation. The difficult problem facing step-parent applicants and their advisers is to forecast to which of the alternatives the court will regard the particular facts of a new case as nearer. It must be remembered that it is on the applicant that the onus lies of showing that adoption is the right course in the child's interest.

(2) Similarly, a court is bound to dismiss an adoption application by a sole applicant who is a step-parent of the child if it thinks the matter would be better dealt with under s 42 of the Matrimonial Causes Act (s 11 (4) of CA 1975). The potential s 42 order in this case might be an order for custody in proceedings concerning the step-parent's own marriage, if he had so treated the child that it had become a child of his family.

(3) Cases (1) and (2) above would each involve the applicant, unless he could persuade the court to prefer adoption to a custody situation, in going back to the divorce court if he wished for any order at all: the adoption court is not given power to make an order *as if* under s 42.

The Association of British Adoption and Fostering Agencies (see p 14) publishes an information leaflet entitled 'Stepchildren and Adoption', of which single copies will be sent on receipt by the Association of a stamped addressed envelope.

(iii) Other cases involving step-parents or relatives

Some step-parent cases are (for the moment: see Appendix II, para 9, as to custodianship provisions yet to come into force) likely to be straightforward, eg those where the child's parent other than the one, if any, who joins in the adoption application has died before the applicant-parent remarried, *leaving no relative with whom the child is likely to maintain contact.* Even before the 1975 Act came into force, Megaw LJ hinted at a criterion based on the probability of advantageous contact between the child and members of the natural father's family (*Re S* (1975) 5

Fam Law 88, the case in which Ormrod LJ first used the symbol of the father-figure). If such contact was likely, the drastic remedy of adoption, which would sever links with the natural father's family, was probably not called for. The case of *Re LA (a minor)* (1978) 122 SJ 417, under the modern legislation, suggests that if the child is already *de facto* integrated into the mother's new family it is not a justifiable course to 'legalise' that integration if it means cutting the child off by adoption from the deceased natural father's parents who are shown to be taking an interest in him.

In relative cases an important question may be whether, in the likely circumstances, the natural parents themselves, or one of them, may continue to have contact with the child (see the distaste with which Harman J contemplated the artificial wrenching away of the child from parents she knew in *Re F (an Infant)* [1957] 1 All ER 819—and that was not a case where the applicants were relatives). *EO (Petitioner)* [1951] SLT (Sh Ct) 11 (sheriff reluctant to authorise adoption by an aunt where the proposal was that the aunt, the children and their father should continue to reside in the same house); *CD (Petitioners)* [1963] SLT (Sh Ct) 7 (grandparents—order refused); and *Re F (T) (an Infant)* [1970] 1 WLR 192, referred to at p 10, are other cases in point.

Nevertheless if, after taking into account the relevant statutory provisions and all the circumstances, giving first consideration to the child's welfare as required by s 3 of the 1975 Act (p 8), a court should conclude that an adoption order in favour of a particular relative or a step-parent ought to be made, it has, and will have, full jurisdiction to make it (cf *Mr & Mrs L, Petitioners*, p 7). And it is pertinent to observe that the Court of Appeal in *Re B (MF) (an Infant); Re D (an Infant)* [1972] 1 WLR 102 held that there is no hard-and-fast rule making separation from the parents a necessary pre-condition for the making of an adoption order. Indeed, in *Re J (Adoption Order: Conditions)* [1973] Fam 106, and also in *Re S (Adoption Order: Access)* [1976] Fam 1, contact between the child and his father was made a condition to be observed by successful adopters; but these were exceptional cases (see further p 52).

2 In Convention Applications in England

The qualifications required of applicants for a Convention adoption order (originally contained in s 3 of AA 1968) are now to be found in s 24 of CA 1975, which was brought into force on 23 October 1978.

This section enacts that an adoption order shall be made as a Convention adoption order if the application is for a Convention adoption order, and if certain conditions are satisfied, both at the time of the application and when the order is made. It is thus clear that the qualifications mentioned above under Age, Number and Status of Applicants and Relationship to Child (pp 16–23) apply as in a non-Convention case. Domicile is irrelevant (ss 10 (2) (*b*), 11 (2) (*b*)).

In addition, at least one of the applicants (or alternatively the child) must *not* be a United Kingdom national (as defined) living in British territory (defined) (s 24 (3)); and the applicant (or applicants) must either:

(*a*) (each) be a United Kingdom national or a national of a Convention country (defined), and (both) habitually reside in Great Britain; or

(*b*) be a United Kingdom national (both United Kingdom nationals), and (each) habitually reside in British territory or a Convention country (s 24 (4), (5)).

A qualified applicant (or applicants) being a national of a (or nationals of the same) Convention country may be affected by a specified prohibitory condition of his (or their) own law (see p 51), with the result that the adoption order cannot be made (s 24 (4), (5), (8)). The definitions referred to above are as follows (s 107 (1) and SI 1978 No 1432 made thereunder):

United Kingdom national: a citizen of the United Kingdom and Colonies who is a 'patrial', ie, who has the right of abode in the United Kingdom by virtue of the Immigration Act 1971, s 2. (This qualification may be founded on birth, adoption, naturalisation, registration, or settlement and at least five years' ordinary residence: see 4 Halsbury's Laws of England, 4th ed, para 975, and Supplement.)

British territory: the United Kingdom.

Convention country: any country outside British territory, being a country for the time being designated by the Secretary of State as a country in which, in his opinion, the Hague Convention (see p 6) is in force. Austria and Switzerland were so designated by SI 1978 No 1431.

Chapter III

Eligibility of Children for Adoption

1 Cases Other than Convention Cases

The persons the adoption of whom is authorised in non-Convention cases are now described in the Acts as children. For the definition of 'child' see pp 6–7. In addition, s 8 (5) of CA 1975 completes the picture for adoption purposes by declaring that an adoption order may not be made in relation to a child who is or has been married. Both as to age and single status the crucial date seems to be that of the order: reaching majority or marrying after the date of the application would rule out an adoption order (cf *S (Petitioner)* [1952] SLT 220, CS).

There is now no express requirement of special circumstances to justify the making of an adoption order in respect of a female child in favour of a sole male applicant.

There are no longer any qualifications concerning the domicile, residence or nationality of the child in cases other than Convention cases.

Specialities do arise, however, if the child is already the subject of an order affecting his person. Thus if it is desired to adopt a child who is a ward of court, application for leave should first be made in the chambers of the Family Division (cf p 66). It was formerly said by the Court of Appeal (*F v S (Adoption: Ward)* [1973] Fam 203) that the test to be applied in deciding whether to give leave did not turn on the child's best interests, but on whether the application to adopt might reasonably succeed. It may be that the welfare principle in s 3 of CA 1975 (see p 8) would now fall to be applied, for that is to be taken into account in reaching 'any decision relating to the adoption of a child'. On the other hand, these words have been held not to be universally applicable, even in questions arising in the adoption application itself (*Re S*, referred to at p 8).

If a custody order relating to the child has been made in divorce proceedings, a court subsequently considering an adoption application is not thereby deprived of jurisdiction, and the custody order will cease on the adoption being made (CA 1975, s 8 (3)). There can be no objection to this, and no preliminary step is necessary, where the adopter is the person already having custody and the other parent does not object, and possibly in other cases in which the adoption is not 'inconsistent' with the existing order. Where, however, an adoption order would conflict with a subsisting custody or access provision, it seems that the applicant should first seek to have the provision discharged by the court having cognisance of it (*Re B (Adoption by Parent)* [1975] Fam 127, disapproving part of *Crossley* v *Crossley* [1953] P 97). Sir George Baker P thought that adoption proceedings after an inconsistent custody order were better brought in the High Court or county court.

Where a child was in the care of a local authority under a resolution assuming parental rights, this was held to be no objection to the making of an interim adoption order which would restrict the effect of the resolution (*S* v *Huddersfield Borough Council* [1975] Fam 113; cf p 53). But it was otherwise where the local authority's care of the child arose by interim delegation in a wardship under s 7 (2) of the Family Law Reform Act 1969 (*Re Clare* (1980) *The Times*, 16 May). It was there held that the authority was under a duty to consult the court of wardship before altering approved arrangements for the child to live with a foster mother who was not the adopter proposed by the authority.

2 Convention Cases in England

An application for a Convention adoption order under CA 1975, s 24 is competent only if, both at the time of the application and of the order, the child:

(*a*) is a United Kingdom national or a national of a Convention country, *and*

(*b*) habitually resides in British territory or a Convention country, *and*

(*c*) is not, and has not been, married (s 24 (2)).

The child must not be a United Kingdom national living in British territory if both the applicants are (s 24 (3)).

For the definition of the constituent terms, see pp 24–25.

If the child is not a United Kingdom national, there is a special code about consents and 'consultations' (see pp 50–51).

Chapter IV

Conditions Precedent to Adoption

1 Trial Period*

Beginning with the Adoption of Children (Regulation) Act 1939, progressively more stringent conditions have been enacted to ensure that the adoptive parents and the child shall have 'tried each other out', under observation where appropriate, before the adoption becomes effective. These requirements will ultimately take the form described in ss 9 and 18 of CA 1975 (Appendix II, para 2). Until those sections come into force the conditions of the trial period are still derived from s 3 of the 1958 Act. They apply to all adoptions, so far as their terms provide, including those privately arranged (so long as private adoptions continue to be possible), and also including English Convention applications under CA 1975, s 24.

(a) Actual Custody

In its present form (ie as amended by CA 1975, Sched 3, para 21), s 3 (1) of AA 1958 requires that at the date of any adoption order other than a provisional order (see s 53 and p 55), the child shall have been continuously in the actual custody of the

---

*The term 'probationary period' was used here in earlier editions of this book. But those words occur in AA 1958, s 8, and in the prescribed form of interim order in a different sense, which has now been judicially explained (see p 53). For the period required under s 3 (1) of the 1958 Act, some writers have used the phrase 'period of care and possession'. But the words 'care and possession' have been changed throughout that Act into 'actual custody'; and since this is only a temporary form of the eventual requirement (see CA 1975, s 9, referred to in the text), the phrase 'trial period' seems now to be the best description of the season for the growth of mutual familiarity which s 3 (1) endeavours to ensure.

applicant for at least three consecutive months immediately preceding that date, not counting any time before the date which appears to the court to be the date on which the child attained the age of six weeks. In the case of an application for a provisional adoption order, the requisite period of custody is six months, again not commencing while the child is under six weeks (s 53 (5)).

(b) Supervision

It is also necessary in certain cases that a local authority should be notified at the beginning of the trial period so as to have the opportunity of exercising such supervision as the Act requires of it. The notice is not required where the applicant or one of two joint applicants is a parent of the child, nor where the child is *not* below the upper limit of the compulsory school age at the hearing of the application. This limit is now sixteen years (Education Act 1944, s 35, and SI 1972 No 444 made thereunder); but note that s 9 of the Education Act 1962 (as amended by the Education (School-leaving Dates) Act 1976, s 1) gives practically all children an artificial birthday for this purpose so that the upper limit is always reached either at the end of the spring term (for those born between 1 September and 31 January) or on the Friday before the last Monday in May (for all others).

In all other cases the applicant must give notice in writing (which may be served by post) at least three months before the date of the order (six months if the application is for a provisional order: AA 1958, s 53 (5)) to the local authority within whose area he then has his home of his intention to apply for an adoption order in respect of the child (s 3 (2)). The words 'has his home' are the result of a transitional substitution effected by Sched 3, para 3, to SI 1976 No 1744, where the section itself says 'resident'.

If the child is for the time being in the care of a local authority when the notice is given, certain consequences follow (s 36, and see p 163); and if the authority which receives the notice knows the child to be in the care of another local authority it must within seven days inform the other authority in writing of the receipt of the notice (s 36 (3), as amended by CA 1975, Sched 3, para 30 (*b*)).

On the notice being given the child becomes, while it is in the actual custody of the person giving the notice, a protected child within Pt IV of the Act, and the local authority will exercise the supervision required of it (see pp 163–167).

(c) Modifications where Applicant in Joint Case has Not Had His Home in Great Britain

Although subs s (1), (2) and (4) of s 12 of the 1958 Act (which made an exception to the former requirement as to the residence in England or Wales of applicants to an English or Welsh court) have been repealed along with the residence qualification itself (see p 16), s 12 (3) has been retained for the present with a consequential adaptation. It now applies generally to joint applications by spouses who have not had their home, or one of whom has not had his home, in Great Britain, and is apt also in joint English Convention cases.

In a s 12 (3) case (competent for the future for magistrates' courts as well as High Court or county court: cf note 13, p 207):

(*a*) either applicant may give the notice under s 3 (2) above; and

(*b*) continuous actual custody of the child by one applicant is sufficient compliance with the conditions described under Actual Custody above if the applicants have been living together in Great Britain for at least one of the three months there mentioned.

Buckley J in *Re M (an Infant)* [1965] Ch 203 was disposed to hold that the phrase 'living together' was here satisfied notwithstanding that the husband had at times been physically separated from the wife because of his business commitments.

The relaxation of the actual custody requirement set out in subpara (*b*) above is permissive, not imperative; that is to say that if applicants who have not had their home here can satisfy s 3 (1) (p 29) in its normal form, it is not fatal to their application that they have not lived together in Great Britain for one of the trial months. In such a case, provided that it is not one in which notice to the local authority is required under s 3 (2), the

Act does not require that the period during which the applicants have continuously had actual custody of the child shall have been spent in England or Wales (or Scotland). So much still seems to survive as law from *Re W (an Infant)* [1962] Ch 918, a case in which Wilberforce J considered the impact of the old s 12 as a whole on the s 3 conditions.

It seems, too, that even in a case in which a notice to a local authority is required, so that the child thereupon becomes a protected child, a reasonably short absence abroad might be possible. There is nothing in the Act which specifically binds a proposing adopter to keep the protected child within the authority's district, or within the country at all. He must give notice of a change of *permanent* address, and must submit to visits by the authority's officers 'from time to time'. Nevertheless, it would, of course, be imprudent not to seek the consent of the authority concerned before taking a protected child abroad (cf their powers under s 43: p 165), and if there was opposition it would be best to take the directions of the court. Moreover, it is important that the guardian ad litem should not be hampered in his duties. Subject to these matters, it may be that foreign holidays and business visits may be undertaken without disqualifying a pending adoption application.

It is to be emphasised, though, that this hypothesis of a permissible absence of the child abroad is directed to the case of an application for full adoption. If the application is for a provisional order as a preliminary to adoption abroad (s 53: p 55) removal of the child would ordinarily fall foul of s 52 (p 170) (*Re M (a Minor)* [1973] Fam 66: but consider the special circumstances outlined by Brandon J at the end of his judgment in that case).

The decision in *Re W* above was strictly speaking confined to a case where the requirement which joint applicants satisfy is the ordinary one contained in s 3 (1). But equally, it would seem, one of two spouses invoking s 12 (3) need not have the actual custody of the child in Great Britain for more than one of the three trial months. Thus, while the ordinary course would be for the wife to bring the child to England (or Scotland) for the purpose of the proceedings including the giving of the notice if necessary, and for the husband (if he chose) to remain abroad except for one of the three months before the order is due to be made, it is conceived that the conditions of the Act would be fulfilled if the arrangement were reversed. The husband might be temporarily in England when the proceedings were commenced, and might give the notice to the local authority if necessary. (This would not seem of itself to make the child a protected child within the definition in s 37, for *he* would probably not have the actual custody of the child: though in some circumstances actual custody may be shared, the need for the latter part of s 12 (3) is not apparent if spouses temporarily separated as there envisaged can both have actual custody.) The wife could continue to have the child with her abroad and bring it to England only for the last of the three months, joining her husband here throughout that month. Again, the work of the guardian ad litem must not be hampered, but though he must see the child and the applicants himself at some time before he reports, he can conduct other enquiries through an agent (Sched 2 to the H Ct R and Co Ct R, para 13; Mag Ct R, Sched 2, para 12).

In *Re M (an Infant)* [1965] Ch 203, where it was held that one of two joint applicants had not fulfilled the condition of s 12 (3), the difficulty was resolved at the suggestion of Buckley J by treating the application as made by the wife alone (who had satisfied s 3 (1)) with the husband's consent. But this does not seem possible in a similar case after November 1976 because of s 11 (1) of CA 1975 (see p 17).

(d) Sanction

Unless these conditions as to actual custody and, if applicable, notice to the local authority are complied with, neither an adoption order, full or provisional, nor an interim order (see p 53) can be made (ss 3 (1), (2), 53 (3), 8 (3)). There seems to be nothing, however, to prevent a proposed adopter making his application during the trial period, securing a date for the hearing after its expiry.

(e) Meaning of 'Actual Custody'

It is enacted by s 87 (1) of CA 1975 that a person has actual custody of a child if he has actual possession of his person, whether or not that possession is shared with one or more other persons. Such possession, in a case where the person has not also the legal custody of the child, imposes the like duties (but not the like rights) as a custodian would have by virtue of his legal custody (s 87 (2)); and by s 86 this includes so much of the parental duties as relate to the child's person, including the place and manner in which his time is spent. Again, s 85 (1) describes parental duties (as part of the phrase 'parental rights and duties') as all the duties which by law the mother and father have in relation to a legitimate child and his property, whether the particular child is legitimate or not.

The distinction which these sections draw between legal and actual custody has been said to derive from the practice of divorce courts (or those exercising guardianship jurisdiction) of making 'split' or divided orders whereby one parent has the custody and the other the care and control of a child (cf *Jussa* v *Jussa* [1972] 1 WLR 881; and see M D A Freeman, *The Children Act* 1975, commentary on s 86). Under such an order the parent with legal custody makes important decisions, and the one with care and control has the duty of seeing to day-to-day matters. But it is respectfully thought that, apt as this analogy may be as regards other parts of CA 1975, it is of very limited assistance in considering the change which that Act has for the time being introduced in s 3 (1) of AA 1958. 'Actual custody' in that amended section replaces 'care and possession'.

Pragmatically, as well as from a reading of ss 85–87 of CA 1975, the statutory alteration seems to emphasise the obligatory side of the relationship which the law now requires. The question in whose actual custody a child is at a given time will clearly be one of fact; but the primary facts must be interpreted in the light of the statutory language, and of the change that Parliament has made in it. The dropping of the word 'care', as well as the reference to sharing the 'possession' of the person of the child, may be seen as rendering the new expression apter than the old to include the type of situation which gave rise to the principal difficulties under the original form of s 3 of the 1958 Act. These cases were, generally, those involving a temporary separation for explicable purposes, such as to enable the child to go to school, including in appropriate cases boarding school or other place of training during the periods usual at such an establishment, or to enable the applicant to go to work, deputing the care of the child to someone responsible for comparatively short periods. There seems no reason to suppose that cases of this sort will not be capable of being comprehended within the term 'actual custody', as they came eventually to be considered covered by 'care and possession' generally speaking. In the classic case on the old wording (*Re B (an Infant)* [1964] Ch 1) Buckley J remarked that continuous physical propinquity was not required, and the same appears to be true of the new provisions, both the transitional one stipulating for actual custody, and the eventual requirement (see Appendix II, para 2) that the child shall have had his home with the applicant.

With the lowering of the maximum adoption age to eighteen, the difficult late-teenager cases may have disappeared in any case.

2 Parental Agreement in Cases Other than Convention Cases, and in English Convention Cases concerning Children who are United Kingdom Nationals

(a) From Whom Required

By s 12 (1) (b) of CA 1975, an adoption order is not to be made unless, in the case of each parent or guardian* of the child, the court is satisfied that:

(i) he freely, and with full understanding of what is

---

*'Guardian' is defined in s 107 (1) of CA 1975, and in s 57 (1) of AA 1958 (as amended by Sched 3, para 39 (*d*), to the 1975 Act):

    (*a*) as meaning a person appointed as such by deed or will in accordance with the Guardianship of Infants Acts or the Guardianship of Minors Act 1971, or by a court of competent jurisdiction, and

    (*b*) in the case of an illegitimate child as including the father where he has its custody by virtue of an order under s 9 of the 1971 Act, or under s 2 of the Illegitimate Children (Scotland) Act 1930. This head abrogates the decision in *Re Adoption Application* 41/61 (*No* 2) [1964] Ch 48, in so far as it was there held that a custody order in favour of a putative father would not give him a *locus standi* as a guardian.

involved, agrees unconditionally to the making of the adoption order, or

(ii) his agreement should be dispensed with on one of a number of specified grounds, as described on pp 42–49.

The consent formerly required of a sole applicant's spouse is not now apposite (see s 11 (1), p 17). When s 14 comes into force, and a child is 'freed' for adoption under its provisions (Appendix II, para 3), that will *ipso facto* satisfy s 12 in regard to subsequent adoption, but only one such adoption (see p 58). Section 12 (1) is excluded and replaced by other requirements (see subheading 3 on p 50) in the case of orders made under s 24 in respect of a child who is not a United Kingdom national, but it will be applicable as it stands in other English Convention cases. As to a United Kingdom national in this context, see p 24.

The putative father of an illegitimate child is not a 'parent' for the purpose of s 12 (see below). Neither does the reference to a parent include a person having the powers and duties of a parent by virtue of CYPA 1969, s 24, or of the corresponding provisions of certain Acts applying in Scotland (1958 Act, s 4 (3) (*a*), (*b*), preserved with amendments by SI 1976 No 1744). But although local authorities, other custodians who are not guardians, and the managers of 'community homes' need not be approached for formal agreement, the rules in all courts either provide that such persons and bodies shall or may in the discretion of the court be respondents to the application, or that notice of the proceedings shall be served on them, so that they may be heard on the question whether an adoption order should be made (see pp 73–74, 88 and 91).

The husband of the child's mother, if married to her at the time when the child was born, is, of course, presumed to be a parent, but evidence in rebuttal of this presumption may no doubt be led to show that his agreement is unnecessary.

A parent or guardian may not, after signifying his agreement to an adoption order, remove the child from the care and possession of the applicant while the application is pending in any court, except with the leave of the court (AA 1958, s 34 (1), and see pp 95–96, where s 34A, forbidding removal by any person, consenting parent or not, in 'five-year' cases, is also set out).

(*b*) *Changed Position of the Putative Father*

The agreement of the natural father of an illegitimate child is not necessary as a 'parent' (*Re M (an Infant)* [1955] 2 QB 479; *Re 'O' (an Infant)* [1965] Ch 23). If, however, he has by virtue of a custody order in his favour become a 'guardian' within head (*b*) of the definition referred to in the footnote on p 35, it is now necessary that his agreement to the adoption should be obtained or dispensed with.

A putative father may, though not a guardian of the child, be liable by order or agreement to contribute to its maintenance. Every person or body so liable is either to be a respondent or to be otherwise notified of the proceedings (subject in the High Court to contrary order), and if the putative father is so notified he will be entitled to be heard on the application (see pp 86, 90 and 91).

In more than one case the putative father of an illegitimate child has sought to disturb the course of adoption proceedings begun by others by applying, during the currency of those proceedings, for custody of the child under the Guardianship Acts. Or the custody application (or one for access) might come first. Where such a custody application was made in an inferior court and the adoption application was pending in the High Court, the latter application was adjourned to enable custody proceedings to come before the High Court at the same time (*Re Adoption Application* 41/61 [1963] Ch 315). In *Re E (P) (an Infant)* [1968] 1 WLR 1913 Pennycuick J dismissed a father's custody appeal without reasons, so that an adoption appeal by the father direct to the Court of Appeal could be heard with it in that court.

It is proper for magistrates to hear an access application and one for adoption by another applicant at the same time if the evidence is the same for both. But if this is done the justices should bear both possibilities in mind and decide the two applications together on a 'balancing test', not grant one first and then treat their decision on that as barring the second (per Balcombe J in *C* v *H* (1979) 123 SJ 537). Circumstances such as these will in practice probably nullify the arrangements for keeping proposing adopters and parents out of contact with each other (see p 89).

But the natural father has no claim to have his proposal considered otherwise than objectively, whether in custody or adoption proceedings or on a concurrent hearing of both (*Re Adoption Application* 41/61 (*No* 2) [1964] Ch 48).

The putative father can ordinarily make his case to the court under the Adoption Rules (see p 74) whether or not he accompanies his intervention with a formal application for custody if the adoption is refused (per Wilberforce J at [1964] Ch, p 59).

The child who was the subject of *Re P (a minor)* (1973) 4 Fam Law 73 had been registered in the name of the mother's husband, and never treated as illegitimate. The natural father was served as a respondent on an application by the mother and her husband to adopt. He was heard by the court and his submissions against the order were rejected. He had not wanted to take the child away, so that to uphold his objection would have been to leave her an unadopted member of an otherwise stable family.

(c) Nature of Agreement

It is clear from a reading of ss 12 and 14 of CA 1975, as well as from the form of documentary agreement scheduled to the rules of court, that an agreement complying with s 12 (1) (*b*) must be to the making of the specific adoption order applied for, not a general consent to *any* adoption. (The Act preserves the word 'consent', in non-Convention cases, for the concurrence of a parent or guardian in a s 14 order freeing the child and vesting the parental rights and duties in an agency, *scilicet* with a view to an adoption not yet arranged: see Appendix II, para 3.) At the same time it is part of the policy of the modern Acts that an adopter who is and who wishes to be anonymous as regards the natural parent may remain so. Accordingly, it is expressly provided that agreement may validly be given by a parent or guardian whether or not he knows the proposed adopter's identity (s 12 (1) (*b* (i)). A system of serial numbers facilitates the giving of specific agreement without disclosure of an applicant's identity (see p 78).

Agreement is usually revocable up to the time when the order is made, for the Act says that an order may not be made without compliance with s 12. This is in line with the previous law (cf *Re F (an Infant)* [1957] 1 All ER 819, in which a deed executed by the parents undertaking not to oppose the application was held not to be binding on them). The court still has, however, in effect a discretion to disregard a withdrawal which it finds to be unreasonable provided it applies proper criteria, because it can then dispense with the agreement in question (see pp 41, 43).

A parent or guardian's agreement must be given freely and with full understanding of what is involved (s 12 (1) (*b*) (i)). Principally involved is the nature of an adoption order, which is conveniently summarised in the explanatory memorandum reproduced at pp 220–221. In *Re P* (1954) 118 JP 139, an inducement was mentioned to the mother by a children's officer, namely, that she would be subject to a claim for maintenance if consent was not forthcoming. The Court of Appeal found this statement to be unjustifiable and regrettable, but held on the facts that it had not affected the free nature of the mother's consent.

The 1975 Act has abolished for the future the possibility of a conditional agreement. Formerly it was recognised that a consent might stipulate the religious persuasion in which a child should be brought up. That potentially very sensitive matter is now dealt with in CA 1975, s 13, which obliges an adoption agency in placing a child to have regard *so far as is practicable* to any wishes of the child's parents or guardians as to religious upbringing (see further pp 52, 158).

(d) Form and Evidence of Agreement

Since the actual agreement of the parent or guardian concerned at the time when the order is made is what the Acts have always required, it may be given in person by a parent or guardian attending in the proceedings, as in *Re P* (1954) 118 JP 139. However, although each parent or guardian either is a party or is to be notified of the proceedings, his attendance (unless he be the applicant) is not normally required.

Accordingly, where a parent or guardian does not attend

(but *only* if he does not: *Re Adoption Application No* 41 *of* 1974, *The Times*, 1 May 1975, per Denning MR), there is provision in s 6 (1) of AA 1958 for his agreement to be received in the form of a document whether executed before or after the proceedings are commenced. The person in whose favour the order is to be made must be named in the document, or be distinguished in the prescribed manner if his identity is not known to the person giving the agreement. In *Y Z, Petitioners* [1954] SLT (Sh Ct) 98 a sheriff's court held a consent bad which did not name either the adopters or the serial number of the proceedings (see p 78).

Forms of agreement scheduled to the respective rules of court may be used (H Ct R r 7 (1); Co Ct R r 6 (1); Mag Ct R r 6 (1): see Forms in Appendix I, pp 181, 207). The form in Mag Ct R differs slightly from the others but all are to the same effect. The present rules make their use optional, using the word 'may'. A document substantially to the like effect may take the place of a scheduled form (see p 63).

If executed before the proceedings are commenced a document signifying parental agreement should be filed with the originating application in county court cases. In the High Court, the rule says that it is to be exhibited to the applicant's affidavit if executed before the date of that affidavit. In magistrates' cases, the documentary agreement, if already given, is referred to in the application and must then be delivered or sent to the court with the application (Mag Ct R r 4 (1)).

The 1975 Act looks forward to a time when agreement to adoption will be witnessed (and other prescribed duties performed) by 'reporting officers' appointed for the purpose of an adoption application (see Appendix II, para 5). In the meantime, a document signifying the agreement of a parent or guardian which complies with AA 1958, s 6 (1), above, is admissible without further proof of signature if attested by a person fulfilling one of a number of specified qualifications according to circumstances. The effect of s 6 (3) of the 1958 Act and of the rules of court (H Ct R r 7 (2); Co Ct R r 6 (2); Mag Ct R r 6 (2)) may be tabulated as follows:

Place of execution	*Person by whom attested*
In England or Wales	An officer of a county court appointed under the County Courts Act 1959, s 87, to take affidavits; or a justices' clerk; or a justice of the peace.
In Scotland	The sheriff or a justice of the peace.
In Northern Ireland	A justice of the peace.
At any other place	Any person authorised for the time being by law in that place to administer an oath for any judicial or other legal purpose; a British consular officer; or a notary public.
	If the person executing the document is serving in any of the regular armed forces of the Crown, a commissioned officer in any of those forces.

A document which purports to be attested as above is to be deemed so attested and to be executed and attested on the date and at the place therein specified unless the contrary is proved: s 6 (4).

The limitations of these evidential provisions must be borne in mind. 'Admissible' does not mean conclusive. Though an agreement is not irrevocable until an adoption order pursuant to it is made, the court has the dispensing power described below, so that withdrawal may in effect be disallowed. Ormrod LJ has pointed out (*Re H (Infants)* [1977] 1 WLR 471) that as time passes withdrawal of agreement becomes more difficult to justify, and has suggested that the prescribed forms ought not to imply that a late change of mind can always be effectively made. The principal type of documentary agreement which is *not* admissible seems to be, reading together the Act and Rules, an agreement to adoption by an unnamed person which does not refer in the prescribed way to the serial number assigned to a specific applicant for adoption.

(e) *Mother's Agreement Not to be Premature*

Both the 1958 and 1975 Acts ensure that a mother shall not be capable of giving an effective agreement until her child is at least six weeks old (s 12 (4) of the 1975 Act). Where she gives her agreement at the time when the order is made, this would in any case be automatically secured by the requirement of a trial period (p 29). Where the mother does not attend and a document is relied on under AA 1958, s 6 (1), s 6 (2) provides that it shall be admissible under the section only if:

(*a*)   the infant is at least six weeks old on the date of the execution of the document; and

(*b*)   the document is attested on that date by a person competent to attest as in (*d*), above.

(*f*)   *Dispensing with Agreement*

As stated above (p 36), the agreement of a particular parent or guardian to the making of an adoption order is not necessary if the court is satisfied that such agreement should be dispensed with (CA 1975, s 12 (1) (*b*) (ii)). But the court's discretion to dispense with a person's agreement is limited as to the grounds on which it may be exercised. The permissible grounds are set out in s 12 (2), and it looks from s 12 (1) (*b*) (ii) as if these were intended to be exhaustive. See, however, *Re F (T) (an Infant)* referred to on p 46. Section 12 (5) must be read into s 12 (2). The grounds of dispensation are here discussed in the order in which subs (2) recites them. For the method of presenting the facts in a dispensation case, see pp 81–82.

(1)   The first ground is put as if it were purely a question of primary fact, namely, that the parent or guardian cannot be found or is incapable of giving agreement (s 12 (2) (*a*)). But on glancing back to s 12 (1) (*b*) (ii) one sees that the court must be satisfied of this state of affairs. In a case of disappearance it should insist that *all* reasonable steps to trace the parent or guardian be taken (*Re F (R), an Infant* [1970] 1 QB 385, where a possible intermediary who was a relative had not been approached for the parent's address and an appeal was allowed). The Department of Health and Social Security, the National Health Service Register, the Ministry of Defence and the Passport Office are examples of sources from which information about missing persons may be sought for proper purposes.

Parents who were in a totalitarian country in which they were 'not sympathetically regarded' by the authorities there, so that they might be endangered if attempts were made to communicate with them, were held incapable of giving agreement (*Re R* [1967] 1 WLR 34). More common cases would be of persons who at the relevant time are mentally ill, or physically ill so as not to be able to receive communications. The court would have to decide whether the evidence satisfied it of the parents incapacity. The subsection does not require *permanent* incapacity.

(2) That the parent or guardian is withholding his agreement unreasonably (s 12 (2) (*b*)). In contrast with former statutes, the 1975 Act does not specify as a special case one where a parent or guardian has already given his agreement in ignorance of the identity of the applicant for adoption, and subsequently withdraws it on the ground only that he does not know that identity. This situation would now stand or fall on the general question whether the parent's attitude at the time of the hearing was reasonable or unreasonable.

It is under this head that most of the case law on dispensation has fallen, and two English cases have been taken as far as the House of Lords. The first was *Re W* [1971] AC 682, the speeches in which may be studied for a comprehensive review of this part of the subject.

Re D (an Infant) [1977] AC 602 applies *Re W* to a particular case and emphasises that the question of reasonableness or otherwise is one of fact and degree, and is to be measured by an objective standard. Lord Wilberforce said that the court must ask itself whether the decision actually made by the parent (a decision to object to the adoption) in his individual circumstances, but assuming him to be endowed with a mind and temperament capable of making reasonable decisions, ranked as a reasonable decision. The factual question in *Re D* turned on the father's confirmed homosexuality. While Lord Wilberforce disclaimed any general principle of dispensing with a parent's agreement on that ground alone, he agreed with the county court judge in thinking that despite changes in legislative or public attitudes the reasonable parent *in the circumstances of the case* would inevitably seek to protect the child from being exposed, at a critical age, to ways of life which might lead to severance from normal society. A majority of their lordships held that the question was one of fact on which at the relevant time no appeal lay from the county court judge. Such an appeal now lies (see p 119).

The question directly in issue in *Re W* was whether withholding of agreement (as it would now be called) could be unreasonable in the relevant sense even though it involved no element of culpability on the part of the parent or guardian or of misconduct by him towards the child. The House held that the test of reasonableness did not necessarily import any element of the sort described. Culpable conduct could, and probably would, be unreasonable, but the converse was not always true. All the circumstances of the individual case should be taken into account. One factor in considering the reasonableness or otherwise of a parent's objection to adoption is his attitude to the child's welfare (see below); others include any blameworthy conduct on the part of the parent, or any 'callous or self-indulgent indifference' shown by him (the phrase is from an earlier Court of Appeal judgment), or failure or the probability of failure of parental duty; while Lord Hailsham LC, at p 700, lists as other factors which 'where carried to excess' would come into play—'sentimentality, romanticism, bigotry, wild prejudice, caprice, fatuousness or excessive lack of common sense'.

In most cases it would be right to disregard completely a mere difference in material circumstances between the facilities which the parent and the adopter had respectively to offer to the child. The judgment of Diplock LJ in *Re C (L) (an Infant)* [1965] 2 QB 449 may be referred to on that point. In the *W* case the evidence showed that the mother might have had to call in aid the social security services, and this was clearly treated as irrelevant; but it seems that the remark of Sellers LJ in *Re B (S)* (1966) 110 SJ 671 holds good. This was to the effect that if a mother had no facilities for bringing up the child or if she was in bad health, it would be unreasonable of her to withhold her agreement.

Obviously in considering the question of reasonableness there may be factors either way interacting, perhaps, one upon another.

The child's welfare   At the time when the House of Lords decided *Re W*, above, it was a statutory requirement, distinct from the question of parental agreement, that before a court could make an adoption order it had to be satisfied in the affirmative that the order if made would be for the welfare of the child (AA 1958, s 7 (1) (*b*)). That provision has now been repealed and replaced by the wider wording of S 3 of CA 1975, set out at p 8 and also referred to at p 96. Section 3 is not in itself relevant to the question of reasonableness now under discussion (*Re S*, cited on p 8). Nor is the well-known 'paramount' principle in the Guardianship of Minors Act 1971, s 1 (applicable in custody and other matters) here in point. Nevertheless consideration of the child's welfare does come into a decision whether to dispense with parental agreement on the ground that it is unreasonably withheld, and has increased in importance in that context over the years (cf per Ormrod LJ in *Re H (Infants)* [1977] 1 WLR 471). *Re W* put it beyond question that the fact that adoption would conduce to the child's welfare does not of itself render the withholding of a parent's agreement unreasonable. The bearing of the child's welfare on parental agreement is explained by Lord Hailsham in a passage which cites and approves as authoritative what Lord Denning MR had said in *Re L (an Infant)* (1962) 106 S J 611. The Lord Chancellor sums up the matter by saying that regard for the child's welfare is a relevant factor in the question of reasonableness if and to the extent that a reasonable parent would take it into account. It is decisive in those cases where a reasonable parent must so regard it. See also *Re S* (1978) 9 Fam Law 88 at p 89.

Earlier cases on reasonableness, many of which have raised this apparent 'conflict between the child's welfare and the rights of an unimpeachable parent' (see per Plowman J in *Re M (an Infant)* (1966) 110 S J 670), and which do not seem to be overruled by the *W* or *D* decisions, are noted below, and should be consulted for their detailed facts. It must be said, however, that the catchwords used in the bracketed indications below merely summarise judicial interpretations of facts in particular contexts: no two cases are truly alike. The courts take account of events and conduct right up to the time when the case comes to be considered, whether on the original application for an order or on review by an appellate court (*Re L*, above; *Re Adoption Act* 1950, *The Times*, 29 July 1958).

The withholding of agreement was found to be unreasonable

in *W* v *D* (1955) 120 JP News 11 (not relevant that adopters might have another child of the same sex, to the material disadvantage of adopted child); in *L* above (lapse of time, vacillation, evidence of possible psychological and physical harm); in *Re C(L)(an Infant)* [1965] 2 QB 449 (lack of plans for future, refusal to comment on evidence of psychological danger); and in *Re W (Infants)* [1965] 1 WLR 1259 (special facts, father had himself initiated adoption proceedings, delay, court thought him to blame for situation). In the extreme case of *Re F(T)(an Infant)*[1970] 1 WLR 192, where one parent had killed the other, the facts were found not to fall expressly within what is now s 12 (2), but the special circumstances rendered it proper for the court to disregard the father's objection.

On the other hand a refusal of agreement was not found to be unreasonable in *Hitchcock* v *WB* [1952] 2 QB 561 (immaterial that magistrates in other proceedings had given the mother custody of the same child against the wishes of the father, who now objected to adoption); in *Re Adoption Act 1950, Re K (an Infant)* [1953] 1 QB 117 (placing with foster parents with mother's concurrence, followed by her change of mind); in *Re L (an Infant)* [1963] CLY 1771 (where father wants his child and can support it, *prima facie* impossible to call his opposition unreasonable); and in *Re M (an Infant)* (1970) 114 S J 264 (father wished to retain child's status and his own rights: immaterial that he had kept away from child).

Of the more recent decisions about dispensing with parental agreement, two stressed the relevance of the effect on the child of a change of surroundings as an element in the reasonableness or otherwise of the parent's attitude. A year-old baby would not, it was thought in *Re PA (an Infant)* (1971) 115 S J 586, be permanently upset by such a change. The mother, whose refusal of her agreement was upheld, had become engaged to be married and the infant would receive love and care from the mother and future stepfather. By contrast the disruptive element involved in moving a three-year-old boy from the applicants' home where he had lived for two-and-a-half years to the company of his natural parents, who were found to be 'not particularly stable individuals', was one of the reasons given for holding as unreasonable a refusal of agreement in the Scottish case in the House of Lords of *O'Connor* v *A and B* [1971] 1 WLR 1227. This was said to mark the first occasion on which a court had dispensed with the consent of *both* natural parents of a child. They had married each other after the child's birth.

In *Re Adoption Application No 41 of 1974, The Times*, 1 May 1975, an Indian mother's apprehension of racial difficulties if her child were brought up by English adopters, notwithstanding that the latter were described as excellent and were already bringing up successfully a half-Ghanaian adopted child, was held not unreasonable even though the judge did not share the mother's anxieties. The question of the reasonableness of a father's objection, when the mother and her second husband applied for adoption, was also referred to in *Re B (Adoption by Parent)* [1975] Fam 127 (cited for its main point on p 27). There Cumming-Bruce J said that it would be quite wrong to use the adoption law to extinguish the relationship between a protesting father and a child unless there was some really serious factor which justified the use of 'the statutory guillotine'. See also *A and B* v *C* [1977] SLT (Sh Ct) 55.

Unussual circumstances were present in *AB Petitioner* [1976] SLT (Sh Ct) 49, in which the mother had consented to a joint adoption of her boy, but withdrew her agreement after the male proposing adopter had died tragically. With obvious hesitation the sheriff dispensed with her consent.

(3) Agreement may be dispensed with if the court is satisfied that a parent or guardian has persistently failed without reasonable cause to discharge the parental duties in relation to the child (1975 Act, s 12 (2) (*c*)). By reference to s 85 (1) (see p 34) we see that the phrase 'parental duties' differs only verbally from the one which appeared in a similar context in the 1958 Act, namely, 'the obligations of a parent or guardian of the infant', and this has received judicial interpretation. It comprehended both moral and financial obligations (*Re P (Infants)* [1962] 1 WLR 1296). The father in *Re B (S) (an Infant)* [1968] Ch 204 was held not to have unreasonably withheld his agreement, and yet to have done nothing to discharge his obligations, so that his agreement could be dispensed with on this ground. The Scottish case of *H and H, Petitioners* [1976] SLT 80 (Court of

Session) was an *a fortiori* case of a father 'washing his hands of' his daughter.

On the other hand, a withdrawal of support of the child associated with the breakdown of his parents' marriage, which was followed by divorce and the remarriage of both parties, was held by the Family Divisional Court not to have amounted to a failure on the father's part to discharge his obligations (*Re D (minors)* [1973] Fam 209). This decision seems, with respect, to be inevitable on its facts, which included the mother's moving away without telling the father, and her unauthorised change of the child's name. But Sir George Baker P made it the occasion for some general observations on the persistent failure of which the Act speaks. These observations have been criticised as too restrictive (eg MDA Freeman, *The Children Act* 1975), but *Re D* was followed in *Re H (minors), The Times*, 26 November 1974. The effect of the President's *dicta* is certainly in keeping with the modern view of adoption as only one of several remedies for the situation of a deprived child (pp 10–12). His lordship said that the Act envisaged a failure of such gravity that there could be no advantage to the child in maintaining contact with the parent in question.

The word 'persistently' should be noted. It implies at least an element of continuity, and in most instances it would have an aspect of duration.

But a mother may change her mind on new circumstances coming to light; for instance, where she had parted with the child to the proposing adopters in order to keep the news of the birth from her parents, this was held not to amount to failure without reasonable cause to discharge her obligations, and she was allowed to object to the adoption on finding that her father was willing to provide a home for the child (*Re M (an Infant)* (1965) 109 S J 574, CA). Somewhat similar facts emerged at a different stage of the proceedings in *Re S (Adoption: Parental Consent)* [1973] 3 All ER 88, in which since the hearing below, a new witness was brought forward who proposed to marry the mother. The Court of Appeal admitted his evidence and took it into account (albeit they thought it made no difference) in dispensing with the mother's agreement.

(4) That the parent or guardian has abandoned or neglected the child (s 12 (2) (*d*)); or

(5) has *persistently* ill-treated the child (s 12 (2) (*e*)).

'Abandoned' bears the same meaning as in the criminal law (*Watson* v *Nikolaisen* [1955] 2 QB 286; see also *Wheatley* v *Waltham Forest LBC* [1979] 2 WLR 543). It is possible that 'neglected' also imports something more than a merely negative attitude (cf the question of the mental constituent in the offence of wilfully neglecting a child which the House of Lords is likely to consider in *R* v *Sheppard* (1980) 70 Cr App R 210). Clearly some distinction between head (3) *ante* and (4) is intended. On this footing, (4) would be a more difficult head to establish than (3), as (from its more specific averment) would also be head (5). It might be thought that 'persistently' ought to be read in a sense corresponding to that of the same adverb in (3) (see p 48); but it is possibly here less susceptible of referring to time than in that paragraph, because in (5) it qualifies a positive verb. The analogy with 'persistent cruelty' in the Matrimonial Proceedings (Magistrates' Courts) Act 1960, s 1 (1) (*b*) (now repealed by DPMCA 1978) seems very strong. In that context mere repetition of a cruel act was often sufficient. Blows are not, of course, the only forms of ill-treatment.

A case in which the child was reported to have suffered severe and repeated assaults over a period of some three weeks is *Re A (a Minor)* (1980) 10 Fam Law 49. The judge's decision dispensing with the natural parents' agreement on the ground that they had persistently ill-treated the child was upheld by the Court of Appeal.

(6) That the parent or guardian has *seriously* ill-treated the child (s 12 (2) (*f*)), and, because of that ill-treatment or for other reasons, the rehabilitation of the child within the household of the parent or guardian in question is unlikely (s 12 (5)). This ground is new in CA 1975. The contrasted adverb clearly distinguishes its prime condition from head (5): provided rehabilitation in the family is unlikely, one cruel act of adequate gravity would seem to satisfy the new ground.

c

3   Consents and Consultations in English Convention Cases concerning Minors who are Not United Kingdom Nationals

To an application under CA 1975, s 24, for the adoption of a child who is not a United Kingdom national (see p 24) the ordinary provisions as to agreement (pp 35–49) do not of themselves apply (s 12 (3)) but undergo the modifications described in the following paragraphs.

The internal law of the country of which the child is a national may contain provisions which require consents to be given and consultations to take place before an adoption can be authorised. Provisions of this kind in the relevant foreign law, so far as they do not refer to consent by and consultation with the applicant and members of his family (including his or her spouse) (see s 24 (7)), are to be observed by the English High Court when seised of an application for a Convention adoption order, for s 24 (6) (*a*) provides that such an order shall not be made except in accordance with such provisions. By s 24 (6) (*b*) it is necessary for the court to be satisfied that each consenting person does so with the full understanding of what is involved (cf p 116).

'Internal law' is defined (AA 1968, s 11 (1)) to mean the law applicable, in the country concerned, in a case where no question arises as to the law in force in any other country. Detailed provisions are to be found in AA 1968, s 9 (2) to (4), as to the treatment of persons appearing to have two nationalities, or to have no ascertainable nationality. By s 10 (1) of the same Act, applied by CA 1975, s 24 (9), if there are in force in that country two or more systems of internal law, the relevant system is ascertained in accordance with any rule in force throughout that country indicating which of the systems is relevant in the case in question, or if there is no such rule, the system is to be that appearing to the English High Court to be most closely connected with the case.

For the purpose of s 24, consents may be proved in the manner prescribed by the Convention Adoption Rules 1978 (see Chapter XI), and the English High Court will have the foreign authority's power to dispense with consent and to effect adoption (s 24 (7)). If the foreign law would ordinarily require the attendance before the authority in question of any person who does not reside in Great Britain, then that requirement is to be taken as satisfied if he has been given a reasonable opportunity of communicating his opinion on the adoption in question to the proper officer of the High Court, or to an appropriate authority of the country in question for transmission to the court; and if, where he has availed himself of that opportunity, his opinion has been transmitted to the court.

4 Home Laws of Non-British Applicants in Convention Cases in England

Certain prohibitions on the making of an adoption order may be contained in the national law of a non-British person who, being qualified, proposes to adopt in England by means of a Convention adoption order. The Hague Convention of 1965 arranged for these to be notified by each signatory country to the other signatories.

The Acts (CA 1975, s 24 (8)) contemplate that the Secretary of State shall specify in an order what provisions have been so notified to him, and that these (defined in s 24 (8) of CA 1975 as 'specified provisions') shall thereupon become in effect binding on the English High Court when seised of a relevant application. The effect of s 24 (4) and (5) is to disqualify an application for a Convention order if the applicant is a national of a Convention country (or if a married couple are applicants and both are nationals of the same Convention country) a specified provision of the internal law of which prohibits the adoption sought. Provisions have been notified and specified for Austria and Switzerland (SI 1978 No 1431, Scheds 1 and 2).

5 Making of Order

The provisions as to the eligibility of the applicants and the child, as to the agreement of parents and guardians, and as to the child's welfare, are supplemented by the only two subsections of CA 1975, s 22, which are yet in force.

These are subs (4), which deals with second applications (see p 57); and subs (5), which directs that the court shall not make an adoption order in relation to a child unless it is satisfied that the applicants have not, as respects the child, contravened s 50 of the 1958 Act. Section 50, as set out on pp 168–169, prohibits unauthorised payments and rewards in connection with adoption.

These then are conditions precedent to the making of an adoption order. Section 8 (7) of CA 1975 also allows a kind of condition subsequent, ie 'such terms and conditions as the court thinks fit' to be contained in the order. An undertaking to bring up the child in a particular religion has sometimes been exacted; and it does not seem that the abolition of the possibility of a parent's consent being subject to a similar condition and the duty now placed on agencies to try to secure placements into families of appropriate religious persuasions (p 39) will necessarily have rendered such a condition obsolete. Conditions as to access may be imposed (cf *Re J (Adoption Order: Conditions)* [1973] Fam 106, and *Re S (Adoption Order: Access)* [1976] Fam 1, both referred to on p 23); but unless such a condition is freely accepted by the adopters, it may not be easily workable (per Dunn J in *Re B (a minor)* (1977) 7 Fam Law 108).

There is no power to revoke the order on the ground of breach of condition. Though the Court of Appeal in *Re G (TJ) (an Infant)* [1963] 2 QB 73 expressed doubts whether conditions could be effectively enforced, if an undertaking by the adopter is invited and given, his compliance with the condition could be indirectly ensured in that way.

Chapter V

Interim Orders

Upon any application for an adoption order, including apparently an application for a Convention adoption order, the court may postpone the determination of the application and make an interim order giving the custody of the infant to the applicant for a probationary period not exceeding two years, on such terms in respect of provision for the maintenance, education and supervision of the welfare of the infant and otherwise as the court thinks fit (AA 1958, s 8 (1), as yet unrepealed: cf Appendix II, para 4). 'Probationary' here imports a process of experiment in relation to all circumstances relevant to the proposed adoption; not merely to the suitability of the applicants (*S* v *Huddersfield Borough Council* [1975] Fam 113, per Buckley LJ at p 124). In the *Huddersfield* case, an interim adoption order was made in favour of foster-parents with staying and visiting access to a natural parent and local authority supervision as a means of trying out the desirability of eventual integration of the child into the natural parent's new family. It is tentatively suggested that such a case might eventually fall to be treated as a custodianship application (see CA 1975, s 37 (3), and Appendix II, para 9). As to the procedure for the determination of the application after an interim order has been made, see p 94, and for the obligation in certain cases to return the infant to an adoption society or local authority, see p 162.

It is expressly provided by s 8 (5) of the 1958 Act that an interim order is not to be an adoption order within the meaning of the Acts (see also CA 1975, Sched 3, para 39 (*a*)), so that, for example, whenever made, it does not affect status, proprietary rights or citizenship. The same agreements are required before an interim order is made as are necessary to an adoption order, and they may be dispensed with by the court in like manner (s 8 (2) as amended by SI 1976 No 1744, Sched 3, para 5; see pp 35–49). An interim order must be preceded by the trial period mentioned in s 3 (1) of the 1958 Act (see pp 29–30), and in appropriate cases notice to the local authority must have been given (see p 30) (s 8 (3)).

Section 8 (4) of the Act of 1958 allows the court to extend up to a total period not exceeding two years an interim order made in the first instance for a lesser period.

As to interim orders in Convention matters, see p 116.

Chapter VI

Provisional Adoption

Until the commencement of s 25 of CA 1975* (see Appendix II, para 7), s 53 of the 1958 Act continues in force so as to authorise provisional orders.

An application for a full order of adoption will not be entertained, in non-Convention cases, unless the proposing adopter is domiciled in a part of the United Kingdom or in the Channel Islands or the Isle of Man (see p 17). However, where an applicant who is not so domiciled satisfies the High Court or the county court within whose district the child is (s 53 (2), as transitionally amended by SI 1976 No 1744, Sched 3, para 8) that he intends to adopt a child under the law of or within the country in which the applicant is domiciled, and desires to remove the child from Great Britain for that purpose either immediately or after an interval, the court may make a provisional adoption order (s 53 (1)). Evidence of the law of adoption in the country concerned must be adduced (see p 79).

A provisional order authorises the applicant to remove the child for the purpose of adoption in accordance with his declared intention, and vests in him in the meantime the parental rights and duties relating to the child (including legal custody). But it does not otherwise create any legal relationship between the provisional adopter and the child (per Buckley J in *Re M (an Infant)* [1965] Ch 203 at p 210). Except under the authority of such an order, a child who is a British subject may

---

*It is in fact with the commencement of s 18 of CA 1975 (notification: see Appendix II, para 2) that ibid, Sched 4, Pt IX, links the repeal of s 53 of the 1958 Act. But CA, s 108 (7), specifies s 25 as being in substitution for AA 1958, s 53.

generally not be removed with a view to adoption (see p 170). Unlike a full adoption order, a provisional order does not affect status, devolution or dispositions of property or citizenship, but otherwise the provisions of the Adoption Acts apply to a provisional adoption order as to a full order (s 53 (4)). A magistrates' court may not make a provisional order (see s 53 (2)).

All the requirements relating to capacity, eligibility and conditions precedent applicable to the making of an ordinary adoption order, apart from that relating to the domicile of the applicant, must be satisfied before a provisional order can be made (s 53 (3); SI 1978 No 1433); the trial period (see s 3 (1) and p 29) is, however, six months and not three, and if notice to the local authority is necessary under s 3 (2) (see p 30), it must be a six months' notice (s 53 (5)). If joint applicants for provisional adoption are not only not domiciled, but also not living in Great Britain, they may avail themselves of the provisions of s 12 (3) (see pp 31–33) equally with non-resident applicants for a full order provided that the child is not a British subject (see p 170); but the one month during which they have been living together in Great Britain must be one of the *three* months immediately preceding the date of the order—not any one of the six months to which the period of actual custody is enlarged in provisional cases (*Re M (an Infant)*, above).

When quashing for want of jurisdiction a full adoption order made by a county court judge, the Court of Appeal, in *Re R (an Infant)* [1962] 1 WLR 1147, substituted a provisional order in favour of the same applicants.

Chapter VII

Fresh Proceedings in respect of the Same Child

1 Same Applicant

By s 22 (4) of CA 1975 (read with s 107 (1)), the court may not proceed to hear an application for an adoption order in relation to a child where a previous application for adoption has been made and refused in Great Britain, Northern Ireland or any British territory outside the United Kingdom by the same person in relation to the same child unless:

(a) in refusing the previous application the court directed that s 22 (4) should not apply; or

(b) it appears to the court that because of a change in circumstances or for any other reason it is proper to proceed with the application. This provision is new as a statutory requirement; previously the gist of it was in the rules of court.

The possibility of s 22 (4) precluding progress with the application is one of the factors the presence of which compels reference of the case to the judge or to the court itself, as the case may be (see pp 85, 88, 91).

2 New Applicant

There is nothing to prevent a second application in respect of the same child by another proposed adopter. Section 8 (8) of the 1975 Act provides for re-adoption orders. Its effect is that a child who is already the subject of adoption (whether under the 1958 or 1975 Acts, or by specified order or overseas adoption) may, nevertheless, be the subject of a subsequent adoption or interim or provisional order.

On an application for a further order a certified copy of the entry of the previous adoption in the Adopted Children

Register (see p 124) is required in place of the birth certificate (p 179, note 7). Moreover, the adopter under the adoption order last previously made is deemed to be the child's parent, so that, for instance it is his agreement and not that of the natural parent which is required (see *Re RM* [1941] WN 244). A sheriff court in *B (Mrs), Petitioner* [1952] SLT (Sh Ct) 48 refused notwithstanding such agreement to make a re-adoption order. The application in that case was put on the grounds that the child had rebelled against her adopted parents.

Chapter VIII

Jurisdiction and Procedure in Non-Convention Cases

1 Courts: Venue

An adoption order may be made by an authorised court within the meaning of s 100 (2) of CA 1975 (ibid, s 8 (1)). Section 100 (2) gives the following courts concurrent jurisdiction in a case where the child is in England or Wales when the application is made:

(*a*) the High Court, ie in practice the Family Division (Administration of Justice Act 1970, s 1 (2) and Sched 1);

(*b*) the county court within whose district the child is;

(*c*) any other county court prescribed by the County Court Rules 1936 (see below); and

(*d*) a magistrates' court within whose area the child is.

When CA 1975, s 14 (as to freeing children for adoption: see Appendix II, para 3) is brought into force, these will also be the authorised courts in respect of an application under that section.

County courts   As regards courts other than the court where the child is at the time of the making of the application (which has jurisdiction by virtue of CA 1975, s 100 (2) (*b*) above), s 100 (2) (*c*) has been implemented in SI 1979 No 1045. Under that instrument a new Ord 2, r 16, is introduced into the County Court Rules 1936, and that adds to the category of authorised courts 'any divorce county court [see Matrimonial Causes Act 1967, s 1 (1)] in which a declaration has been made under s 41 (1) (*b*) or (*c*) of the Matrimonial Causes Act 1973 in respect of' the child in question. Thereby, in appropriate s 10 (3) and s 11 (4) cases (see pp 20, 22) the same county court may be asked to deal with the adoption application as has the power to make the custody order which the subsections cited require to be considered as an alternative.

It may also be noted that the general county court rules are applied to adoption matters (see below), so that a matter may be transferred from one county court to another under Ord 16, rr 1 to 9. Such a transfer may be made, for instance, if the judge or registrar is satisfied that the proceedings can be more conveniently or fairly tried in some other court (r 1 (1)), a condition that might be considered fulfilled in a s 10 (3) or s 11 (4) case. There may also be a transfer where the case has been commenced in the wrong court (r 4), but in that event the rule gives the judge or registrar the alternative of retaining the proceedings instead of transferring them to the court for the child's district: it is unlikely that the court would order the proceedings to be struck out for a wrong choice of district, though that course, too, would be open to the judge or registrar on the terms of Ord 16, r 4, and might be followed if it were apparent on the face of the application that it could not succeed.

Magistrates' courts   In references to magistrates' courts, CA 1975 uses the word 'area' in the sense of the commission area for which justices are appointed under s 1 of the Administration of Justice Act 1973 (s 107 (1) of the 1975 Act), and not the petty sessions area indicated by the term 'jurisdiction' in the former legislation. It is thus now possible for an applicant who wishes to apply to a magistrates' court for an adoption order to choose any court within the commission area where the child is (usually coincident with a county under the Local Government Act 1972) instead of being obliged to go to the court for a particular petty sessions area.

All proceedings before a magistrates' court under AA 1958, AA 1960 or CA 1975, Pt I, are included in the definition of 'domestic proceedings' in MCA 1980, s 65 (1), with the exception only of proceedings under AA 1958, s 42 or s 43 (protection of certain children: see p 166), which are retained by the juvenile court. This is the result of s 79 of DPMCA, which Act also repealed s 21 (3) of CA 1975.

Domestic proceedings come before what the Act now describes as 'domestic courts', consisting entirely of justices qualified by membership of a domestic court panel as set out in MCA, ss 66 and 67, and SI 1979 No 757 made thereunder. So far as is consistent with the due dispatch of business, the hearing and determination of domestic proceedings must be separated from other business (s 69 (1)). The court hearing domestic proceedings must be composed of not more than three justices, including so far as practicable both a man and a woman, except that a stipendiary magistrate who is a member of a domestic court panel may sit alone (s 67 (7)); as may a metropolitan magistrate in an Inner London Petty Sessions area, whether or not he is a panel member, if it is not practicable to assemble a mixed bench; though he more usually chairs a bench consisting of himself and two members of the panel (s 66 (2)). Where, despite resonable efforts, the clerk had failed to secure the attendance of a woman justice, a court consisting of three men was held not to be improperly constituted (*Crowe* v *Crowe* (1962) 106 SJ 432), but a fourth member of the bench, or the inclusion of a justice not belonging to a domestic panel, would invalidate the hearing, it seems.

In domestic proceedings the court ought to assist an unrepresented party, where it appears necessary, with examination or cross-examination of witnesses (s 73).

Section 9 (5) of AA 1958 (as amended) remains operative. It provides for rules under which adoption applications to a magistrates' court would lie to a juvenile court, and be heard in closed court. The Magistrates' Courts (Adoption) Rules 1976 (p 62) were made under it, but the 1979 amendment referred to later has translated juvenile court to domestic court. Juvenile courts now play a small part in adoption law (see p 166). They are constituted under CYPA 1963 and orders effective thereunder determine the composition of the bench, it being generally necessary to ensure that not more than three persons, of whom one is a man and one a woman, shall sit.

Special cases   A magistrates' court must decline jurisdiction, by refusing to make an order on any application to it under CA 1975, if it considers that the matter is one which would more conveniently be dealt with by the High Court (s 101 (3); cf the reference on p 27 to *Re B (Adoption by Parent)*). Thereupon the magistrates' proceedings will lapse: nothing in the nature of the removal of the same proceedings is provided for, and the applicant must begin again. On the other hand, the complementary provision in relation to county court applications (s 101 (1)) is exercisable, not by the county court of its own motion, but by the High Court at the instance of a party. The power given by this subsection is to remove an application under CA 1975 or, as the case may be, under s 34 or s 34A of AA 1958 (see pp 95 and DPMCA 1978, Sched 2, para 49) to the High Court, where it is to be proceeded with. See further p 91.

Only the High Court or the county court within whose district the child is may make a provisional order under AA 1958, s 53 (see p 55), or a parental rights order under CA 1975, s 25, when in force (Appendix II, para 7).

Authorised courts in the case of an application under CA 1975, s 30, for the return of a child taken away from the person with whom he has his home in breach of AA 1958, s 34 or s 34A (see p 97) are:

(*a*) if there is a pending application for adoption or for freeing the child, the court in which that application is pending;

(*b*) in any other case, the High Court, the county court within whose district the applicant lives, and the magistrates' court within whose area the applicant lives, 'area' bearing the wider meaning mentioned above (s 100 (8) of the 1975 Act).

The provision for applications to free a child for adoption (CA 1975, s 14) is not yet in force (see Appendix II, para 3).

Rules   The rules now in force are the Adoption (High Court) Rules 1976, SI 1976 No 1645 (amended by SI 1978 No 1519), the Adoption (County Court) Rules 1976, SI 1976 No 1644 (amended by SI 1978 No 1518 and SI 1979 No 978), and the Magistrates' Courts (Adoption) Rules 1976, SI 1976 No 1768 (amended by SI 1979 No 1222).

The present rules lay down a procedure which is fundamentally uniform in all the courts, and use the modern vocabulary consonant with CA 1975 (cf p 6). Their full texts may be found in the Supreme Court Practice, the County Court Practice, or Stone's Justices' Manual, as the case may be. Each set of rules refers to schedules and forms for use at the several stages of an adoption matter. These forms, or forms substantially to the like effect, are to be used with such variations as the circumstances may require (H Ct R r 2 (2); Co Ct R r 2 (2); Mag Ct R r 2 (3)). Together with their footnotes, the scheduled forms seem to illustrate the procedure sufficiently graphically to warrant reproducing them in Appendix I, abbreviated where possible for reasons of space.

Where the rules prescribe requirements as to the time within which steps are to be taken (eg H Ct R r 6) these ought to be strictly observed (cf *Practice Direction* [1966] 1 WLR 706); and indeed the desirability of settling a child's future as quickly as possible has been stressed in several cases (eg *Re W (Infants)* [1965] 1 WLR 1259).

Subject to the special sets of Adoption Rules enumerated above, the Rules of the Supreme Court and the County Court Rules 1936 respectively apply with the necessary modifications in the appropriate courts to proceedings under AA 1958 and CA 1975 (H Ct R r 3 (2); Co Ct R r 3 (2)). In a similar sense it is provided by Mag Ct R r 35 that, save in so far as special provision is made in Mag Ct R, proceedings on an application under those rules are to be regulated in the same manner as proceedings on complaint (*scilicet* under the Magistrates' Courts Rules 1968), the statement of application being regarded as a complaint, the respondents as defendants, and any notice issued under the special rules to a respondent as a summons; but no warrant lies for failure to appear in answer to any such notice. For appeal procedure, see p 118.

By the Legal Aid Act 1974, s 7 and Sched 1, Pt I, legal aid is available in appropriate cases in any adoption proceedings in the House of Lords, the Court of Appeal, the High Court or a county court; and in any case in a magistrates' court in which the making of an order under Pt I of CA 1975 is opposed by any party to the proceedings (1975 Act, Sched 3, para 82 (*a*)), or which relate to a removal application under ss 34 or 34A of AA 1958 (DPMCA 1978, Sched 2, para 45 (*b*)). An unrepresented party who contests the order but is not told that legal aid is available may on appeal be allowed a new trial, if his circumstances were such that he would have been eligible for aid (*Re*

M (an Infant) [1973] QB 108, per Sachs LJ).

In the remainder of this section the basic procedure is described under subject headings, the wording of the relevant rules being followed so far as applicable, and differences occasioned by variations in jurisdiction and procedure as between the respective courts being noted. Following the Act, the orthodox course is taken of dealing first with the High Court procedure; but it may here be noted that the most common forum for adoption proceedings is the county court, with the magistrates' courts substantially ahead of the High Court in the number of applications.

In cases in which there is a choice of court, the additional expense of proceeding in the High Court is undoubtedly a factor to be considered. But High Court proceedings may, in the long run, be better in a case involving a new or difficult legal point or a predictable contest of complicated fact (see also the comment of Sir George Baker P in *Re B*, cited on p 27). Moreover, applicants who are well-known in a particular locality may prefer not to have their affairs canvassed, even in judicial confidence, by a local bench and local officials. There is the further point that, whereas in the inferior courts the attendance of the child and the applicants is normally necessary, that is not so in the Family Division (cf p 86).

In the Family Division of the High Court, initiating and interlocutory proceedings are conducted at the Principal Registry of that Division at Somerset House, Strand, London WC2R 1LP, and a registrar of the Division may, unless a contrary intention appears in the rules, exercise any powers conferred on the court (H Ct R r 3 (4)). But the application is heard by a judge (see p 85). Adoption proceedings may be conducted in chambers (see p 75), and hearings before a judge will usually take place at the Royal Courts of Justice in the Strand. In special circumstances, on application to the registrar, the hearing of an application can be referred to a Crown Court where a judge of the Family Division sits.

2   Guardian ad litem

For the purposes of any application for an adoption order, the court must appoint some person to act as guardian ad litem of the child* upon the hearing of the application, to safeguard his interests before the court (AA 1958, s 9 (7)). If an officer of a local authority is appointed the court may authorise the authority (whose consent to the appointment is essential) to incur any necessary expenditure (s 9 (8)). As to local authorities, see p 13.

In the High Court the Official Solicitor is normally the guardian if he consents, but there are provisions enabling some other person to act, the procedure in that regard being referred to at p 66. In the inferior courts the director of social services of a local authority (see p 156) or a probation officer is usually assigned. A probation officer takes no fee for acting as guardian ad litem. A director of social services appointed as guardian may carry out his duties and appear before the court personally or by any other officer or servant of the same local authority who assists him in the exercise of his functions (H Ct R r 12 (4); Co Ct R r 10 (4); Mag Ct R r 9 (3)). But the rules applicable in the inferior courts generally prohibit the appointment as guardian of an officer of a *respondent* authority (see p 67).

See Appendix II, para 5, as to eventual changes whereby the appointment of a guardian ad litem may become discretionary, a reporting officer (see p 40) may be appointed, and the guardian and reporting officer may also be concerned in 'freeing' applications and in applications for vesting of parental rights and duties with a view to adoption abroad (Appendix II, paras 3 and 7).

---

*Where a parent was a minor and consented to the adoption, no separate guardian ad litem was appointed for him in the Chancery Division, which formerly dealt with adoption applications (see *Re K (an Infant)* [1952] 2 All ER 877 at p 887). In the county court the situation is the same unless the judge otherwise directs (Co Ct R r 34). As to mental disability of a respondent, see note † on page 71.

The court in *Re R* [1967] 1 WLR 34 asked for counsel to be briefed by the Treasury Solicitor as *amicus curiae* in addition to counsel for the parties. It was a case which had what Buckley J described as a security aspect.

(*a*) Appointment

(*i*) Family Division

Official Solicitor　Unless the applicant desires otherwise, the Official Solicitor, if he consents to act, becomes the guardian ad litem of the child without any express appointment (r 12 (1)). His consent should be obtained before the issue of the originating summons, since if he does not consent the summons must ask for the appointment of some other person (r 12 (2)).

The necessary consent may be applied for by letter addressed to The Official Solicitor to the Supreme Court, 48–49 Chancery Lane, London WC2A 1JR, setting out the full circumstances. A copy of the proposed summons and a draft of the supporting affidavit (see below) might be supplied to the Official Solicitor at this stage. Pressure of work in the Official Solicitor's office is understood to be considerable.

The consent will usually be given in consideration of an undertaking by the applicant to pay the Official Solicitor's proper costs in the matter. The rules do not prescribe a form of undertaking, but an appropriate document will be prepared in the Official Solicitor's Department if the case is approved for consent, and sent to the solicitor for completion by his client, or to the applicant if acting in person. The wording differs according as it is, or is not, a legal aid case. An undertaking is not normally asked for where the adoption application relates to a ward of court, and is made pursuant to leave to apply granted in the wardship proceedings.

If the Official Solicitor signifies that he is willing to act, the applicant issues the originating summons and serves on the Official Solicitor a copy of it (r 12 (1)), and also a copy of the affidavit in support (see p83) as soon as that affidavit is filed (r 12 (3)).

Other guardian ad litem　If the Official Solicitor does not consent to act, or if the applicant desires that some other person should be appointed, the originating summons must ask for such appointment, and must be supported by an affidavit (additional to the affidavit required in support of the application for adoption) sworn by the applicant and stating the facts. The court may then appoint as guardian any person who appears to be suitably qualified, and the applicant must serve on him a copy of the summons (r 12 (2)). The applicant must also serve on the guardian a copy of the affidavit supporting the summons as soon as it is filed, or as soon thereafter as the guardian is appointed (r 12 (3)).

As to the appointment being a matter of public policy, see the observations of Roxburgh J in *Re DX (an Infant)* [1948] WN 377; *sub nom Re AB (an infant)* [1948] 2 All ER 727, a case under an older rule which required 'special reasons' for the appointment of a guardian other than the Official Solicitor. These observations could still be relevant if the proposal were to have a private person appointed, not an officer of a local authority, particularly if he were related to any of the persons concerned· in the application.

(ii) Inferior courts

In the county court and magistrates' court a guardian ad litem is to be appointed by the court as soon as practicable after the making of the application, a copy of which, with the documents attached thereto, is then served on him (Co Ct R r 10 (1)) or furnished to him (Mag Ct R r 9 (1)). The registrar makes the appointment in the county court. The appointment is subject to the rule requiring a preliminary examination of jurisdiction in certain cases (see p 88).

The guardian ad litem is to be:

(*a*) if the local authority concerned consents, the director of social services of a local authority or an officer or servant of that authority who assists the director in the exercise of his functions;

(*b*) a probation officer; or

(*c*) if in any particular case the court considers it not reasonably practicable or that it would be undesirable to appoint one of these persons, some other person who appears suitably qualified (Co Ct R r 10 (2); Mag Ct R r 9 (2)).

But by Co Ct R r 10 (3) a person is not eligible for appointment in a county court case if he is a respondent, or is a member, officer or servant of a respondent body other than a local authority which is a respondent merely because of Co Ct R r 4 (2) (*f*), as the recipient of a notice of intention to adopt. As to who are respondents, see p 74. In the domestic court, a proviso to Mag Ct R r 9 (2) (*c*) prohibits the appointment as guardian ad litem of:

(*a*) a person who has the parental rights and duties in respect of the child or who has taken part in the arrangements for the adoption; or

(*b*) a member, officer or servant of a local authority, adoption society or other body of persons having such rights and duties or which has taken part as aforesaid.

(*b*) *Duties*

In all courts, a guardian ad litem is under duty, so far as reasonably practicable, with a view to safeguarding the interests of the child before the court:

(*a*) to investigate all the circumstances relevant to the proposed adoption, including all matters alleged in the application or affidavit and those specified in (*c*) below; and

(*b*) to perform such other duties as are specified in (*c*) below, or as the court may direct (H Ct R r 13 (1); Co Ct R r 11 (1); Mag Ct R r 10 (1)).

On completing his investigations, the guardian must make a confidential report in writing to the court, and he may at any time make such interim report (which may be oral, although the main report must be in writing) as appears to him necessary with a view to obtaining the court's directions on any particular matter (H Ct R r 13 (2), (3), (4); Co Ct R r 11 (2), (3), (4); Mag Ct R r 10 (2), (3), (4)). But the guardian takes no part in the court's decision, and should not be seen to appear to do so (cf *Re B (Adoption by Parent)*, referred to at p 92). It will be the guardian's duty, where an application is by a parent and stepparent, to draw the court's attention to the disadvantages as well as the advantages of adoption, as compared with the other courses which the court must consider (see pp 20–23) (*Re S (Infants)* [1977] Fam 173). As to the use to be made of a guardian's report, see pp 72 and 81. Though it has been said that the report is not a substitute for necessary evidence, the context of that warning was dispensation with parental agreement; there is no doubt that the judge can rely on the contents of the report for those matters which are directed to be covered by it (see below), at all events in the absence of contrary indications, and can have regard to it in coming to his decision (cf *Re G (TJ) (an Infant)* [1963] 2 QB 73). In its nature it will consist of, or be based on, hearsay to a large extent, but in regard to controversial matters *Thompson* v *Thompson* [1975] 2 WLR 868 (a matrimonial case in which a welfare officer's report was used) suggests that the guardian should report his own observations and assessments explicitly indicating second-hand matter.

*(c) Particular Duties of Guardian ad litem**

1 The guardian ad litem shall interview the applicant and shall ascertain:
(*a*) why the applicant wishes to adopt the child;
(*b*) whether the applicant understands the nature of an adoption order and, in particular, that the order, if made, will render him responsible for the maintenance and upbringing of the child;
(*c*) in the case of an application by the mother or father of the child alone, what reason there is justifying the exclusion of the other natural parent;
(*d*) in the case of an application by one only of a married couple, why the other spouse does not join in the application;
(*e*) in the case of an application by a married couple, the state of the marriage, and, in particular, whether it has the stability which is likely to provide a sound basis for a secure parental relationship with an adopted child;

---

*As in Sched 2 to the respective rules. The schedule here copied is that to Co Ct R. In the other sets of rules the schedule shows slight incidental variations. For instance, account is taken in H Ct R of the fact that interested individuals other than the applicant and the child are notified, but are not respondents. Paragraph 5 (2) of H Ct R refers to an individual under any disability, whereas (perhaps surprisingly) under Co Ct R minority is the only disability of a respondent that the guardian is specifically enjoined to report (but see note † on p 71) and Mag Ct R contain no mention of a respondent's disability. The excepting words at the beginning of para 2 are not applicable to magistrates' cases, and are therefore absent from Mag Ct R, as also is the para printed here as 12.

(*f*) such other information, including an assessment of the applicant's personality and, where appropriate, that of the child, as has a bearing on the mutual suitability of the applicant and the child and on the ability of the applicant to bring up the child;

(*g*) whether the applicant suffers or has suffered from any serious illness and whether there is any history of tuberculosis, epilepsy or mental illness in the applicant's family;

(*h*) particulars of all members of the applicant's household and their relationship (if any) to the applicant;

(*i*) particulars of the accommodation in the applicant's home and the condition of the home;

(*j*) the means of the applicant and, where appropriate, the rights to or interests in property (under dispositions already made) which the child stands to obtain if adopted;

(*k*) the applicant's religious persuasion, if any:

(*l*) whether any person specified in the application as a person to whom reference may be made is a responsible person and whether he recommends the applicant with or without reservations.

2 Except in the case of an application for a provisional adoption order, the guardian ad litem shall forthwith inform the court if it appears to him that the applicant or both applicants may not be domiciled in a part of the United Kingdom, the Channel Islands or the Isle of Man.

3 The guardian ad litem shall ascertain and inform the applicant:

(*a*) whether the child has been baptised and, if so, the date and place of baptism;

(*b*) what treatment the child has received with a view to immunising him against disease;

(*c*) what, if any, rights to or interests in property the child stands to retain or lose if adopted;

(*d*) whether an insurance policy for the payment on the death of the child of money for funeral expenses has been effected.

4 (1) The guardian ad litem shall, as soon as is reasonably practicable, ascertain whether the child is able to understand the nature of an adoption order.

(2) If, in the guardian's opinion*, the child is able to understand the nature of an adoption order, the guardian shall forthwith inform the court.

(3) The guardian shall, so far as practicable, ascertain the wishes and feelings of the child regarding the decision.

5 (1) The guardian ad litem shall interview either in person or by an agent appointed by him for the purpose every individual who is a respondent or who appears to him to have taken part in the arrangements for the adoption of the child.

(2) The guardian shall forthwith inform the court if, in his opinion, any respondent is under the age of majority†.

6 (1) The guardian ad litem shall obtain from every respondent, not being an individual, such information concerning the child as they have in their possession and which they consider might assist the court in deciding whether or not the child should be adopted by the applicant.

(2) Where such information is given in the form of a written report, the guardian ad litem shall append it to his own report to the court.

7 The guardian ad litem shall ascertain who has had actual custody of the child throughout his life and for what period or periods.

8 The guardian ad litem shall ascertain that every agreement to the making of an adoption order in pursuance of the application is freely and unconditionally given and with full understanding of what is involved.

9 Where either parent of the child is dead, the guardian ad

---

*The task of evaluating the extent of the child's understanding is thus put on the guardian. In a Scottish case the court said that a child of eight was too young to appreciate what was involved in adoption as distinct from custody (*AB, Petitioners* [1959] SLT (Sh Ct) 49).

†Cf the notes * on pp 65 and 69. A guardian ad litem of a respondent under a mental disability is necessary in the county court (CCR 1936, Ord 5, r 11; Co Ct R r 3 (2)). The usual procedure is explained in the County Court Practice, note to r 34 of the Co Ct R.

litem shall forthwith inform the court if he learns of any relation of the deceased parent who wishes to be heard by the court on the question whether an adoption order should be made.

10 Where the child is illegitimate but the putative father is not the guardian of the child or is not liable to contribute to his maintenance by virtue of any order or agreement the guardian ad litem shall forthwith inform the court if he learns* of any person, claiming to be the father, who wishes to be heard by the court on the question whether an adoption order should be made.

11 The guardian ad litem shall forthwith inform the court if he learns of any person who is or has been married to the mother or father of the child and who may have to be joined as a respondent.

12 The guardian ad litem shall forthwith inform the court if he learns of any other person or body who wishes or ought in his opinion to be heard by the court on the question whether an adoption order should be made.

13 Where appropriate, the guardian ad litem shall endeavour to obtain a report on the applicant's home and living conditions from a suitable agency in any country outside Great Britain in which the applicant is or has been living or resident.

(d) Information to be Confidential

The guardian's report, whether interim or final, is expressly declared to be confidential in H Ct R r 13 (4), Co Ct R r 11 (4) and Mag Ct R r 10 (4), and the rules are not in that respect *ultra vires (Re PA (an Infant)* [1971] 1 WLR 1530). This constitutes an exception to the general proposition that all facts presented to the court must be known to all parties, though in all proceedings concerning infants, not only adoption cases, that proposition is to be subordinated to the infant's welfare (*Official Solicitor* v *K* [1965] AC 201). As to information obtained by an agency, see p 160. Nevertheless, the judge has a discretion to

---

*This paragraph does not require the guardian to *seek out* the putative father (per Wilberforce J in *Re Adoption Application* 41/61 (*No* 2) [1964] Ch 48 at p 58).

disclose the contents of the report at the hearing (*Re G (TJ) (an Infant)* [1963] 2 QB 73; *Re M (an Infant)* [1973] QB 108); but the difficulties encountered in those cases because of allegations made in the report against a non-consenting parent are now alleviated by the rule (p 82) requiring the service of statements of fact where application is to be made for agreement to be dispensed with.

3 Parties

In the Family Division, the proposed adopter is described in the rules (and in the documents and the proceedings generally) as the applicant, and the child as the respondent (H Ct R r 4 (2)). There are no other respondents, as such, but by r 18 the proceedings are notified by the registrar to:

(*a*) each parent or guardian, not being an applicant, of the child;

(*b*) any local authority having the powers and duties of a parent or guardian of the child by virtue of CYPA 1969, s 24;

(*c*) any local authority in whom the parental rights and duties with respect to the child are vested, whether jointly or not, by virtue of CA 1948, s 2 as substituted by CA 1975, s 57;

(*d*) in the case of an application made after the future date from which CA 1975, s 60, is brought into force, any voluntary organisation in whom the parental rights and duties with respect to the child are vested, whether jointly or not, by virtue of that section;

(*e*) (unless otherwise directed) any person liable by virtue of an order or agreement to contribute to the maintenance of the child;

(*f*) the local authority to whom notice has been given at the commencement of the trial period (see p 30);

(*g*) any local authority or adoption society named in the application or in any form of agreement as having taken part in arrangements for the child's adoption;

(*h*) any local authority or voluntary organisation in whose care the child is under CA 1948, s 1, or under or within

the meaning of any other enactment;
- (*i*) (unless otherwise directed) in a case where a sole applicant is married and proposes to rely on the ill-health of his spouse as qualifying him as an applicant (see p 17), the applicant's spouse; and
- (*j*) any other person or body who in the registrar's opinion ought to be served with notice of the hearing of the application.

Head (*j*) might include the putative father of an illegitimate child if he did not fall within (*a*) or (*e*). He would not fall within (*a*) as a parent, but would do so as a guardian if he had been given custody by order under the Guardianship Acts (see p 37). If it appeared from the guardian's report (see para 10 under 'Particular Duties', above) that the father wished to be heard, he could be given his opportunity under this rule.

In *Re R* [1967] 1 WLR 34 Buckley J had to consider the contemporary rule corresponding to r 18 (*a*) in the case of parents to whom, for political reasons, danger might lie in an attempt to communicate with them. His lordship held that the rule related to practice and procedure and not to jurisdiction. It was intended for the benefit of the person to whom the notice was ordinarily to be given, and the court could at its discretion excuse compliance with it.

In the other courts the proposed adopter is the applicant and the respondents are the persons and bodies described in (*a*) to (*i*) above (Co Ct R r 4 (2); Mag Ct R r 4 (2)*), with the addition of any other person or body, *not being the child*, who the court at any time directs to be made a respondent (Co Ct R r 4 (3); Mag Ct R r 4 (3)). This might include, for example (as might (*j*) above as regards notification), the person who was the mother's husband at the time of the child's birth, where

---

*Mag Ct R r 4 (2) divides head (*h*) into two, without affecting the general correspondence of the two sets of rules in the inferior courts. (It slides Co Ct R r 4 (2) (*i*) down to Mag Ct R r 4 (2) (*j*).) But the change does draw attention to the fact that a voluntary organisation which has had actual custody of a child and then transfers him to an individual who does not have legal custody (as would be the situation of most proposing adopters) continues to have the child in its care by virtue of CA 1975, s 88 (*b*).

someone else is in fact the father (see 117 JP News 418, and cf 118 JP News 554), or, as suggested by Lord Parker CJ in *R* v *Liverpool City Justices* [1959] 1 All ER 337 at p 340, a close relation who is known to have sought custody of the child. Compare paras 9–12 of the guardian's particular duties, set out above.

The child is the sole respondent (in form) in the High Court. In the other courts he is not automatically to be made a respondent, but where he is considered by the guardian ad litem to be of sufficient age and understanding to understand the nature of an adoption order, the applicant in county court cases is to be given notice by the registrar in a prescribed form that the child's presence at the hearing will be necessary unless the judge, in special circumstances, should be prepared to waive the requirement (Co Ct R r 14 and Form 6). In the magistrates' court the notice to the applicant of the hearing is in similar circumstances to include a clause requiring the child's presence (Mag Ct R r 13 and Form 5).

4 Secrecy

(a) *General*

Section 21 (1) of CA 1975, as amended by DPMCA 1978, s 73, allows adoption proceedings in the High Court to be disposed of in chambers, while s 21 (2) declares that such proceedings in the county court shall be heard and determined *in camera*. 'Adoption proceedings' here include proceedings under Pt I of the CA 1975 or under AA 1958, 1960 or 1968 (s 21 (2A) of CA, added by DPMCA). Removal proceedings under s 34, 34A or 35 of the 1958 Act, and provisional applications under ibid, s 53, are now therefore included. Section 9 (5) of the 1958 Act, as extended by CYPA 1963, s 54, so as to cover removal and provisional proceedings, has, however, been left unrepealed (cf p 61).

Section 21 of CA 1975 no longer covers magistrates' courts. But, adoption proceedings before them now being domestic proceedings (see p 60), s 69 (2), (3) and (7) of MCA 1980 come into play. By these subsections, no person may be present during the hearing and determination by the court of adoption proceedings except officers of the court and parties to the case before the court, their solicitors and counsel, witnesses and other persons directly concerned in the case.

Publication of reports in a newspaper or periodical is restricted by s 71 of the 1980 Act. In adoption matters the only publication allowed is of submissions on any point of law which arises and the court's decision on them, and of the decision of the court on the case, including any observations made by the court in giving it. The section specifically mentions as being among the particulars which may *not* be given in any such publication (*a*) the child's name, address or school, (*b*) any picture as being or including a picture of the child, and (*c*) any other particulars calculated to lead to the identification of the child.

Note, too, the restriction on publishing information about proceedings relating to adoption where the court sits in private (Administration of Justice Act 1960, s 12 (1) (*a*), (4); and see *Re F (otherwise A) (a minor)* [1976] 3 WLR 813, CA). Parties to High Court proceedings may obtain transcripts without leave (Practice Note [1972] 1 WLR 443), and the court may for good reason, after taking account of all the circumstances, allow publication (*Re R (MJ) (a minor)* [1975] Fam 89).

Appeals to the Court of Appeal, whether from a High Court judge or from the county court, and appeals to the High Court from magistrates, whether by case stated or otherwise, were formerly, as a rule, heard in open court. Now, by s 1 of the Domestic and Appellate Proceedings (Restriction of Publicity) Act 1968, an appeal court may, on an application to it heard in private, in its discretion sit in private during the whole or part of a case in which the court below could sit in private. But, unless there are good grounds (which must be stated in public) to the contrary, the court's decision on the appeal and the reasons for it must be given publicly. A case stated is an appeal for this purpose.

In all the courts of first instance, all documents relating to proceedings under the Acts are to be kept in a place of special security while they are in the custody of the court (H Ct R r 30 (1); Co Ct R r 30 (1); Mag Ct R r 32). That part of the

Magistrates' Court Register kept under r 54 of the Magistrates' Courts Rules 1968, which relates to adoption proceedings, must be kept in a separate book (the Register of Adoptions) following Form No 17 in Mag Ct R (r 31).

Moreover, the rules provide that any information obtained by any person in the course of, and relating to, any proceedings under the Acts shall be treated as confidential and shall be disclosed if, but only if, the disclosure is necessary for the proper exercise of his duties; or if the information is requested by:

    (*a*) a court or public authority (whether or not within Great Britain) having power to authorise an adoption, for the purpose of its duties in that behalf; or

    (*b*) the Registrar General, or a person authorised in writing by him, where the information requested (i) relates only to the identity of any adoption society or local authority which made arrangements for the child's adoption or of a local authority which was notified of the applicant's intention, or (ii) is to the effect that no such adoption society or local authority so acted or no such notice was given in that case; or

    (*c*) a person authorised in writing by the Secretary of State to obtain it for the purposes of research (H Ct R r 29; Co Ct R r 30 (2); Mag Ct R r 33).

The instance at (*b*) above is consequential upon CA 1975, s 26 (p 130) as to an adult adopted person's right of access to his birth records.

These rules do not protect from disclosure in affiliation proceedings a statement made to a social worker four months before the birth of the child, though made with a view to adoption proceedings (*R* v *Nottingham Justices; ex parte Bostock* [1970] 2 All ER 641). But local authority records kept under the Boarding-Out Regulations are not to be produced in custody proceedings (*Re D (Infants)* [1970] 1 WLR 599) and the same would presumably be true in an adoption case. For the confidentiality of the guardian's report, see pp 72–73; and as to a member of a local authority seeing confidential papers, see pp 156–157.

(b) Serial Numbers

Apart from these precautions against general publicity, the Act and Rules allow the concealment of the identity of the applicant from the natural parent, in any case in which the applicant so desires. Thus, not only is the agreement of a necessary party not invalidated by his ignorance of the identity of the adopter (see p 38), but it is provided as follows:

(1) If any person who proposes to apply for an adoption order wishes his identity to be kept confidential, he may, *before* making or filing his application or issuing his summons, apply to the court for a serial number to be assigned to him for the purposes of the proposed application. The application for a serial number should be made to:

    (*a*) the Senior Registrar of the Family Division;
    (*b*) the registrar of the county court in question; or
    (*c*) the clerk to the appropriate justices;

and a number will be assigned to him accordingly (r 5 of the respective Rules).

(2) If a serial number has been so assigned, notices and documents supplied to parents and guardians must refer to the applicant only by that number, and the proceedings shall be conducted with a view to securing that he is not seen by or made known to any party not already aware of his identity, except with his consent (H Ct R rr 8 (2), 16, 20; Co Ct R rr 7 (2), 13 (2), 18; Mag Ct R rr 6 (4), 12 (2), 17). The procedure is designed to facilitate separate attendances by the applicant and by any such party (see pp 86–89).

5   Special Points of Evidence

(a) Medical

In certain cases the rules require a certificate as to the applicant's health and a report on the health of the child to be filed with the application, being exhibited to the applicant's affidavit in those Family Division matters in which they are required.

The certificate and report must be given and made by a fully registered medical practitioner. The cases in which they are required are those where no applicant is the father or mother of the infant *and* where the infant has not reached the upper limit of the compulsory school age (H Ct R r 9; Co Ct R r 8; Mag Ct R r 7). As to school age, see p 30. Forms of certificate and report, which are optional, are set out in the respective rules (see pp 182–183).

The report on the child's health must be made during the month preceding the date of the application if the child is less than a year old on that date, and in any other case during the six months before the application.

(b) Foreign Law

Where the application to the High Court or a county court is for a provisional order (see p 55), evidence of the law of adoption in the country of the appellant's domicile must be provided (H Ct R r 10; Co Ct R r 22 (3)). In the High Court an affidavit of expert evidence of the foreign law must be filed with the affidavit supporting the application. The expert must be a person who is suitably qualified on account of his knowledge or experience to give evidence as to the relevant law. No doubt he could be called to give oral evidence, and if there are opposing experts it may be necessary to require this. But ordinarily an affidavit by the expert will suffice. In the county court Ord 20, r 5, of the County Court Rules 1936, as to notice and supply of a copy of the affidavit, would ordinarily have to be complied with; but if the affidavit is sworn by a person qualified as mentioned in s 4 (1) of the Civil Evidence Act 1972, Co Ct R r 22 (3) makes this unnecessary, and the affidavit is admissible without notice.

Exceptionally an applicant might avail himself of s 4 (2) of the 1972 Act mentioned, under which previous recorded decisions or findings on foreign law of certain courts in this country, or of the Privy Council, are made prima facie binding if adduced in civil proceedings after prescribed notice.

(c) Identity of Child

It is, of course, necessary in all cases to identify the child referred to in the various forms of agreement and in the information obtained with the child to whom the order is to relate.

The exhibiting of birth or former adoption certificates to both application and agreement will, it is thought, in most cases be sufficient, and if this is done, Co Ct R r 19 (1) and (2) deems this procedure to be adequate to establish identity unless the contrary appears. Where any further proof is required it may apparently be given, in all courts, by affidavit; and there is a rule (Mag Ct R r 19 (1) and (2), authorised by s 9 (6) of the 1958 Act) expressly allowing this method of proof in the domestic court. The rule also provides that where such an affidavit is used the attendance of a witness at the hearing to prove the same fact is not to be compelled unless the fact is disputed or unless for some special reason the court so requires.

(d) Paternity

If it is necessary to determine whether or not some person is a parent of the infant, the evidence of a husband or a wife is now both admissible and compellable to prove that marital intercourse did or did not take place, and there is no longer any privilege, in civil proceedings, for communications during coverture (Civil Evidence Act 1968, s 16 (3) and (4)). The Family Law Reform Act 1969, Pt III, enables blood tests to be directed in accordance with RSC Ord 112; CCR Ord 46, r 23; and the Magistrates' Courts (Blood Tests) Rules 1971. For the method of taking, testing and reporting on samples, see SI 1971 No 1861, and the *Law Society's Gazette*, 23 February 1972, p 10. The present fee-scale for sampling and testing is in SI 1978 No 1266.

(e) Admissibility of Evidence

The rules normally contemplate the personal attendance of the applicant and of the guardian, and sometimes of the child. Any respondent (in the inferior courts) or person required to be served with notice of the proceedings in the High Court (see p 73) may also attend, or be heard at a special appointment (pp 86, 89). Any person attending may be allowed (in the court's discretion) to tender evidence *viva voce*, so long as the affidavit evidence which the rules require is complete and the guardian has reported as required.

No doubt the rule excluding hearsay evidence applies

generally to testimony about any matter that is in dispute. But that rule does not exclude evidence of an admission by a person who is a party if given against his own interest. In *Humberside County Council* v *DPR (an infant)* [1977] 1 WLR 1251 Lord Widgery CJ observed that in *non-adversary* proceedings (he was dealing with an application for a care order) it could not be right that the admissibility of a statement should depend on whether a person was formally a party or not, provided it was direct evidence of an admission by someone who was concerned with, or had control of, the child. It might be that this decision could have some relevance in adoption proceedings.

Evidence may possibly be given in documentary form if the conditions of s 1 of the Evidence Act 1938 (applicable in the magistrates' court) are fulfilled; or, in the High Court or the county court, under the more liberal provisions of Pt I of the Civil Evidence Act 1968, and the rules of court made thereunder, or (as regards expert evidence) under s 4 of the Civil Evidence Act 1972 (see also 'Foreign Law', p 79). Part I of the Civil Evidence Act 1968 has not, however, yet been applied to magistrates' proceedings. Neither has any part of the 1972 Act.

Questions which cannot be answered without acknowledging or referring to a conviction which is spent within the meaning of the Rehabilitation of Offenders Act 1974 are inadmissible in most kinds of judicial proceedings, and the spent conviction is in effect to be disregarded for most legal purposes. However, by s 7 (2) (*c*) of the Act, this does not apply to the determination of any issue, nor prevent the admission or requirement of any evidence as to convictions, or ancillary thereto, in any proceedings relating to adoption.

(*f*) *Grounds for Dispensing with Parental Agreement*

Where it is desired that the court shall dispense with the agreement of any parent or guardian on one or more of the grounds discussed at pp 42–49, admissible evidence in support must be adduced. The guardian's confidential report (see p 68) will no doubt contain material relevant on this matter, but it has been said in several cases that the report should not be accepted as such evidence, at all events unless the non-consenting parent is given an opportunity of rebutting any

D

allegations which it contains; and the difficulties of giving such an opportunity while respecting the confidential nature of the report have been emphasised (see eg *Re M (an Infant)* [1973] QB 108). It is for the proposed adopters to show that consent ought to be dispensed with, and in *Re F (R) (an Infant)* [1970] 1 QB 385, a case which was to be remitted for a rehearing, Salmon LJ said that it was vital for the court to see the adoptive parent, and the natural parent, who was objecting, and not simply to rely on affidavit evidence.

On the other hand, all the rules of court now require the scene to be set, at least, by the lodgment of documentary evidence. An applicant who intends to ask the court to dispense with a parent or guardian's agreement must do so (unless otherwise directed) either in his original application or by a subsequent notice to the court, supported in either case by a statement of the facts on which he intends to rely. In the High Court two copies of the statement must be exhibited to the supporting affidavit, if the dispensation is requested at the time of the original application, or *three* copies attached to the notice in other cases (H Ct R r 8 (1)). The rules in the county court require three copies of the statement in all cases, either attached to the originating application or to the notice (Co Ct R r 7 (1)). The statement itself, attached to the application or notice as the case may be, is all that the domestic court requires (Mag Ct R r 6 (3)). The statement must not disclose the applicant's identity if the case is one working under a serial number (see p 78). The parent or guardian in question is given notice of the dispensation application and a copy of the statement of facts (pp 84–85).

6   The Application and Subsequent Proceedings

(a) *Family Division*

(i) *Form of application*

An application to the High Court for an adoption order is made by originating summons issued out of the Principal Registry of the Family Division (H Ct R r 4 (1)). The form is numbered 1 in the Schedule to the Rules and is reproduced in Appendix I at p 175. Note that the names of the child to be given in the originating summons and in the supporting affidavit are the names by which the child is to be known if adopted. Notwithstanding the Rules of the Supreme Court (Writ and Appearance) 1979, the form of originating summons in the High Court Adoption Rules has not been amended so as to require the child (through the guardian ad litem or otherwise) to give any acknowledgment of service. Despite the wide wording of the new RSC Ord 7, r 2, and Ord 12, r 9, the Adoption Rules and form of summons prevail and no acknowledgment is necessary, for the RSC are applied only subject to the Adoption Rules (see H Ct R r 3 (2)). For the procedure by originating summons generally, see RSC Ords 7 and 28, particularly r 2 (2) of the latter. Form 1 provides, in case of need, for an application to appoint a guardian ad litem other than the Official Solicitor (see p 66), but the clause formerly included for second applications is now omitted in view of the new procedure provided for the jurisdiction to be examined by a judge in 'second bite' and step-parent cases (see p 85).

(ii) Service of summons

A copy of the summons must be served on the Official Solicitor, if he consents to be the guardian ad litem (H Ct R r 12 (1); see p 66), or on any other person appointed as guardian pursuant to an application contained in the originating summons (r 12 (2)). There is no provision for service on or notice to any other person at this stage. For mode of service, see p 93.

(iii) Evidence in support

This is to be given by affidavit in Form 2 (r 6; see Appendix I, p 176). It will be seen that the form calls, in addition to formal and historical particulars, for certain certificates to be exhibited; for the name and address of a referee as to the applicant—but this is required only when the applicant is not a parent or relative (as defined in the footnote on p 18) of the child; for an election as to the names and surname by which the child is to be known after adoption (see p 155); and for particulars of any proceedings relating wholly or partly to the child which have been completed or commenced in any court in England or Wales or elsewhere. The notes to the form are copious and instructive, and should be carefully studied.

The written agreement of all parents and guardians should be obtained in Form 3 (see Appendix I, p 181) and, if executed before the date of the application, should be exhibited to the affidavit (r 7 (1)). The name applied to the child in the agreement form is naturally that by which the person giving the agreement knows him, so that the surname at least will ordinarily differ, in High Court cases, from that used in the formal title of the proceedings.

If it is desired to ask the court to dispense with any person's agreement, the affidavit may be completed accordingly, two copies of the statement of facts (p 82) being exhibited; though the request for dispensation may alternatively be made by separate subsequent notice attaching three copies of the statement (r 8 (1)). There seems no time limit for a dispensation application by separate notice, but since a copy of it has to be sent to the guardian ad litem (r 15 (2)), it seems important that it shall be made in time not to hold up his report to the court. A sole married applicant, or one who is applying alone to adopt her or his own child, should state in the affidavit the grounds relied on (see pp 17, 19) and should exhibit any documentary evidence where appropriate.

If the date or country of the child's birth is uncertain, any relevant information should be collected and filled into para 6 of the affidavit. In the case of a child who is one of twins, the hour as well as the date of birth may become relevant. See also 'Special Points of Evidence', pp 78–81.

The evidence supporting the application is to be filed in the Registry within fourteen days (r 6) and copies served by the applicant on the guardian ad litem at the same time, or as soon thereafter as the guardian is appointed (see p 67) (r 12 (3)). On the filing of the affidavit the registrar notifies any consenting parent or guardian and *any* parent or guardian in a case to which s 34A of the 1958 Act applies (application by person with whom child has had his home for five years: see p 95) (r 14). The notice must inform the addressee of the making of the application and of the statutory prohibition on removal of the child imposed by s 34 or s 34A of the 1958 Act, as the case may be. The registrar must also, where practicable, inform a parent or guardian of any request made under r 8, above, to dispense with his agreement, sending him a copy of the statement of facts (r 15 (1)).

(iv) *Directions, appointment and notice of hearing*

When the guardian ad litem has completed his investigations and has made his report to the court (p 68), the registrar (subject to (v) below) fixes a date for the hearing of the application by a judge, first, however, giving such directions (if any) as he, the registrar, thinks necessary (r 17). When he has fixed the date, he must serve notice of the hearing on the applicant and the guardian, and on the persons mentioned in r 18, which is set out and discussed on pp 73–74.

(v) *Preliminary examination of jurisdiction*

There are two special cases, however, in which the registrar's course of action, as described, is arrested by r 11. This applies, in a High Court case, if it appears to the court that it *may*:

(a) be required to dismiss the application pursuant to s 10 (3) or s 11 (4) of CA 1975 (step-parent cases: see pp 20–22); or

(b) be precluded by s 22 (4) of that Act from proceeding to hear the application (second applications by the same person in respect of the same child: p 57).

In these cases, the application must thereupon be brought to the attention of a judge, and must not be proceeded with unless he or another judge gives directions as to the further conduct of the application.

A case affected by r 11 may be capable of being identified from the evidence which is lodged in support of the application, or its nature in the relevant sense may not come to light until the guardian reports on his investigation. A Practice Direction at [1976] 1 WLR 1267 lays down the procedure under r 11 as follows:

'All applications which appear to be governed by the rule will automatically be referred to a judge for his directions once the guardian has made his report to the court pursuant to r 13 (2). But if the applicant for the adoption order or the guardian ad litem wishes to apply to have this preliminary issue as to jurisdiction determined at an earlier stage, he may do so by applying ex parte to the registrar. The registrar will fix a date for the hearing of the preliminary examination by a judge in chambers and notice of the date will be sent by the court to the applicant and the guardian ad litem.'

In uncontested cases it is usually possible in practice for arrangements to be made to enable the judge, if he decides the preliminary question in the applicant's favour, to go on immediately to deal with the substantive application.

(vi) The hearing

Rule 20 in the H Ct R has to be observed in a serial number case (see p 78). The ordinary method of ensuring that the proceedings are conducted so as to secure that the applicant is not seen by or made known to any person who is not already aware of his identity, except with his consent, is for the registrar's notice to an individual in such a case *not* to disclose the day and time of the hearing, since that information might lead to the identification of the adopter, but by an alternative clause to advise the addressee, if he wishes to attend and be heard, to notify the registrar so that a further appointment may be fixed for his attendance.

At the hearing, or at such further appointment, any person entitled to notice under r 18 (p 73) may attend and be heard on the question whether an adoption order should be made; and local authorities and other bodies may be represented by authorised officers or servants (r 19). The applicant may be allowed to give oral evidence at the judge's discretion in addition to that put in by affidavit (cf Re W (Infants) [1965] 1 WLR 1259 at p 1284); and it may be that in some applications by a parent and step-parent it would be right for the judge to hear the other natural parent (cf *Re S (Infants)* [1977] Fam 173 at pp 178–179).

Order 32, r 5, of the RSC (applied by Ord 28, r 1, via H Ct R r 3 (2)) declares that where any party fails to attend, the court may proceed in his absence, if it thinks it expedient, after being satisfied as to service. It is considered preferable for the applicant to attend, but the court will proceed on the affidavit evidence if his attendance is shown to be impracticable or inconvenient. In that case there must be lodged a letter from the applicant confirming that the child has been continuously in his actual custody for three months preceding the hearing, in compliance with AA 1958, s 3 (see p 29, and the direction of Russell J referred to in the Supreme Court Practice at para 4305).

(b) *County Court*

(i) *Form of application*

An application for a full adoption order is made by filing an originating application in Form 1 (p 190) in the office of any county court authorised by or under CA 1975, s 100 (2) (see p 59) (Co Ct R r 4 (1), substituted by SI 1979 No 978). Some courts make a practice of explaining to an applicant in person, before the application is accepted, any difficulty which appears on its face, such as the possible relevance of CA 1975, s 10 (3) or, s 11 (4), or the need for a particular consent. Consultation at this stage with the social services department of the local authority may save the application fee.

The form of application is generally similar to the affidavit required in the High Court (see above), and is just as generously annotated. A point of difference, however, is that the county court form is headed with the child's birth certificate name; in the county court and the domestic court it is in the Schedule to the adoption order that the adoptive name is first officially applied to the child.

The form must be filed in duplicate, but no duplicates are required of the various documents that are required to be attached, except that three copies of the statement of facts are required in a dispensation case (rr 4 (4), 7 (1); see p 82). As to application for a number when it is desired to keep confidential the identity of the applicant, see p 78.

There is a special form (Form 7, p 192) for applications for a provisional order (Co Ct R r 22 (1)). This declares the applicant's intention to adopt the child under the law of (or within) the country of his domicile and his desire to remove the child from Great Britain for the purpose of adoption. The procedure in provisional cases continues as in others (Co Ct R r 22 (2)).

Apart from the case of a joint application in which it is desired to have the personal attendance of one of the applicants dispensed with (see *(iv)* below), it is not necessary to verify the application by affidavit.

As to originating applications generally, see Ord 6, r 4, of the County Court Rules 1936. Those rules apply subject to the modifications contained in the adoption rules (see p 63).

The requirements as to medical evidence, and in provisional order cases of evidence of foreign law, should be noted (see pp 78–79).

(ii) Preliminary examination of jurisdiction

As in the High Court, the Co Ct R contain a new provision (r 9) requiring the registrar to bring to the attention of the judge any matter falling within certain descriptions, and providing that in such a matter the application shall not be proceeded with unless the judge gives directions as to its future conduct. This situation arises if it appears that the court *may* be required to dismiss, or be precluded from hearing the application under CA 1975, s 10 (3), s 11 (4) or s 22 (4) (step-parent cases and second applications: cf pp 20, 57); or may for any other reason appearing in the application have no jurisdiction to make an adoption order. A county court may lack jurisdiction on geographical grounds, or because the application is expressed to be a Convention one, or discloses a lack of the conditions as to capacity applicable in non-Convention cases (see pp 16–23).

The terms of the Practice Direction (p 85) relating to this stage of High Court proceedings may be noted. That direction is not binding in county court matters, but there seems no reason why a county court judge should not follow it in so far as it postpones the preliminary examination required by r 9 until after the guardian's report is received. Cf also the High Court practice in uncontested cases of dealing with the substantive application immediately after the preliminary point is decided in the applicant's favour (p 86).

(iii) Appointment for hearing: notices

At the time of appointing the guardian ad litem (see p 67) the registrar fixes a date and time for hearing of the application and must serve notice on all the parties (see p 74), the notice for each respondent being in Form 5 (p 190), with a copy to the guardian ad litem. A note of service or non-service must be indorsed on a copy of Form 5 (Co Ct R r 12, and see County Court Rules 1936, Ord 8, r 9).

Form 5 contains alternative clauses, and also two optional ones. If addressed to a local authority, an adoption society, any other body of persons, or the spouse of the applicant, or in any case where the applicant does not desire anonymity, the notice shows the time and place for the hearing, and gives the addressee an opportunity of attending and being heard. But where the addressee is an individual other than the applicant's spouse, and the application is made under a serial number (see p 78), the day and time of the hearing are not disclosed but the addressee is invited, if he wishes to attend and be heard, to notify the registrar before a named day, so that a special time can be fixed for his appearance. The notice also recites the prohibition against removal of the child by parents or guardians who have agreed to the order, and in appropriate cases against removal where the child has had his home with the applicant for five years (see p 95); and if addressed to a parent or guardian with whose agreement the court has been asked to dispense, notice of that fact, a copy of the statement of facts being attached in that event. A perforated attachment to the form provides for an acknowledgment and reply.

Only the guardian ad litem is to be served with a copy of the application itself (Co Ct R r 12 (3)), and he is to receive also the attached documents (r 10 (1)). If a person files in the court office any notice or document copies of which are to be served by the registrar, a sufficient number of copies must also be lodged for service on the other parties and the guardian (Co Ct R r 32); but this does not apply to the applicant when lodging the application (p 87) or when applying to dispense with a parent's consent (p 82).

Where the court is notified by the guardian that he considers the child to be of sufficient age and understanding, as set out at p 71, the registrar must also serve on the applicant a notice in Form 6 (p 192) (Co Ct R r 14).

(iv) Hearing and attendance of parties

The proceedings must be heard and determined *in camera* (CA 1975, s 21 (2), as amended by DPMCA 1978, s 73).

Applicant The judge is not to make an adoption order or an interim order except after the personal attendance before him of the applicant, save that, if the application is made jointly under CA 1975, s 10, the judge may dispense with the personal attendance of one of the applicants if the originating application is verified by an affidavit sworn by him in the usual manner for county court affidavits (see s 87 of the County Courts Act 1959), or, if made outside the United Kingdom, attested by any person competent to attest an admissible form of agreement (see p 41) (Co Ct R r 15).

Child   If a notice in Form 6 (see above) is served, an adoption or interim order cannot be made unless:

(*a*) the judge is satisfied that the child has been informed of the nature and effect of the order, if made, and has been given an opportunity of expressing his wishes and feelings regarding the decision; *and*

(*b*) the child has personally attended before the judge, or it appears to the judge that there are special circumstances making that attendance unnecessary (Co Ct R r 16).

But where the judge had decided on consideration of the guardian's report and other matters *not* to make an adoption order, the Court of Appeal held that the fact that he had not seen the infant gave no ground for alleging a disregard of this rule (*Re G (an Infant)* [1963] 2 QB 73).

Respondents   They are given, by service on them of the notice in Form 5 (see above), an opportunity of attending and being heard, but their attendance is not essential to the making of the order, and by analogy with *Re R* (p 74), the judge could presumably in special circumstances dispense with service on a respondent. Local authorities and other bodies which are respondents may appear and be heard by authorised officers or servants (Co Ct R r 17). See p 86 as to the desirability, in many s 10 (3) cases (p 20) of hearing the non-applicant parent.

Guardian ad litem   There is now no rule requiring the guardian's presence at the hearing. Obviously, however, he may be ordered to attend, and Co Ct R r 11 (3) in effect gives him access to the court at any time (see p 68).

(v) Adjournment

The rules no longer prohibit the adjournment of the application at the instance of the applicant, but it is conceived that some adequate reason for such an adjournment would be required.

As to copies of an adoption order, costs, form and communication of an adoption order to the Registrar General, see pp 101–107 and 126.

(vi) Removal of proceedings to High Court

This course is open, under CA 1975, s 101 (1) (see p 62), on application to the High Court by any party, on such terms as to costs as the High Court thinks proper. The ex parte form of originating summons (Appendix A, No 11, unchanged by the new Writ and Appearance Rules) should be used, and the further procedure is detailed in RSC Ord 90, r 10, as supplemented by a Practice Direction at [1978] 3 All ER 960.

(c) Domestic Court

An application for an adoption order is made to a domestic court acting for the commission area (see p 60) within which the child is at the date of the application, by delivering or posting to the justices' clerk a written application in duplicate in Form 1 (see p 203) accompanied by all documents referred to in the application as being attached (Mag Ct R r 4 (1)). The documents attached need not be in duplicate or copied. They, and the contents of the form, are similar to those required in the High Court and county court (see above). The application must be signed by all applicants. As to keeping the applicant's identity confidential by means of a serial number, see p 78.

The rules as to:

(i) preliminary examination of jurisdiction (r 8);

(ii) appointment of guardian ad litem and date for hearing (rr 9, 11);

(iii) evidence of health (p 78) (r 7), documentary evidence of agreement, and statement of facts in a dispensation case (r 6);

(iv) notices (rr 11–13), attendance of parties (rr 14, 15, 17), and right of address (r 16)

correspond with the County Court Rules summarised above and the observations made on them are relevant also to domestic court matters. The verification of the statement of application necessary if the court is to dispense with the personal attendance of one of two joint applicants is to be by a declaration made by that applicant and attested by a justice of the peace or a justices' clerk or, if made outside the United Kingdom, by a person qualified to attest agreements (r 14, and see p 41).

The applicant is notified of the hearing in Form 5 (see p 209). If the child's attendance is required, this form includes an additional clause to that effect (r 13). Form 6 (p 210) is sent to respondents, and a copy of Form 6 must be endorsed with a note of service or non-service. The guardian is served by the court with copies of Forms 5 and 6, as well as of the application and with the documents attached thereto (r 11). It is not permissible for the guardian, or his representative, to retire with the justices (*Re B (Adoption by Parent)* [1975] Fam 127 at p 137). A note should be taken of any oral evidence (*Re JS* [1959] 1 WLR 1218 at pp 1222–3).

A magistrates' court may sit on any day of the year (MCA 1980, s 153).

See p 80 as to affidavit of identity.

7   Supervision or Care after Refusal of Adoption

Section 17 (1) of the 1975 Act confers on the court the power, when it refuses an adoption order in relation to a child under sixteen, to order:

(*a*) that the child be under the supervision of a specified local authority or probation officer, or

(*b*) that the child be committed to the care of a specified local authority.

DPMCA, s 72 (1), abrogates, as from 1 February 1981, the upper age limit of sixteen, so that thereafter the power to make an order under CA, s 17, is exercisable on any refusal of an adoption order.

To justify such an order it must appear to the court that there are exceptional circumstances. For a supervision order these must be exceptional circumstances making it desirable that the child should be under the supervision of an independent person; a care order may be made if the circumstances (being exceptional) make it impracticable or undesirable for the child to be entrusted to either of the parents or to any other individual.

In *Re S (a minor)* (1978) 122 SJ 759, a temporary care order was made so that the hand over from the unsuccessful applicant for adoption to the mother (who was taking the child abroad) could be achieved under supervision.

The cases envisaged will usually be non-agency cases. By s 17 (2) a care order may require the payment by either parent to the local authority of maintenance for the child in such weekly or other periodical sums as the court thinks reasonable. The supplementary provisions in ss 3 and 4 of the Guardianship Act 1973 (prospectively enlarged by CA 1975, Sched 3, para 80, and DPMCA, s 44 (2) and Sched 2, paras 41 to 43) are applied to a s 17 order as they apply to an order under s 2 of the 1973 Act (s 17 (3)).

Where a court proposes to make a *care* order under s 17 (1) (*b*), it must give the local authority in whose area the child is resident an opportunity of making representations. Where that authority has been served with notice (in the High Court) or is a party (in the inferior courts) and is before the court when the adoption order is refused, the court may proceed forthwith to hear its representations as to the making of a care or maintenance order (H Ct R r 22 (1), (2); Co Ct R r 20 (1), (2); Mag Ct R r 20 (1), (2)). If the authority is not a party or is not before the court, or if it makes representations about a maintenance order, sub-r (3) of the respective rules just mentioned obliges the registrar or the justices' clerk, as the case may be, to fix a time for the hearing of any representations from the authority and from each parent of the child; and to send notice thereof to the authority, the applicant, each parent and the guardian ad litem. Notice to an authority not a party or not already notified must be accompanied by a copy of the notice served under H Ct R r 18 (see p 73) or, in the inferior courts, on respondents (p 74).

8 Mode of Service

Any notice or information under the 1958 Act or under Pt I of CA 1975 may be given by post (AA 1958, s 55; 1975 Act, Sched 3, para 37).

Unless otherwise directed, any document under the rules may be served:

(*a*) on a corporation or body of persons by delivering it at or sending it by post to its registered or principal office;

(*b*) on any other person by delivering it to him or sending it by post to him at his last known or usual address (H Ct R r 31), place of abode (Co Ct R r 33), or place of residence (Mag Ct R r 34).

On principle a notice of adjourned hearing is to be served as for the original notice of hearing (cf *Unitt* v *Unitt* (1980) 124 SJ 80, decided on a different rule).

9   Proceedings after Interim Order

Where the determination of an application is postponed and an interim order made (see p 53):

In the Family Division the registrar, at least one month before the interim order expires, fixes a date for further hearing and, unless otherwise directed, serves notice of that hearing on all persons who were notified of the original hearing, including the applicant and the guardian (H Ct R r 28).

In the inferior courts also a time is fixed for the further hearing of the application. The registrar in the county court must do this not less than one month before the order's expiry if no time has been previously fixed (Co Ct R r 29 (1)). The rule in the domestic court requires the court to fix the further appointment on making the interim order or at any time thereafter but not less than a month before the expiry of the period named in the order, whether or not the applicant applies for the purpose (Mag Ct R r 21 (1)). There is no discernible substance in the variation of wording. The county court registrar serves notice of the hearing on the applicant and on the guardian (Co Ct R r 29 (2)) and, according to Co Ct R r 29 (3), serves every respondent with a notice in Form 5. But that form, when used after an interim order, needs adaptation as described in a general note to it (see p 191). The domestic court is to serve the applicant with Form 7 (p 211) and every respondent with Form 8 (p 212) (Mag Ct R r 21 (2)), the guardian being served with a copy of each.

If an interim order in respect of a child placed for adoption by an adoption society or local authority expires without an adoption order being made, the child must be returned to the society or authority (AA 1958, s 35 (4), and see p 162).

10   Applications concerning the Removal or Return of a Child

(a) Restriction where Adoption Agreed

Section 34 of the 1958 Act, as substituted by CA 1975, s 29, prohibits any parent or guardian, except with the leave of the court, from removing a child in respect of whom an application for adoption is pending from the custody of the person with whom the child has his home, against that person's will, when once that parent or guardian has agreed to the making of an adoption order, whether or not he knows the identity of the applicant for adoption (subs (1)).

Subsection (2) extends the restriction so that it will cover, when CA 1975, s 14 ('freeing' applications) is operative, a child in respect of whom a s 14 application is pending, if the child is in the care of the applicant-agency and there is at least one consenting parent or guardian. In a s 14 case, however, the prohibition against removal will operate only on a parent or guardian who has *not* consented. See further, and as to s 14, Appendix II, para 3.

(b) Restriction where Child Five Years with Applicant or Prospective Applicant

A further restriction is introduced in s 34A of the AA 1958 (see CA 1975, s 29). In form this protects the position of persons who have fostered a child for at least five years and who wish to adopt him: but the true purpose of the provision has been said to be to promote stability for the child himself. The period of five years is variable by statutory instrument subject to the affirmative procedure (s 34A (7)).

By s 34A:

(1) During the pendency of an adoption application by a person with whom the child has had his home for the five years preceding the application, no person may remove the child from the applicant's custody against the applicant's will, except with the leave of the court, or under authority conferred by any enactment (eg if the child has to be removed to a place of safety under the appropriate legislation) or on the arrest of the child (subs (1)).

(2) The same protection may be obtained temporarily by a *prospective* adopter who gives written notice to the local authority within whose area he has his home of his intention to apply for an adoption order, provided that the child has had his home with him for the five years preceding the notice. This protection lasts for three months from the giving of the notice, but continues under subs (1) above if the prospective adopter makes his adoption application within that time and so becomes an applicant (subs (2)). The effect of s 34A (5) is that a fresh notice cannot be given until after twenty-eight days from the expiry of the first.

The section clearly restrains principally parents or guardians who may find their recollections of the child stirred by being asked to agree to an adoption. But, subject to ss 35 and 36 of AA 1958 (see pp 162–163), local authorities in whose care (as distinct from actual custody) the child was before beginning to have his home with the foster parent are also prevented from removing the child without leave from the latter if the child remains technically in the care of that or any other local authority (s 34A (3), as amended by DMPCA 1978, Sched 2, para 18). In contrast to the position under s 34 (above), it is immaterial whether or not parents or guardians have agreed to an adoption, or are or are not prepared to do so.

The notice to the local authority seems to be distinct from that required in some cases under s 3 (2) (p 30), but it may presumably be given at the same time. The authority must within seven days of the receipt of a s 34A notice inform any other authority or voluntary organisation in whose care the child is known by it to be.

An application for leave to remove a child despite s 34 or 34A will be one of the many occasions on which courts, in reaching their decision, must observe the welfare principle enjoined by s 3 of CA 1975 (see p 8).

Though examples will be rare, ss 34 and 34A no doubt apply to cases where the adoption application is a Convention one under CA 1975, s 24.

(c) Breach of Restrictions

Where a child has been removed from the custody of a person contrary to s 34 or s 34A of the 1958 Act, that person may apply to the court (see p 62), which may then order the remover to return the child (1975 Act, s 30 (1)). If a person protected by s 34 or s 34A has reasonable grounds for believing that another person is intending to remove the child from his custody in breach of either of those sections, the court may, on his application, by order direct that other person not to remove the child contrary to the section in question (subs (2)).

Section 30 (3) and (4) provide auxiliary sanctions for the enforcement of orders under the section. The ordinary powers of enforcement will apply, varying as the order is mandatory or prohibitory. In addition, if the High Court or a county court has made an order for return of a child and the court which made the order (or, in the case of a county court order, any county court) is satisfied that the child has not been returned, it may make an order authorising one of its officers to search specified premises and to return the child, if found, to the applicant. A justice of the peace who is satisfied by information on oath that there are reasonable grounds for believing that a child to whom a return order relates is in specified premises may (by whichever court the order was made) issue a search warrant to a constable, who is to return the child to the applicant if he finds him.

(d) Procedure

Applications under s 34 (1) or s 34A (1) or (2) of the 1958 Act, or under s 30 (1) or (2) of CA 1975, are regulated by H Ct R r 23; Co Ct R r 21; and Mag Ct R r 28 or r 29 according to circumstances. All such proceedings in the High Court are now within s 21 (1) of CA 1975, and may therefore be disposed of in chambers; in the county court they fall within the amended version of ibid, s 21 (2), and must therefore be heard and determined *in camera*; while magistrates' proceedings under the sections mentioned are included in the new definition of domestic proceedings (see p 62).

In appropriate cases a wardship application in the High

Court may be found to be more effective or convenient as a method of countering a threatened or apprehended removal attempt. In the wardship proceedings the court's leave may be sought to make or pursue an adoption application (see p 26).

A *High Court* application under r 23 is made by summons in the proceedings if an application for an adoption order is pending; otherwise by an originating summons or, if an originating summons under the rule is already pending, by a summons in the proceedings so constituted (r 23 (2)). By r 23 (3) (as slightly amended by SI 1978 No 1519) the registrar is to give such directions as he thinks necessary before fixing a date for the hearing by a judge; this sub-rule is amplified by a Practice Direction at [1976] 1 WLR 1267 which directs an applicant under r 23 to lodge in the registry two copies of the summons or originating summons, endorsing thereon an estimate of the likely length of the hearing. No date of hearing will be allotted until the summons has been considered by the registrar. After fixing the date and giving necessary directions, the registrar notifies the applicant and serves a copy of the summons or originating summons:

(a) where adoption proceedings are pending (and this includes a case where they have been commenced after the summons), on the applicant in those proceedings and the guardian ad litem and every person entitled to notice under r 18 (see p 73);

(b) in any other case, on any person against whom an order is sought, on any local authority notified under AA 1958, s 3 (see p 30), and on any other person or body who, in the registrar's opinion, ought to be served.

In the *county court*, if adoption proceedings are pending, the application under s 34, s 34A or s 30 (above) is made in the same proceedings on notice to the registrar under Ord 13, r 1, of the County Court Rules 1936; in any other case, by an originating application, filed in the office of the court within whose district the applicant lives or, in s 34A cases, where the child is (Co Ct R r 21 (2)). (Rule 21 (2) (b) refers to an originating application as being filed under Ord 6, r 1; but presumably Ord 6, r 4, is intended.) A respondent to such an originating application who wishes to claim relief (for instance, in an 'intended removal' case under s 30 (2) the respondent may want to cross-apply for leave to remove) must do so by means of an answer to the application made within seven days of service of a copy of the application on him (r 21 (3)).

On the filing of an originating application, the registrar fixes a day for the hearing; in the case of an interlocutory notice in existing proceedings, the court office should be consulted as to the date, time and place to be inserted in the notice as particulars of the appointment for hearing (cf Ord 13, r 1 (1) (*b*) (ii)).

The registrar must serve a copy of the application, and of any answer, and a notice of the time of the hearing:

   (*a*) if the application is made in pending proceedings, on all other parties and on the guardian ad litem;

   (*b*) in the case of an originating application:

     (i) under s 34 (1) or s 34A (1) or (2) on the prospective adopter and on the local authority to whom he has given notice;

     (ii) under s 30 (1) or (2) on the person against whom the order is sought, and on the local authority to whom the prospective adopter has given notice;

   (*c*) in the case of an answer, on all the other parties to the application under r 21, and on the guardian ad litem, if any (r 21 (4)).

The court may at any time give directions as to the conduct of any application or answer under r 21 (r 21 (7), (11)). In particular, directions may be given as to the appointment of a guardian ad litem of the child. Unless directed otherwise, a prospective adopter (see s 34A (2) of the 1958 Act: p 96) who is served with a copy of a r 21 application or answer and who wishes to oppose it, must file his adoption application within fourteen days, or before or at the time when he is heard on the r21 application, whichever the sooner (r 21 (6), (11)). If a special direction is given under r 21 (6), the court must give further directions under para (7) as to the conduct of the application or answer (r 21 (7), (11)).

In the *domestic court* an essentially similar procedure is laid down, as regards applications for removal. Form 15 or Form 16 (pp 218–219) as the case may be, must be delivered or posted to the justices' clerk of the court hearing the adoption application (Mag Ct R r 28 (1): ss 34, 34A (1)), or of the court within whose commission area the child is or, if that is not known, where the applicant for removal lives (r 28 (2): s 34A (2)); unless, in either of the cases mentioned, proceedings have already been begun for an order for the return of the child, or for his removal to be prohibited. Return and prohibition proceedings are to be by way of complaint (r 29 (1)), the appropriate court being the domestic court in which any adoption application is pending, or, if none, that in whose commission area the complainant lives. If any such complaint is pending, removal applications under s 34, s 34A (1) or s 34A (2) must be made to the court which is dealing with it (r 28 (3)). Other sub-rules of r 28 describe the persons to be served, deal with directions and other matters, and apply the ordinary adoption rules as to fixing and notifying the hearing, costs, confidentiality etc (r 28 (11)). A justice's search warrant under CA 1975, s 30 (4) (above), is to be in Form 10 of the Magistrates' Courts (Children and Young Persons) Rules 1970, or to the like effect (r 29 (2)).

In *all courts* there are rules designed to ensure that the serial number system (p 78) protects the proceedings on the application for removal etc (H Ct R r 23 (5); Co Ct R r 21 (5) ; Mag Ct R r 28 (6)); and in addition the High Court and county court rules allow a person who proposes to apply for an adoption order but has occasion earlier to seek an order for return, or restraint of removal, to obtain a serial number for the purposes of the s 30 application, with the same consequences as if it had already been assigned to him in adoption proceedings.

Events on and after the determination of the application for removal or return are dealt with in H Ct R r 23 (6) and (7), in Co Ct R r 21 (9) and (10) and in Mag Ct R r 28 (9) and 29 (3). A court which grants leave to remove a child from the custody of a proposing or prospective adopter, or which refuses to order the child's return or to prohibit its allegedly intended removal, may pursue the logic of its decision by treating the application as the hearing of the adoption proceedings (if these are in being) and refusing an adoption order accordingly. A parent or guardian whose application for leave to remove the child has failed is not precluded as a matter of law from objecting in the adoption proceedings, withdrawing any agreement he may have given, but in those circumstances he perhaps runs a special risk of having his agreement dispensed with as being unreasonably withheld.

Notice of the effect of the determination of any application falling within H Ct R r 23, Co Ct R r 21 or Mag Ct R r 28 is to be served by the court on all parties, or persons served with notice of the application, except, in the domestic court, any parties who were present at the determination.

A point of jurisdiction needing to be watched may arise if it becomes necessary to enforce before magistrates an order made in an adoption matter, for instance one concerning the removal of a child. Whilst original proceedings under the Adoption Acts are domestic proceedings (p 60), that is not so in the case of proceedings for the enforcement of an order made under those Acts (MCA 1980, s 65 (1) (i)), unless the court thinks fit to make a positive order to that effect under s 65 (2); or unless, exceptionally, s 65 (3) applies because the enforcement proceedings are heard with ordinary domestic proceedings between the same parties. A separate bench sitting in public may, therefore, have to be constituted for enforcement purposes.

11 The Order

(a) Form and Copies

Adoption, provisional adoption, and interim orders made in a county court are to be drawn up in the forms numbered 8 and 11 in Sched 1 to the rules (Co Ct R rr 25 (1), 27). The corresponding forms in the domestic court are numbered 9 and 13 in Sched 1 to the relevant rules (Mag Ct R rr 22 (1), 24). (See pp 195, 201, 212 and 216, and as to recall of an order before entry, see p 105.) A feature introduced in 1976 is the inclusion, as part of the order, of an Appendix recording certain matters which ordinarily merge in the making of the order, but which may nevertheless need to be referred to in the future. These are the grounds on which the court decided to dispense with the agreement of a named parent or guardian, or was satisfied that a married sole adopter or a parent who is a sole adopter fulfilled the terms of s 11 (1) (b) or (3) of CA 1975.

The function of the Appendix is to meet a suggestion made by members of the Court of Appeal in *S* v *Huddersfield Borough Council* [1975] Fam 113 at pp 119 and 125, where it was said that, dispensing with consent being a judicial act bearing directly on the propriety of making an adoption order, it should be recorded in the order. The prescribed forms go further, indeed, and provide for the record to show the grounds on which the dispensation with agreement was based. The Appendix, as a result of Co Ct R r 31 (5) and Mag Ct R r 25 (3), is excluded from any copy or abridgement of the order supplied to the applicant or to any person other than the Registrar General.

An abridged copy of a full or provisional order in Form 9 (p 198) is prepared for the applicant in the county court. In the juvenile court it is in Form 10, and is signed by a member of the court or the clerk (Co Ct R r 25 (2); Mag Ct R r 22 (2)).

Where an adoption order is made by a court sitting in Wales in respect of a child who was born in Wales (or who is treated under r 19 (4) of the respective rules (see p 105) as having been born in the district in which that court sits), then if the adopter so requests before the order is drawn up the order and the abridged copy must contain a prescribed bilingual schedule in Form 10 instead of the schedules in Forms 8 and 9 (Co Ct R r 26 (1)); or, as the case may be (in domestic court cases), bilingual schedules in Forms 11 and 12 instead of the schedules in Forms 9 and 10 (Mag Ct R r 23 (1); for the forms, see pp 215, 216). In such cases the order and the abridged copy must each specify in both English and Welsh the particulars to be entered under headings 2 to 6 of the bilingual schedule to the order, the English text prevailing in case of any discrepancy between the two texts (Co Ct R r 26 (2); Mag Ct R r 23 (2)).

No special form of order is prescribed for High Court cases. The ordinary practice of the Family Division applies; though it may be noted that the 'sweeping-up' reference in H Ct R r 3 (2) is to the RSC, and not (as in the case of orders drawn up in the same Division on adoption appeals from magistrates) to the Matrimonial Causes Rules (see p 63). There is no mention in the High Court rules of an abridged copy, or of the Appendix, but by r 25 (3) the registrar may omit from the copy order sent to the applicant any information which, in the registrar's opinion, need not appear in the copy; and r 25 (4) contains a provision corresponding with Co Ct R r 26 to ensure that at the option of the adopter under an order made by the High Court sitting in Wales in respect of a Welsh child, or one treated as such, the particulars in the order required for registration purposes shall be specified in both English and Welsh.

By the combined effect of several rules, no copy or abridged copy of any order made under the 1958 or the 1975 Act, or any previous enactment relating to adoption, may be supplied by the registrar or justices' clerk except:

(*a*) to or at the request of the Registrar General (H Ct R rr 25 (1), 26 (*b*); Co Ct R rr 25 (1), 31 (2); Mag Ct R rr 22 (1), 25 (1) (*b*)); or

(*b*) to an applicant, or on his request (H Ct R rr 25 (1) (2), 26 (*c*); Co Ct R rr 25 (2), 27 (abridged copies), 31 (3); Mag Ct R rr 22 (2) (abridged copy), 24, 25 (1) (*b*)); or

(*c*) on the application of any other person, under an order of the judge in the High Court or the county court or, in the magistrates' court, a domestic court for the same petty sessions area as the court in which the order was made (H Ct R r 26 (*d*); Co Ct R r 31 (4); Mag Ct R r 25 (1) (*c*)); or

(*d*) to any person entitled to request or authorised to obtain information under H Ct R r 29; Co Ct R r 30 (2); or Mag Ct R r 33 (see p 77).

Except under (*a*) and (*d*) the rules in the inferior courts require the omission of the Appendix from any copy supplied in accordance with these exceptions.

Within seven days of the making of an order or interim order, as the case may be, the applicant is to be sent or handed a copy or abridged copy (see above) (H Ct R r 25 (1), (2); Co Ct R rr 25 (2), 27; Mag Ct R r 22 (2), 24).

Notice of the making of or refusal to make an adoption order, or of the making of an interim order, is to be given to all the persons on whom notice was served under r 18 (H Ct R r 24 (1): see pp 73–74), on every respondent (Co Ct R r 24 (1)), or in the domestic court on all persons who were served with notice under r 11 (1) (pp 91–92) but were not present when the court made its determination or order (Mag Ct R r 26 (1)). In the domestic court, too, notice to the same persons must be given if the application is withdrawn or not proceeded with (r 26 (2)). All the sets of rules require the notice of a refusal to make an adoption order to include particulars of any order made under CA 1975, s 17 (H Ct R r 24 (2); Co Ct R r 24 (2); Mag Ct R r 26 (1)). In addition, notice of an *adoption* order must be served on any court in Great Britain which appears to have made an order of the kind referred to in s 8 (3) of CA 1975, namely, one vesting in a person other than a parent or guardian any parental right or duty relating to the child, or imposing a duty to make maintenance payments for the child (H Ct R r 24 (3); Co Ct R r 24 (3); Mag Ct R r 26 (3)). The obvious example is an affiliation order, but cf p 152.

In the Family Division and in the county court the registrar serves these notices; in the domestic court, the justices' clerk.

(b) *Directions to Registrar General*

By s 21 (1) of the 1958 Act, as amended by CA 1975, Sched 3, para 24, every adoption order must direct the Registrar General to make an entry in the Adopted Children Register (see p 124) in such form as the Registrar General may by regulation specify. The relevant regulations are the Forms of Adoption Entry Regulations 1975 (SI 1975 No 1959) and set out two schedules of particulars to be entered pursuant to orders made by courts sitting in England or Wales, as the case may be. The schedules correspond exactly with those pre-scribed by Co Ct R and Mag Ct R as part of the forms of order to be drawn up in the inferior courts (see pp 197 and 214). Thus the court initiates the particulars to be entered.

The English form requires (*inter alia*):

(a) Date and country of child's birth with the registration district and sub-district if the birth was in England or Wales. All the rules of court provide that where the precise date is not proved to the satisfaction of the court, the court shall 'give the child a birthday' by determining the probable date of his birth, and may specify it in the order (H Ct R r 21 (1); Co Ct R r 19 (3); Mag Ct R r 19 (3)). The country may be omitted if not proved to the court's satisfaction; except that if it is proved to the court's satisfaction that the child was born in England or Wales, or if it appears probable that the child was born within the United Kingdom, the Channel Islands or the Isle of Man, he may be treated as born in the registration district and sub-district in which the court sits (H Ct R r 21 (2); Co Ct R r 19 (4); Mag Ct R r 19 (4)).

(*b*) Name and surname of child. The notes to the form of order show that the names to be specified are the name or names and surname stated in the adoption application, or, if none is there stated, the child's original name or names and the applicant's surname. 'Name' and 'surname' appear here to be distinguished the one from the other so that 'name' must refer to a Christian or forename (see further p 155).

(*c*) Sex of child.

(*d*) Name, surname, address and occupation of adopter or adopters.

(*e*) Date of order and description of court making it.

As to directing the marking of birth registers, see pp 125–127.

12 Alteration and Amendment of Orders

The court may change its mind, at any rate in the High Court or county court, and recall its order at any time before it is passed and entered. But, just as the making of the order is discretionary in a judicial sense so any change must be arrived at by a judicial exercise of discretion (*R* v *Colchester and Clacton County Court* (1979) 9 Fam Law 155, in which, in the absence of reasons given by a county court judge the Queen's Bench Divisional Court directed him by mandamus to perfect his order).

The court has statutory power to amend an adoption order which it has made by correcting errors and, as regards pre-1950 orders, by inserting certain particulars. The possibilities may be summarised as follows:

Provision of AA 1958	Nature of amendment	On whose application	Court must be satisfied:
1 s 24 (1)	Correction of any error in the particulars contained in the order	Adopter or adopted person	No specific requirement, but the power appears to be discretionary (see below).
2 s 24 (1) (a)	Substitution or addition of new name (see below) in particulars to be entered in Adopted Children Register	Adopter or adopted person	That within one year from date of order a new name has been given to the adopted person (whether in baptism or otherwise), or taken by him, either in lieu of or in addition to a name specified in the particulars.
3 s 24 (1) (b); Sched 5, para 6 (1)	Revocation of a direction for marking an entry in Registers of Births or Adopted Children Register included in the order under s 21 (4) or (5) of the Act (see p 125) or under s 18 of AA 1950	Any person concerned	That the direction was wrongly included in the order.
4 Sched 5, para 6 (2)	Amendment of particulars specified in an order made under previous Adoption Acts to bring the order into the form it would have taken if s 21 of the Adoption Act 1958 (see 'Directions to Registrar General' above) had applied to it	Adopter or adopted person	No specific requirement, but the paragraph is permissive. If the application is for amendment of an order not specifying the surname of the adopted person, his surname one year after the order may be added in the particulars instead of the adopter's surname (if different).

These powers are conferred in each case only on the court by which the original order was made (s 24 (1)), but, in relation to a magistrates' court, that expression includes a court acting for the same petty sessions area (s 24 (7)). Under the rules, the application may be made ex parte in the first instance, but the court may require notice to such persons as it thinks fit. A form is prescribed for use in the domestic court (Form 14, p 217) (H Ct R r 24 (1); Co Ct R r 28 (1); Mag Ct R r 24 (1), (2)).

Head 1 is a wide power, not merely a jurisdiction to correct slips. Thus, justices were directed by the Divisional Court in *R v Chelsea Juvenile Court Justices (Re an Infant)* [1955] 1 All ER 38 to hear and determine an application under the subsection to substitute in the order a new recital of the identity and a different date of birth on information not previously before the court.

Under head 2 the power is apparently confined to forenames and Christian names, to judge from the context and from the absence of any reference to surname, a word used distinctively in other provisions of the 1958 Act.

13 Costs

On the determination of an application for an adoption order, and on the making of an interim order, an inferior court may make such order as to costs as it thinks just, and in particular may order the applicant to pay:

(a) the out-of-pocket expenses incurred by the guardian ad litem;

(b) the expenses incurred by any respondent in attending the hearing or such part of those expenses as the court thinks proper (Co Ct R r 23; Mag Ct R r 30 (1)).

The 'determination of an application' includes, on the ordinary meaning of the words, a refusal of an application. In the domestic court the expression is extended also to cover a refusal by an applicant to proceed with his application, or his withdrawal of it (Mag Ct R r 30 (2)).

There is no express mention of costs in the H Ct R, except that the form of originating summons asks that they be provided for. They are therefore in the complete discretion of the judge. In the ordinary way they will be payable by the applicant. As to the costs of the Official Solicitor as guardian ad litem, see p 66.

Chapter IX

Revocation of Adoption after Legitimation

A power which the court still possesses despite the modern rationalisation of legitimacy law is that of revoking adoption orders made in favour of parents of children who, subsequently to the adoption, become legitimated on the marriage of the parents. Such legitimation is now possible, in the case of an adopted person, only if either natural parent is the *sole* adoptive parent (CA 1975, Sched 1, para 3 (2); Legitimacy Act 1976, s 4 (1)). But the court's power of revocation under AA 1958, s 26, as originally enacted was, in any event, limited to a case of a person adopted by his father or mother alone. (For revocation in similar circumstances of Convention adoptions effected overseas, see p 113.)

The application to revoke an adoption order made in the United Kingdom, whether as a Convention adoption order or otherwise,* may be made by any of the parties concerned and lies to the court by which the adoption order was made (AA 1958, s 26 (1)); or, in the case of an order made by a magistrates' court, to any court for the same petty sessions area (s 26 (3)). The procedure is the same as on an application to amend an order (H Ct R r 27; Co Ct R r 28; Mag Ct R r 27: see p 106).

The adoption may have been at any time. But s 26 applies only where the legitimation takes place *on the parents' marriage*. Legitimation did not so take place, by English law, in the case

---

*Convention adoption orders are put on the same footing as other United Kingdom orders in this respect by DPMCA 1978, Sched 3, repealing CA 1975, Sched 3, para 26.

of any marriage before 29 October 1950 either party to which was married to a third person when the child was born. In those circumstances, the child became legitimate on the date mentioned, ie on the passing of the Legitimacy Act 1959.

Standing by itself, then, s 26 of AA 1958 did not cover *past* adoptions by parents whose marriage derived its legitimising force from the reform introduced by the Legitimacy Act 1959, s 1. This was thought to discriminate unfairly against some adopted persons who wished to have the record of their adoption *by their natural parents* expunged from the public registers (see p 125) for personal reasons. Accordingly s 1 (1) of AA 1960 extended s 26 of AA 1958 so as to authorise a revocation order in a case where a person legitimated *by s 1 of the Legitimacy Act 1959* had been adopted by his father *and* mother before 29 October 1959. This obsolescent instance is the only joint case in which revocation is possible.

The case that would stand to benefit in a material sense from a revocation order under s 26 of the 1958 Act is that of a child adopted in 1974, say, by its mother only, the mother then marrying the father and both parents dying before 1 January 1976. In that case Sched 1 to CA 1975 would not apply and if the adoption order persisted, the adopted child would not be entitled to share in its father's estate on intestacy. The child would become legitimate, but under AA 1958, s 16, would fall to be treated as 'not the child of any other person' than his mother for the purposes of intestate succession, not (eg) of his father. As regards events after 1975, however (eg if the father in this example had died in January 1976 or later), CA 1975, Sched 1, para 13 (2) (a) (repealed by the Legitimacy Act 1976, and re-enacted as s 4 (2) (a) of that Act) preserves the child's relationship to its natural father despite adoption by its mother (and vice versa), so that revocation under s 26 is henceforth unnecessary so far as concerns disposition or devolution of property (cf s 5 of the Legitimacy Act 1976).

Revocation of the adoption order, whether under s 26 of the 1958 Act or under s 1 of that of 1960, does not affect the operation of the proprietary rights provisions of CA 1975, Sched 1 (see p 145) as they apply to an intestacy occurring or a

disposition made before the date of the legitimation
(Legitimacy Act 1976, s 4 (2) (*b*)).

Chapter X

Jurisdiction to Neutralise Overseas Adoptions

1   Definitions

The 1968 Act, pursuant to the Hague Convention (see p 6), contains provisions with regard to adoptions effected in countries outside Great Britain. It distinguishes and specially defines two categories of such adoptions, as follows:

1 'Overseas adoptions', namely, adoptions of such a description as the Secretary of State may by order specify, being a description of adoptions of infants appearing to him to be effected under the law of any country outside Great Britain (s 4 (3)).

The only order so far made under the section is the Adoption (Designation of Overseas Adoptions) Order 1973 (SI 1973 No 19). Its schedule lists many Commonwealth countries and United Kingdom dependent territories and also a number of other countries and territories, and should be referred to for its contents. Article 4 specifies the manner in which evidence of an overseas adoption may be given, namely, by production of a document purporting to be a certified copy of an entry in a public register of adoptions made according to the law of the country or territory concerned, or a certificate of adoption purporting to be signed as authorised by the appropriate law, or a certified copy of such a certificate. Proof by other means that an overseas adoption has been effected is not precluded.

2 'Convention adoptions', a narrower class, which by virtue of SI 1978 No 1432, art 3 (made under s 5 (2)) are overseas adoptions regulated by the Hague Convention. Again an authorised method of giving evidence that an overseas adoption which has been effected is so regulated is specified. Article 4 of SI 1978 No 1432, while not precluding proof by other means

allows proof by the production of a certified copy or certificate
as described in para 1 above relating to 'overseas adoptions',
provided that the document shows, or certifies as the case may
be, that the adoption is regulated by the Convention. Clearly
only adoptions effected in Convention countries (see p 25) can
be regulated by the Convention.

As a matter of distinctive terminology, the term 'Convention
adoption order' is used to mean an English or Scottish adoption
order made as mentioned in s 24 of CA 1975 (s 107 (1)) (ie, in
practice, a Convention adoption order made in Great Britain);
while 'Convention order' is simply a marking pursuant to AA
1968, s 8 (1), placed in the register to denote a Convention
adoption order (see p 124).

2   Annulment, Revocation etc in England of Overseas Adoptions

Schedule 1 to CA 1975 includes overseas adoptions with
adoptions of other kinds in describing the status conferred by
adoption and its other effects in English law (see p 136).
Overseas adoptions have been generally recognised since 1
January 1973 (the date when s 4 of the 1968 Act, now absorbed
in CA 1975, was brought into force); and AA 1968, ss 6 and 7,
did not become operative until 23 October 1978. Under s 6 the
High Court may review on stated grounds certain overseas
adoptions and determinations related to them. As to the
validity of such adoptions etc in default of (or subject to the
result of) such review, see p 142.

The court's positive powers under the 1968 Act may
generally be described as powers of annulment, revocation and
invalidation in Great Britain, annulment and revocation
applying only to Convention adoptions of which it can be
postulated that immediately before the application to the
English court the person adopted or the adopter resides in
Great Britain or, as the case may be, both adopters reside there
(s 7 (2)).

By s 24 (8A) of the 1975 Act (added by DPMCA 1978, s 74
(1)) the power of annulment under s 6 (1) of AA 1968 is conferred on the High Court in relation to a Convention adoption
order which it has made. There is no such extension to United

Kingdom Convention adoption orders of the other powers here under discussion.

(a) Annulment

The grounds on which the court may so annul a Convention adoption are set out in s 6 (1). They are:

(*a*) that at the time the adoption took effect, it offended a prohibition contained in the national law of the adopter or adopters as notified to or by the United Kingdom government as being then in force, and specified in an order of the Secretary of State, if the adoption could have been impugned on that ground under that law (for notified and specified provisions in the cases of Austria and Switzerland, see SI 1978 No 1431, Scheds 1 and 2);

(*b*) that at the time the adoption took effect it contravened the consent provisions of the adopted person's national law, if under that law the adoption could have been impugned on that ground;

(*c*) that on any other ground the adoption can be impugned under the law in force for the time being in the country in which it was effected.

An application for an order *under s 6 (1)* is not to be made (except with the court's leave) later than two years after the date of the adoption to which it relates (Convention Adoption Rules 1978, r 13 (2)).

(b) Revocation

The High Court may revoke a Convention adoption upon an application by the parties concerned if, having been adopted by his father alone or his mother alone, a person has subsequently become legitimated on the marriage of his father and mother (s 6 (2)). This complements the power of revoking United Kingdom orders (whether made under the Convention or otherwise) on the same ground, as discussed on p 108. The use of the word 'revoke' rather than 'annul' underlines the distinction between s 6 (2), which applies only to (overseas) Convention adoptions, and s 6 (1), which is applied also (by CA, s 24 (8A)) to Convention adoption orders made here.

E

(c) Invalidation in Great Britain

By s 6 (3) the High Court has control over any overseas adoption and over certain determinations by an authority of a Convention country or specified country; namely, determinations to authorise or review the authorisation of a Convention adoption or a specified order, or to give or review a decision revoking or annulling such an order or an adoption order made under the 1968 Act. The reference here to a determination of a *specified* country (Northern Ireland has alone been specified to date: SI 1978 No 1432, art 6) relies on the definition of 'determination' in s 7 (4) as bringing into s 6 (3) by a side wind the terms of s 5 (1) (see pp 136–137). Section 6 (3) thus covers determination by specified as well as Convention authorities.

The power of the High Court extends to ordering that such an overseas adoption or such a determination shall cease to be valid in Great Britain, or to deciding the extent, if any, to which such a determination has been affected by a subsequent determination (s 6 (3)). The grounds on which an order invalidating an adoption or determination in Great Britain may proceed are that it is contrary to public policy, or that the authority in question was not competent to entertain the case, and for this purpose the court is bound by any finding of fact made by the authority and stated to be so made for the purpose of determining the authority's competence to entertain the case (s 7 (3)).

(d) Validity of Overseas Adoption etc in Particular Proceedings

In addition to these general powers given to the High Court, any court in Great Britain before which proceedings are pending has a power, limited to those proceedings, to treat as invalid an overseas adoption, or a determination by an authority of a Convention country or a specified country as in (c) above (s 6 (4)). The grounds on which a court can so treat an adoption are the same as would justify the High Court in invalidating the adoption or determination as set out in (c).

Chapter XI

Procedure in Convention and 1968 Act Applications

Applications for Convention adoption orders under CA 1975, s 24, are regulated by the provisions of the section (see pp 24 and 27) and by the Convention Adoption Rules 1978 (SI 1978 No 417). These cross-refer to the Adoption (High Court) Rules 1976, as amended, as 'the general rules,' for the only court for such applications when the child is in England or Wales is the High Court (CA 1975, s 100 (2), (5)). Correspondingly, by force of the definition of 'court' in s 11 of AA 1968, proceedings in England and Wales under s 6 of that Act (see p 112) for annulment, revocation etc of certain adoptions and determinations made abroad are possible only in the High Court. The Convention Adoption Rules 1978 deal also with these 1968 Act proceedings. All proceedings may be disposed of in chambers (CA 1975, s 21 (2) as amended, (2A): see p 75). The rules are set out at para 4433A of the Cumulative Supplement to the Supreme Court Practice 1979, and in view of the small number of cases which are likely to arise under them (cf p 1), only a few points will be made here.

1 Section 24 Applications

The originating summons, which is a modified version of that printed at p 175, must state that the application is for a Convention adoption order (r 4 (1)), para 2 of the affidavit in support is omitted (r 4 (2)), and fresh paragraphs 23, 24 and 25, printed with their proper notes at pp 184–185, take the place of the normal paragraphs 23 and 24. These modifications in the form meet the terms of s 24 (2), (3), (4) and (5) of CA 1975 (see pp 24, 27), but r 6 requires (pursuant to the wording of s 24 (1)) positive evidence that the conditions stated in these subsections are fulfilled *immediately before the order is made.* This may be shown by oral evidence, or by a document executed by the applicant and supplied at the hearing. Rule 21 lays down a method of rendering such a document admissible, by attestation according to a scheme corresponding with that tabulated at p 41.

The court may postpone the application and make an interim order, but it must first take account of any specified provision (see p 51) of the internal law of a Convention country of which the applicant or both applicants are nationals (r 20).

There are special requirements (see the notes to the form on p 184) where the child is not a United Kingdom national. Consents etc must comply in form with the foreign internal law, and the High Court may call for further evidence if not satisfied that a person consents with full understanding (r 10; and cf s 24 (6) (*a*), p 50).

Subject to any necessary modifications to take account of s 24 (6) (*a*), the general rules about agreement to adoption (p 35) and paras 9 to 13 of Form 2 (p 176) apply (r 10 (4)).

Notice of hearing is given as in the general rules, but where the child is not a United Kingdom national, the registrar must also serve the notice on any person whose consent is required but who is not an applicant, and on anyone who has to be consulted under the Convention country's internal law (r 11).

2   1968 Act Applications

The Convention Adoption Rules also contain forms of application (see pp 185–189) under s 6 (1), (2) or (3) (see pp 112–114). The person whose adoption is in question and any adopter other than the applicant are to be respondents (rr 13, 14). As to the time limit *for s 6 (1) applications,* see p 113. Evidence is to be filed within fourteen days of the issue of the originating summons, but the court may direct a deponent to give oral evidence (r 15).

The provisions relating to dual nationality and conflicts of internal laws apply (AA 1968, ss 9, 10; see p 50).

3   General

A guardian ad litem is required in Convention adoption applications, and (by r 16) also in 1968 Act cases in which the adopted person is under eighteen at the date of the application. Appointment is in accordance with r 12 of the general rules (see p 66).

Other rules deal with expert evidence about specified or notified provisions (see p 51) (r 19); and translations (rr 22 and 23).

4   Notification of Orders

When a Convention adoption order is made, the direction to the Registrar General which it must contain pursuant to s 21 of the 1958 Act (see p 124) includes an instruction to have the entry in the Adopted Children Register marked with the words 'Convention order' (AA 1968, ss 8 (1), 11 (1); CA 1975, Sched 3, para 64 (a)). Moreover, within seven days after a Convention adoption order has been drawn up, the Senior Registrar of the Family Division requests the Registrar General, by notice, to send the information to the designated authorities of any Convention country of which the child or the applicant is a national, or in which the child was born or the applicant habitually resides (r 7).

Where the court has, under s 6 of the 1968 Act, ordered annulment or revocation, or has by order invalidated an adoption or determination, the Senior Registrar notifies the Registrar General, specifying the date of the adoption, the name and address of the authority which granted it, and the names of the adopter or adopters and of the adopted person (r 18 (1)). The notice to the Registrar General in an annulment or revocation case (including the revocation under s 26 (1) of the 1958 Act of a Convention adoption order: see p 108n) requests that the information be sent to the authorities of any Convention country of which the adopted person is a national or in which he was born; and in s 6 cases to the country in which the adoption was granted (r 18 (2) (3)).

Chapter XII

Appeals

1 High Court and County Court

An appeal lies to the Court of Appeal from an order of the High Court or of a county court authorising an adoption or from the refusal to make such an order. The procedure is to be found in RSC, Ord 59, the time for service of notice of appeal being six weeks (fourteen days if the order is interlocutory), reckoned, in the case of a High Court order, from the date on which it was signed, entered or otherwise perfected (r 4 (1)), but in a county court case from the date of the judgment or order (r 19). The time may be extended by the court (Ord 3, r 5), but exceptional circumstances must be shown (eg that the appellant's agreement had been dispensed with on the factually doubtful ground that she could not be found: *Re F (R) (an Infant)* [1970] 1 QB 385). The Court of Appeal may remit the case for a fresh hearing on it appearing that information before the court below was incorrect, even though the decision appealed from may have been the right one on the materials before the judge (ibid). The court may admit fresh evidence, in a proper case, of events since the hearing below (*Re S (an Infant)* [1973] 3 All ER 88; see p 48). As to sittings in private, see p 76 (cf also 'Finality of Order', p 140).

Though there have been many appeals against decisions dispensing with parents' or guardians' agreements, or refusing such dispensation, an appellate court should be slow to interfere on such a question, unless it has been tainted by error of law or decided on inadequate evidence (see the cases discussed at pp 42–49).

If a High Court order has been made by consent, the leave of the judge making it is necessary before there can be an appeal

118

(Judicature Act 1925, s 31 (1) (*h*)). Formerly, if the matter was a county court one, only a party who was dissatisfied with the determination or direction of the judge in point of law or equity or upon the admission or rejection of any evidence might appeal, according to the County Courts Act 1959, s 108; though in *Re B (an Infant)* [1958] 1 QB 12 the court admitted an appeal by a mother who had taken no part in the proceedings below, holding that their jurisdiction to do so derived from what is now RSC, Ord 59, whether or not the mother was a party.

However, by inserting a new sub-paragraph (*h*) into s 109 (2) of the County Courts Act 1959, CA 1975, Sched 3, para 41 (amended by DPMCA 1978, Sched 2, para 19) has added proceedings under CA 1975 or under AA 1958, s 34 or s 34A, to those particular categories of case in which any party dissatisfied with the determination of a county court judge *on any question of fact* may appeal to the Court of Appeal. Circumvention of the appeal procedure by an application under the wardship jurisdiction is not encouraged (*Re S (a minor)* (1978) 122 SJ 759). The prerogative orders lie in appropriate cases, however (see *R* v *Colchester and Clacton County Court*, in the Queens Bench Divisional Court, narrated on p 105).

On appeal from an inferior court, the local authority representative or other person who was guardian ad litem in the proceedings below should remain in the same capacity for the purpose of the appeal (per Roxburgh J in *Re S (an Infant)* [1959] 1 WLR 921); though it is understood that in some exceptional cases the Court of Appeal has asked the Official Solicitor to act as guardian, or to brief counsel as *amicus* to argue a novel point, as in *Re S (Infants)* [1977] Fam 173.*

2 Domestic Court

Until 1959 the only right of appeal from magistrates in an adoption matter lay in the right of a person who was a party to the proceedings or who was aggrieved by the magistrates' order

---

*Both the *Re S* cases mentioned in this paragraph were appeals by unsuccessful applicants. There is some doubt whether the guardian ad litem in a county court case has a right to appeal either in his own capacity or on behalf of the child. The child himself is not a party in the county court, and by Co Ct R r 4 (3) cannot be made so.

to apply to them for the statement of a case on a question of law or jurisdiction under what is now s 111 of MCA 1980. This procedure does not seem now to be generally open. The 1958 Act introduced an express right of appeal to the High Court from a magistrates' court which had made or refused to make an adoption order, and so by the terms of s 111, *pro tanto* ousted the right to demand a case. CA 1975, s 101 (2), has generalised this express right so as to make it apply to an order made or refused on any application under that Act. But since AA 1958, s 10, has been repealed, and not all applications to magistrates in adoption matters are made under CA 1975, it may be that a case may still be demanded, eg where a point of law arises in connection with an application under s 34 or s 34A of the 1958 Act (see p 95). The case stated must be requested by written notice addressed to the clerk to the justices within twenty-one days of the decision questioned (1980 Act, s 111 (2)), a time limit which cannot be extended. In proper cases a prerogative order would no doubt lie.

An appeal under CA 1975 is assigned to the Family Division, and is heard by a Divisional Court of that Division.

Section 101 (2) does not confine the appeal to one on law; but it was held in the Chancery Division (which formerly heard adoption appeals from magistrates) that the discretion of the justices will not be interfered with unless they have taken a wrong view of the law or their findings of fact are not justified by the evidence, or unless they have clearly not exercised the discretion in the way most beneficial to the infant (*Re G (DM) (an Infant)* [1962] 1 WLR 730).

The procedure is stated in RSC, Ord 90, r 9, in such a way as to incorporate r 16 of that Order. The time for appeal is thus six weeks from the date of the order or determination appealed against, within which period a notice of motion must be served and the appeal entered (r 16 (2), applying Ord 55, r 4 (2), with a modification). But, though not in terms mentioned in Ord 90, r 9, the remainder of Ord 55 (which governs appeals to the High Court generally) clearly applies in so far as it is not inconsistent with the particular rules laid down for adoption appeals from magistrates (see Ord 55, r 1 (4)), and rr 11 and 12 of Ord 90 are also relevant.

As a result, the motion must be an originating one (Ord 55, r 3 (1)); the notice must state the grounds of the appeal and whether the whole or part of the magistrates' decision is appealed against (r 3 (2): for instance, a condition imposed under s 8 (7) of the 1975 Act might be all that was objected to); and the bringing of the appeal does not, unless otherwise ordered, operate as a stay (r 3 (3)). It was said in a case under the Chancery procedure (*Re B (an Infant)* (1960) *The Times*, 25 March) that if a new trial may be required it is better to include a request for it in the notice of motion.

The notice must be served on the clerk of the domestic court together with sufficient copies for all other parties affected by the appeal. The clerk should be requested to serve the parties other than the appellant (Ord 55, r 4 (1); Practice Direction, 7 December 1972). Personal service is not necessary (Ord 90, r 16 (3)). The guardian ad litem who acted below is also the guardian for the purpose of the appeal and he must be served (cf pp 64 et seq).

The appeal is entered (Ord 90, r 16 (1)) by lodging three copies of the notice of motion in the principal registry of the Family Division (see p 64). On entering the appeal, or as soon as practicable thereafter, the appellant must, unless otherwise directed, lodge in the principal registry three copies of certain documents, and a certificate, as described in r 16 (4). The copies required in triplicate are of the summons and order appealed against (these must be certified copies), the clerk's notes of the evidence, and the justices' reasons for their decision. Magistrates' names should appear at the head of the statement of reasons, with the explanation why any justice has not signed. But dissenting reasons are not required (*Re Nicoll* [1972] 2 All ER 232).

The Practice Direction referred to above states that the clerk to the justices should be asked to forward the application and exhibits, notice of determination, guardian's report and any other exhibits used at the hearing to the principal clerk of the Contentious Department at the Principal Registry, together with a certificate of service of the notice of appeal, stating the persons or bodies to whom it was sent. If the clerk's notes are not produced, the court may hear and determine the appeal on any other evidence or statement of what occurred below as appears to the court to be sufficient (r 16 (5)). In a case where the clerk's notes are not available, it seems prudent to explore in advance the possibility of agreeing with the other parties a note of the evidence given.

The certificate required from the appellant is as to service of the notice of motion on the justices' clerk and on the guardian ad litem. If an extension of time for appeal is to be asked for, an additional certificate and a copy thereof must be lodged. This must be signed by the appellant's solicitor (or the appellant if he is acting in person) and must set out the reasons for the delay and the relevant dates (r 16 (4) (*d*), (*e*)).

There is no rule requiring an appointment for directions to be taken in every case, but interlocutory applications may be heard by a single judge (Ord 90, r 16 (8)). And by r 12 a registrar has the authority of a judge in chambers except as may be reserved by the judges. It was held in Chancery chambers that leave to adduce further evidence should be asked for on a preliminary appointment, and that if it relates to facts anterior to the hearing before the magistrates, special ground must be shown as in the case of appeals to the Court of Appeal (*Re J S (an Infant)* [1959] 1 WLR 1218 at p 1224).

Order 90, r 16 (7), deals further with a registrar's powers in the case of an adoption appeal. He may dismiss it for want of prosecution or by consent, and may deal with any question of costs thereby arising. Orders on appeals are drawn up and served in accordance with the rules as to matrimonial causes (Ord 90, r 11). The court is not bound to allow an appeal on the ground merely of misdirection or improper reception or rejection of evidence unless, in its opinion, substantial wrong or miscarriage of justice has been thereby occasioned (r 16 (6)). As to the court's discretion, on application being made, to sit in private, see p 76.

A further Practice Direction at [1977] 2 All ER 543 supplements r 16, and gives a form of notice of motion for use in (*inter alia*) adoption appeals. Lodgment is required of three copies of any manuscript document and two copies of any typescript document put in as an exhibit below. Original exhibits (transmitted by the justices' clerk) are not handed out by the

Principal Registry for copying, but copies can be bespoken there.

Chapter XIII

Adopted Children Register

1 Contents

The Registrar General is required to keep a register, called the Adopted Children Register, at the General Register Office, in which entries of adoptions are recorded as directed by adoption orders (see p 104). According to s 20 (1) of the 1958 Act, no other entries are to be made in the register, but this is qualified by s 8 (2) of the Act of 1968, which requires certain overseas adoptions to be entered (see below). The form of entry to be made in the register is prescribed by the Registrar General as described on pp 104–105. In the case of Convention adoption orders made under CA 1975, s 24, there must be added the words 'Convention order' (see p 117).

Amendments of the Adopted Children Register are to be made as ordered (AA 1958, s 24 (2)).

By AA 1968, s 8 (2) (in force from 1 February 1973), if the Registrar General is satisfied that an entry in the Register of Births relates to a person adopted under an overseas adoption (defined as on p 111) and that he has sufficient particulars relating to that person to do so, he is to make an entry in the Adopted Children Register. He may require an English translation of a certificate or certified copy presented as evidence of an overseas adoption or a convention adoption, as the case may be, if that document is not in English (SI 1973 No 19, art 4 (2); SI 1978 No 1432, art 4 (2)).

Entries may be corrected following annulment of the adoption, or on it otherwise ceasing to have effect (s 8 (3)).

2 Marking of Birth Registers

By s 21 (4) of the Act of 1958, if upon an application for an adoption order, there is proved to the satisfaction of the court the identity of the child with a child to which any entry in the Registers of Births relates, the Registrar General is directed in the adoption order to cause such entry in the Registers of Births to be marked with the word 'Adopted'. Similarly with the Adopted Children Register in the case of a re-adoption (s 21 (5)). Scottish adoption orders are similarly noted if they affect the English Registers of Births or of Adopted Children (s 24 (4)) and there are reciprocal provisions for marking entries in the Scottish registers where those entries relate to children adopted in England (s 24 (5)).

In the case of a provisional adoption order, the marking is to be 'Provisionally adopted' or 'Provisionally re-adopted', as the case may require (s 53 (6)).

Effect must be given to any directions of a court on the quashing of an adoption order or the allowing of an appeal against it by cancelling the markings in the Registers of Births and the entry in the Adopted Children Register, and both markings and cancellations are in that event to be omitted from all copies of the entries affected in those registers (s 24 (3), (6)). Similarly, where the court, under s 24 (1), amends an order or revokes a direction for marking (s 24 (2), (6)).

There are certain cases in which the Registrar General has a duty or power to mark Birth Registers otherwise than pursuant to literal directions in an order of an English court. These are comprised in AA 1964, s 3 (Northern Ireland, Isle of Man or Channel Islands adoption or cancellation orders identifiable with births registered here) and s 8 (2) and (3) of AA 1968 (overseas adoptions etc similarly identifiable: cf pp 111–114).

Section 14 of the Births and Deaths Registration Act 1953 provides for the re-registration, on certain conditions, of the births of legitimated persons. If such re-registration takes place *after* the original entry in the Registers of Births has been marked 'Adopted', the entry made on re-registration is to be similarly marked (AA 1958, s 27; 1964 Act, s 3 (4); 1968 Act, s 8 (4), applying to entries of overseas adoptions). The 1958 provision is stated to be without prejudice to the court's power to revoke an adoption order in consequence of legitimation (s 26; and see p 108). Where that power is exercised the fact is communicated to the Registrar General (see below), and the entries and markings in the Adopted Children Register and the Registers of Births, respectively, must be cancelled; and this will now apply when the order revoked is a Convention adoption order, for CA 1975, Sched 3, para 26, which avoided this result, is repealed by DPMCA 1978, Sched 3. As to notification in Convention matters generally, see p 117.

As to local registers, it is provided by reg 37 of the Registration of Births, Deaths and Marriages Regulations 1968 (SI 1968 No 2049) that a superintendent registrar or registrar must, on being directed by the Registrar General, mark any entry specified in the direction with the word 'Adopted', or, as the case may be, 'Provisionally adopted', adding his signature and official description, and send to the Registrar General a certified copy of the entry showing the marking. By reg 38, any certified copy of such entry given under the provisions of the Registration Acts must include a copy of the marking. There are provisions for cancellation of markings on the direction of the Registrar General (reg 37 (2)).

3   Communication of Adoption Order to Registrar General

The prescribed officer of the court is responsible for communicating every adoption order to the Registrar General, who must then comply with the directions to him contained therein (AA 1958, s 21 (6)). This duty is performed in the Family Division by a registrar of that Division (see p 64), in the county court by the registrar and in the domestic court by the justices' clerk. The rules require a copy of the order to be sent to the Registrar General within seven days after it has been drawn up (H Ct R r 25 (1)) or made (Co Ct R r 25 (1); Mag Ct R r 22 (1)). See also as to the supply of copies pp 102–104.

Where an adoption order is quashed, or an appeal against an adoption order allowed by any court, *that* court is to give directions to the Registrar General to cancel any marking of an entry in the Registers of Births and any entry in the Adopted Children Register which was effected in pursuance of the order (s 24 (3)).

On amendment of an adoption order or revocation of a direction under s 24 (1) or under para 6 of Sched 5 to the Act (p 106), or on revocation under s 26, the prescribed officer of the court is to cause the amendment, or the fact of revocation, as the case may be, to be communicated to the Registrar General (s 24 (2); s 26 (2)) by notice as described in the rules (H Ct R r 27 (2); Co Ct R r 28 (2); Mag Ct R r 27 (3)).

4   Evidence of Adoption and Date and Place of Birth

A certified copy of an entry in the Adopted Children Register bearing the seal of the General Register Office is evidence:
  (*a*) of the adoption to which the entry relates; and
  (*b*) where the entry contains a record of the adopted person's date of birth or country or district and sub-district of birth, of that date or country or district and sub-district, as though it were a certified copy of an entry in the Registers of Births (AA 1958, s 20 (2)).

By s 2 (1) of the 1964 Act, a similar document receivable as evidence under the adoption legislation applying in Scotland or Northern Ireland is also receivable in England.

Any certified copy of the entry relevant to an adoption order which has been amended must be a copy of the entry as amended, without any note or marking being reproduced relating to the amendment or any cancelled matter (1958 Act, s 24 (6)).

A copy of any entry in the Registers of Births or the Adopted Children Register, the marking of which is cancelled on the quashing of an adoption order or on a successful appeal or on revocation of an order after legitimation (see p 108) is to be deemed to be an accurate copy if and only if both the marking and the cancellation are omitted therefrom (ss 24 (6), 26 (2)).

5   Inspection of Register, Copies, and Fees therefor

By s 20 (3) of the 1958 Act every person is entitled to search the indexes of the register at the General Register Office (part of the Office of Population Censuses and Surveys), St Catherine's House, 10 Kingsway, London WC2 and to have a certified copy of any entry in the register on the same conditions as are applicable under the Births and Deaths Registration Act 1953, and the Registration Service Act 1953. (Registers of adopted children are not kept locally.)

The General Register Office is open for searches of the indexes from 8.30 am to 4.30 pm on Mondays to Fridays, but is closed on Saturdays. No fees are payable for searching in the indexes at the General Register Office. A certified copy of an entry may be obtained on personal application at a fee of £3.50 (£1.50 if applied for within 28 days of first registration). If applied for by post, the sum of £8 should be sent for each certified copy, with crossed postal order or cheque payable to the Registrar General and stamped addressed envelope.

Certain other registers or books must be kept in order to link the entries in the Adopted Children Register with those in the Registers of Births (AA 1958, s 20 (4)). But these books are not open to public inspection nor may any information contained in them be divulged to any person, except in accordance with s 20A (see p 130), or by order of any of the courts specified in s 20 (5). It is tentatively suggested that the court might so order, for instance, if a question of the adopted person's nationality turned on natural parenthood, not being covered by s 19 (see pp 143–144) because the adopter was not a United Kingdom citizen. See also *Lawson* v *Registrar General* (1956) 106 Law Journal 204 (county court), where it was the adopted person who was sought, so that she could be paid a legacy from a god-mother. The courts in question are:

(*a*) the High Court;
(*b*) the Westminster County Court or such other county court as may be prescribed*;
(*c*) the court by which an adoption order was made in respect of the person to whom the information, copy or extract relates. In the case of an order made by a magistrates' court, this includes a court acting for the same petty sessions area (s 20 (6)).

Section 33 of the Births and Deaths Registration Act 1953 and regulations (SI 1968 No 2050) made thereunder provide for a shortened form of birth certificate at a fee which is now £6.50 (£2 on personal application). Such a certificate will include only the name and surname (see reg 6), sex, date of birth (reg 8)

---

*No other county court has so far been prescribed.

and place of birth (reg 9), but will *not* include any particulars relating to parentage or adoption. When application is made for a short certificate from an entry in the Adopted Children Register, the particulars given by the applicant should include the date of birth, the names and surname of the adopted person and the adoptive parent or parents, the date of the adoption order and the court by which it was made. The short certificate is in the same form as a short birth certificate and contains no details of adoption. The fee is the same as for a short birth certificate, but is reduced to £1.25 if applied for personally within 28 days of registration.

Chapter XIV

New Provision for Access to Birth Records

Section 26 of CA 1975 may be said to have effected a partial breach in the system described on p 128 whereby the links between the Registers of Births and of Adoptions formerly in England and Wales remained screened. In Scotland disclosure to an adopted person was always allowed when he reached seventeen years of age, and there were no doubt many cases of adoption in England in which the person concerned came, by endeavour or chance, to know, not only that he was adopted—which practically everyone has always agreed should be disclosed to him in due season—but also what his origins were. The sociological, and the present official, view on the subject is that an adopted person who has come of age should have the right to know, if he chooses, his natural parentage. There are implications of the situation which may not always be apparent to the adopted person, and skilled social workers acting as counsellors are available to give advice in the matter. But to endeavour to trace his birth particulars remains the person's absolute right. There is no compulsion on him to accept or follow any advice he may be given.

Accordingly, s 20A of the 1958 Act (added by CA 1975, s 26), by subs (1) obliges the Registrar General, on application made by an adopted person a record of whose birth is kept by the Registrar General and who has attained the age of eighteen, to supply to that person on payment of the prescribed fee (if any) such information as is necessary to enable the applicant to obtain a certified copy of the record of his birth.

Subsection (2) deals with a different type of case, namely, that of an adopted person under the age of eighteen whose birth record is kept by the Registrar General and who is intending to be married in England or Wales. Such a person is entitled, on application made and fee paid as prescribed, to be informed by the Registrar General whether or not it appears from information contained in the registers of live births or other records that the applicant and the person whom he intends to marry may be within the prohibited degrees of relationship for the purposes of the Marriage Act 1949.

The forms for both types of application are prescribed by the Adopted Persons (Birth Records) Regulations 1976 (SI 1976 No 1743). Under subs (1) two alternative forms are prescribed, their applicability depending on whether the person was adopted before the 12 or after the 11 November 1975. This is because the Registrar's obligation—and indeed his authority —to supply information to a person adopted before the *passing* of the CA 1975 (despite the fact that s 26 of that Act did not become operative until 26 November 1976) is conditional upon the applicant having attended an interview with a counsellor (s 20A (6)). In other subs (1) cases the interview with a counsellor is optional, but the Registrar General must inform the applicant that counselling services are available, and where (s 20A (4)). Counselling is not required or provided for in the case of an application under s 20A (2).

Fewer persons than had been expected took advantage of s 20A (1) in the early years of its operation, while s 20A (2) had not been invoked at all up to the end of 1978 ('First Report', referred to at p 12).

The Registrar General and each local authority are under a duty to provide counselling for subs (1) applicants, and when the comprehensive adoption service is in being under ss 1 and 2 and 4 to 7 of CA 1975 (see Appendix II, para 1, p 227), approved adoption societies must provide it also (AA 1958, s 20A (3)). Application forms for access to birth records can be obtained from the General Register Office (CA Section), Titchfield, Fareham, Hants, Box 7, PO15 5RU, and when completed should be returned to that address. Applicants are asked to indicate on the form their choice of one of three alternative places where they would prefer to meet a counsellor by appointment; these are the General Register Office, London, or at the social services department of the local authority for the area in which the applicant lives, or for the area where the court sat when making the adoption order (cf s 20A (4)). There is no fee for counselling, but if the applicant wishes to proceed he will be charged a fee of £3.50 for the birth certificate.

If the applicant chooses to receive counselling from a local authority, the Registrar sends to that authority the information to which the applicant is entitled under subs (1) (s 20A (5)). But further information may in some cases be available. It may, in other words, be possible to give information beyond the purely nominal links which lead from the Adopted Children Register to the Register of Births, to which s 20A (1) gives the applicant a legal right. Counsellors are, it is understood, able to help the applicant to find out through which agency (if any) his adoption was arranged, if he wishes to do so after hearing their advice on his particular circumstances. This is the key to the relevance of H Ct R r 29 (*b*) (ii) and the other rules of court to the like effect cited on p 77. The counsellor holds an authorisation to the court to bring these sub-rules into play if necessary. But the official leaflet warns applicants that there can be no certainty that any information outside the birth certificate still exists.

Chapter XV

Effects of Adoption

1   General

(a)   Development of the Present Principle

Adoption by formal process of law necessarily entails certain effects on the rights and obligations of the adopter, the adopted person and the natural parents. The early English statutes expressed these effects in quite general terms, which were at first selectively interpreted (see eg *Coventry Corporation* v *Surrey County Council* [1935] AC 199); and an additional limitation lay in the fact that they applied only on an adoption ordered by a court in England or Wales. Over the years the situation was broadened by amending legislation, and gradually a position was reached in which it could be generally said that the effects of the completed adoption process were either actually or (taking into account the prospective provisions of AA 1968) potentially similar in most important respects as between one adoption and another, wherever authorised; and such effects had come to cover a wider range of legal rights and obligations than formerly. The latest stage in this progress towards complete catholicity was reached in CA 1975. Schedule 1 to that Act replaced the piecemeal enumeration of the particular effects of adoption which made up the pre-1976 law by one general proposition designed in the fullness of time to embrace all adoptions which English law recognises and to admit of only a few stated restrictions in scope.

The general proposition of Sched 1 is that an adopted person is to be *treated in law* as if

(*a*)   he had been born to the adopter in wedlock, and

(*b*)   he were not the child of any other person.

This goes farther in scope, in uniformity and in precision than the previous enactments, which used a variety of formulae, none taking the hypothesis quite so unequivocally back to the adopted person's birth as does the new one. The hypothesis does not look to any particular marriage of a sole adopter; but where the adopters are a married couple, it is of their marriage that the child is treated as having been born, whether or not he was in fact born after that marriage was solemnised (Sched 1, para 3 (1), (2)).

As to legitimacy, see p 143.

(b)   Application of the New Principle: Relevance of Dates of Events

The scope of the general principle just set out is confined to events occurring after its introduction. For CA 1975, Sched 1, para 3, has effect from 1 January 1976 in the case of an adoption carried through before that date, and in the case of any other adoption, from the date of the adoption (para 3 (4)). Although the principle applies (subject to any contrary indication) for the construction of enactments or instruments passed or made before the adoption or later (para 3 (5)), it has effect only as respects things done, or events occurring, after the adoption, or after 31 December 1975, whichever is the later (para 3 (6)). As regards events before 1976 it will be necessary to consult the contemporary legislation, discussed in earlier editions of this book; some of it is more summarily referred to in appropriate places below. The width of the new principle has emboldened Parliament to repeal some enactments which covered (perhaps superfluously, in some cases) particular topics: for instance, it is no longer necessary to mention specifically adopted children as being among the members of a person's family for the purpose of his entitlement to certain compensatory payments and supplements in housing law, and CA 1975, Sched 3, paras 15, 66 and 83, amend the text of the Housing Acts 1957, 1969 and 1974 accordingly, without affecting their meaning; and AA 1958, s 25, which in effect said that an existing adoption was to be recognised when compiling a baptismal register, is now

---

*Among similar examples which figured expressly in editions of this book .

allowed to go without saying, and is repealed.* But there are nevertheless some areas of law in which Sched 1, or some other provision of CA 1975, has explained, exemplified, modified, or even excluded the application of its general proposition, and these will be set out in the following pages.

(c) Relevance of Date of Order and Enabling Authority in Some Cases

The general principle applying to post-1975 events obtains, on its own terms, whenever the adoption took place (Sched 1, para 1 (4)); and whether the adoption is or was one authorised under the Adoption of Children Act, 1926, AA 1950 or 1958, or by s 8 (1) of CA 1975, which covers adoption orders of the Scottish courts besides those effected in England and Wales as dealt with in this book (para 1 (2) (*a*) and (*b*)); or is a Northern Irish, Isle of Man or Channel Islands adoption order (para 1 (2) (*c*)); or is an overseas adoption (para 1 (2) (*d*): see below); or an adoption recognised by English law though effected abroad (para 1 (2) (*e*): see below). But because this comprehensive position has been reached only by legislative degrees, and because the modern principle has also developed in stages, it is always necessary, in assessing the effects of a pre-1976 adoption as regards an event occurring, a thing done or a disposition of property contained in an enactment or instrument passed or made before 1 January 1976, to know both the country in which the adoption took place and the date of it. The territorial considerations are briefly summarised under heads (*d*), (*e*) and (*f*) which follow.

---

up to and including the seventh are the references to adoption in the Army Act 1955, s 150 (5), the Air Force Act 1955, s 150 (5) (the Queen's Printer's copy of CA 1975 misprints this as s 15 (5)), the Fatal Accidents Act 1959, s 1, the Mental Health Act 1959, s 49 (2) and (5), and the Pensions (Increase) Act 1971, s 3 (7), all which specific references are among those repealed as respects events after the end of 1975. Other topics of which particular discussion seems now unnecessary in view of the breadth and comprehensiveness of the general principle are taxation, security of tenure under the Rent Acts, and superannuation schemes. Family provision is now dealt with by the Inheritance (Provision for Family and Dependants) Act 1975, which brings in any person who was treated by the deceased as a child of his family, and that would include an adopted child in normal circumstances.

(*d*) English Orders

As indicated above, the 1958 Act set out in detail some of the
legal results which flowed from an adoption order made under
it, and other incidents were added by statutes on specific
subjects. As regards Convention adoption orders made in
England, the 1968 Act originally provided that they should
have, generally, the same effect as 1958 Act orders. A
corresponding result is now achieved directly by bringing all
orders made in England or Wales, whether under the normal or
the Convention adoption order provisions of CA 1975, s 24,
within the definition of adoption for the purposes of Sched 1
(para 1 (2) (*a*)). The English courts, indeed, make but one kind
of adoption order (cf p 12).

(*e*) Adoptions Outside England: Effect Given by Statute

(*i*) Orders made in the British Islands

By AA 1958, ss 1, 9, 11 and 57 (1), Scottish adoption orders
had the same effect in English law as have those made in
England or Wales. So, since the beginning of 1950, had orders
made in Northern Ireland in some respects; and AA 1964
advanced the process of equating in this respect the orders of
neighbouring jurisdictions by giving effect to a certain extent in
English law to adoption orders made in the Isle of Man or in
any of the Channel Islands, and by extending the effect of
Northern Irish orders.*

These British adoptions have the same effect in English law
as regards events after 1975 as those carried through in
England or Wales (CA 1975, Sched 1, para 1 (2) (*c*)). (The
effect of adoption in Scots law is stated in Sched 2.)

(*ii*) Overseas adoptions

Section 4 (1) of the Act of 1968 applied to an overseas
adoption, as defined in the Act (see p 111), certain provisions of
English law as respects anything done or any event occurring *on
or after* 1 February 1973, the date when s 4 came into force.

---

*By SI 1978 No 1432, Northern Ireland has become a 'specified country'
within AA 1968, s 11 (see p 114) and its authorities' determinations are
therefore within ibid, s 5 (1) (see *(ii)* on this page).

Applied in this way was any provision (however expressed) in any enactment passed *before* the date mentioned under which a person adopted in pursuance of a 1958 Act order was for any purpose treated as the child of the adopter, or any other relationship was deduced by reference to such an order (see now pp 145–150). In addition, some particular provisions of the 1958 Act were specifically applied to overseas adoptions by s 4 (2) of the Act of 1968.

As respects things done, or events occurring after 31 December 1975, s 4 (1) and (2) are repealed and overseas adoptions as defined rank with English adoptions as regards their effect on status, property and other matters falling within CA 1975, Sched 1.

Southern Rhodesian adoptions were cognisable as overseas adoptions despite our law's non-recognition of that country's independence (see the Southern Rhodesia (Marriages, Matrimonial Causes and Adoptions) Order 1972, SI 1972 No 1718). This order came into force on 11 November 1965 and was repealed on the coming into effect of the Zimbabwe Act 1979, namely from 18 April 1980).

As from 23 October 1978, when ss 5 and 6 of the 1968 Act were brought into force, there are further points to note about decisions in adoption matters abroad. Section 6 is principally dealt with at pp 113–114. Section 5 refers not to all overseas adoptions and orders, but only to those which are Convention adoptions (see p 111), or, as the case may be, orders made under the Hague Convention in specified countries (see p 114). The section gives effect in English law to determinations made by competent authorities of Convention countries or of specified countries in the exercise of a power to authorise or review the authorisation of a Convention adoption or an order made either in a specified country or in Great Britain in pursuance of the Hague Convention.

Any court in Great Britain has jurisdiction to decide that an overseas adoption or such a determination as is last mentioned shall, for the purpose of proceedings before it, be treated as invalid on the ground that it is contrary to public policy, or on the ground that the authority purporting to make it was not competent to entertain the case (s 6 (4), and see p 114). Except as provided by s 6, the validity of an overseas adoption or determination is unassailable in our courts (s 6 (5)).

(f) Adoptions Outside England: Effect Given by Common Law

Foreign adoptions which are not within the statutory provisions discussed above (eg because they are not made in the United Kingdom or the British Islands, or are not overseas adoptions as defined, or because the adoption or some relevant event antedates the effective commencement of a provision which might otherwise be applicable) may nevertheless have some force in the English conflict of laws. Paragraph 1 (2) (e) of CA 1975, Sched 1 brings within that Schedule foreign adoptions if recognised by the law of England and Wales; and as regards previous periods and events AA 1968, s 10 (2), repealed for future happenings (CA 1975, Sched 4, Pt I and note), establishes clearly that any recognition due to such adoptions apart from statute is preserved.

The topic of foreign adoption conditions was extensively canvassed in *Re Valentine's Settlement* [1965] Ch 831, a case raising the question whether a person, South African born, was the child of his adopter for the purpose of construing an English settlement made before 1950. The adoption had been effected in South Africa, the adopter, a British subject, being domiciled in Southern Rhodesia. These conditions were not such as to deprive the South African court of jurisdiction under its own law.

In these circumstances (which, it must be emphasised, arose before the somewhat liberalising influence of the Hague Convention, and before the CA 1975 had equiparated for the future foreign adoptions recognised in English law with English adoptions) it was unanimously accepted that English law would generally give effect to an adoption order made by a court within whose jurisdiction English law regarded the adopting parent as domiciled. Two members of the Court of Appeal thought that in addition it was necessary for the child to be ordinarily resident in that jurisdiction. The majority of the court decided, however, that English law would not so recognise the adoption if the adopter's domicile was elsewhere;

and further that English law's recognition of a foreign adoption did not confer on the adopted person the rights given by the foreign law, but only the same rights as under an English adoption, which at that time fell short of those foreign rights.

2 Parental Rights and Duties

It is implicit in the definition of 'adoption order' as used in CA 1975 (s 107 (1)) that such an order vests in the adopter or the adopters the parental rights and duties (as to which, see p 34) relating to the child (s 8 (1)). For the present a provisional adoption order has the same effect (AA 1958, s 53 (4), adapted by SI 1976 No 1744, Sched 3, para 10). But no adoption order affects the parental rights and duties so far as they relate to any period before the making of the order (CA 1975, s 8 (2)). Thereafter the order operates to extinguish:

(*a*) any parental right or duty relating to the child which:
    (i) is vested in a person (not being one of the adopters) who was the parent or guardian of the child immediately before the making of the order*, or
    (ii) is vested in any other person by virtue of the order of any court; and
(*b*) any duty arising by virtue of an agreement or the order of a court to make payments, so far as the payments are in respect of the child's maintenance for any period after the making of the order or any other matter comprised in the parental duties and relating to such a period (s 8 (3)). But (*b*) does not apply to a duty arising by virtue of an agreement which constitutes a trust, or which expressly provides that the duty is not to be extinguished by the making of an adoption order (s 8 (4)).

These provisions, supplementing the general principle

---

*In so far as one of these duties may consist in a duty to register the child's birth, this may be the place to remark that CA 1975, Sched 3, para 13 (6), contains what is surely a purely precautionary definition, which stands out as a curious reversal of the general principle of the 1975 Act as to imputed relationship. The qualification and duties of 'fàther' and 'mother' under the Births and Deaths Registration Act 1953 are in consequence not the adopter's but the natural parents', as one would indeed expect.

discussed in **1** above, operate technically from 26 November 1976, when SI 1976 No 1744 brought them into force. But the previous corresponding provisions (ss 13 (1) and 15 (1) of AA 1958) had stood repealed as from the preceding 1 January, so far as concerned things done after 31 December 1975. It is thought that the general principle was strong enough to tide over the intervening period and to produce broadly the result now detailed in CA, s 8. Only so far as a particular thing or event was done or occurred before 1976 would the repealed ss 13 and 15 be relevant. As to s 15, see also p152. Section 13 (1) and (2) corresponded, using contemporary phraseology, with s 8 (1), (2) and (3) (*a*) of CA 1975 as set out above.

Thus it always appears to have been the case, and CA 1975 can only have placed it quite beyond doubt, that an adopter may appoint a testamentary guardian of the child to act after the adopter's death under the Guardianship of Minors Act 1971; and that the survivor of a husband and wife who have jointly adopted a child becomes its statutory guardian under s 3 of the same Act. An order for the maintenance of an adopted child may be made under the 1971 Act against its adopter (see eg *Skinner* v *Carter* [1948] Ch 387).

Section 13 (1) and (2) of the 1958 Act covered only English and Scottish adoption orders. Since s 13 was a provision under which an adopted person is 'for any purpose treated as the child of the adopter, or any other relationship is deduced' by reference to an adoption order, s 1 (1) (*b*) of the 1964 Act (now repealed) extended it to Northern Ireland, Isle of Man and Channel Islands adoptions, as respects anything done or any event occurring between 16 July 1964 and 1 January 1976; and s 4 (1) of the 1968 Act extended it to overseas adoptions as defined (see p 111) as respects anything done or any event occurring after 31 January 1973.

3   Finality of Order

A pronounced distinction emerges from the 1968 Act between adoption in Convention cases and in others as regards the possibility of their being annulled or otherwise invalidated.

(*a*) *Orders in Cases Other than Convention Cases*

Subject always to the court's powers of amendment (see p 105) and revocation after legitimation (p 108), such an order, though founded on an error of fact, has to be acted on unless and until a competent court sets it aside. Thus in *Skinner* v *Carter* [1948] Ch 387 it was held that, so long as the order stood, it could not be disregarded by justices seised of a maintenance application against a 'husband' as adopter and guardian of a child, despite his subsequent conviction of bigamy in respect of his 'marriage' with his co-adopter. Lord Greene MR said that it might be that only by certiorari could an order made without jurisdiction be impeached (p 394); and that it was by no means certain that non-compliance with the statutory directions would necessarily have the result of making the order—of which the important effect was the consequence it had on the status of the infant—void or voidable.

The point has recently been taken a stage further in *Re F* (*Infants*) [1977] Fam 165. Joint adopters had subsequently discovered that the prior marriage of one of them had not been dissolved as they and the court believed at the time of the adoption, and (having regularised the matrimonial position) they sought to appeal out of time against the adoption order by way of testing its validity. The Court of Appeal held that an adoption order made in those circumstances was not *void* (in which case a court before which it was questioned would have had no option but to ignore it or—given jurisdiction—set it aside), but at most voidable on appeal by an aggrieved party; and in a case where justice so required the time for appeal might be extended. In the case in question no one came forward with an interest to challenge the order, which was therefore in effect confirmed by the refusal of the leave sought.

In *Re RA* (*minors*) (1974) 4 Fam Law 182, the Divisional Court set aside an order which had been obtained by false representations to the magistrates including statements that the applicants were married to each other and the female applicant (in fact the child's mother) was the child's aunt.

The Scottish decision in *J and J* v *C's Tutor* [1948] SC 636 is worth noting. There the Court of Session held that an adoption was not a matter of contract between the adopters and the natural parent. Accordingly it refused to reduce an adoption order on grounds of essential error in the application induced by innocent misrepresentation on the part of a charitable organization acting on behalf of the child's mother. The court remarked that there was nowhere any provision for the suspension or (at that time) for cancellation of adoptions.

Orders effective in English law under the 1964 Act (see p 136) or by reason of the principles of private international law are presumably final or otherwise according to the provisions of the law under which they were made.

An adopted child remains within the ambit of potential wardship, and even a parent who had agreed to the adoption would be able, for good cause (such as the death or prolonged incapacity of the adopter), to apply to the court. A strong prima facie case for investigation in the best interests of the child must be made out, as it was in *Re O (a minor)* [1977] 3 WLR 732, CA, reversing the decision cited in the last edition of this book.

(b) Convention Orders

The Act of 1968 contemplates at various points that a Convention adoption, whether made in England or elsewhere, or an overseas adoption or a specified order, may be subject to review and it both gives our courts certain jurisdiction to effectuate such review (see s 6 and pp 112–114) and provides for the recognition in England of the results of such a review competently made elsewhere (see s 5 and p 137). Subject as stated, however, the validity of an overseas adoption, or of a determination in exercise of proper powers of review of Convention orders etc, is not to be impugned in any court in Great Britain (s 6 (5)).

4   Status of Adopted Person

It is now beyond dispute that adoption is capable of affecting the status of the child who is the subject of it, though whether in a particular case it gives the child a status afterwards different from that which was his before it must depend on the facts. When CA 1975, Sched 1, para 3, which is headed 'Status conferred by adoption', is examined, it appears to be concerned less with legitimacy, domicile and nationality than with conferring a notional lineage in place of the natural one, and this may or may not affect one or more of the incidents which are usually comprehended within 'status' as that word is used by most lawyers.

(a) Legitimacy

It is, at all events, declared by para 3 (3) that para 3 prevents an adopted child from being illegitimate. He is treated in law as if born in wedlock to the adopter or adopters (see p 133). Nevertheless an adopted person can become legitimated as the child of *both* his parents after sole adoption by one of them (see p 108).

(b) Domicile

The situation before 1 January 1974 was that an adopted child's domicile became that of the adoptive parent, and changed during minority with any change of that parent's domicile (see the observations of Lord Denning MR in *Re Valentine's Settlement* [1965] Ch 831 at p 842; *Re B (S) (an Infant)* [1968] Ch 204). The Domicile and Matrimonial Proceedings Act 1973 shortened the period of dependent domicile by declaring that the time at which a person first becomes capable of having an independent domicile should be the attainment of the age of sixteen, marriage under that age, or 1 January 1974 in the case of a dependent person who was then already sixteen or had been married (s 3). Section 4 specifically included an adopted child, with regard to whom its leading proposition was that if his adoptive parents were alive but lived apart, his domicile was dependent on that of the female adopter in certain circumstances.

But the general principle of Sched 1 (p 133) for the future covers domicile as well as other matters, and the reference to an adopted child in s 4 of the 1973 Act has been repealed without changing the effect of the section.

(c) Nationality

This topic is partly covered by s 19 (1) of the Act of 1958, which declares that, where an adoption order is made in respect of a child who is not a citizen of the United Kingdom and Colonies, then, if the adopter or, in the case of a joint adoption, the male adopter is such a citizen, the child shall be a citizen of the United Kingdom and Colonies as from the date of the order. Orders made in England, Scotland or Northern Ireland (see s 19 (2)) have had this effect since 1 January 1950; but s 19 (1) has never applied to an overseas adoption as defined at p 111. The reference to it in s 4 (2) of the 1968 Act was never brought into force when the remainder of s 4 was activated by SI 1973 No 18, and the whole of s 4 (2) is now repealed. By s 1 (3) of the 1964 Act, an Isle of Man or Channel Islands adoption order made on or after 16 July 1964, when the Act came into force, has a similar effect as from the date of the order; and if it was previously made in respect of a person who would have become a United Kingdom citizen at the date of the order had the Act been then in force, he is such a citizen as from the commencement of the Act.

Section 9 (5) of the 1968 Act (in force from 23 October 1978, as amended by CA 1975, Sched 3, para 63) contains a provision confined to orders made in Convention cases or in specified countries (see p 114). It provides that where such an order ceases to have effect (either on annulment or otherwise) the cesser shall not affect the status of United Kingdom citizenship acquired under s 19 (1) of the 1958 Act.

Section 19 does not apply to provisional adoptions (s 53 (4)). Nor does it affect the nationality of persons, whether British subjects or not, who are adopted by aliens or by British subjects who owe their nationality solely to Dominion citizenship. The section is not repealed or amended by CA 1975. Indeed, the general principle (p 133) treating the child in law as if he had been born to the adopter is expressly stated not to apply to any provision of the British Nationality Acts 1948 to 1965, the Immigration Act 1971 or any other legal provision determining citizenship of the United Kingdom and Colonies (CA 1975, Sched 1, para 7 (2)). A British child will thus, on general principles, remain British after adoption by an alien, even if his nationality depends on descent from a British natural parent, subject to the provisions of the British Nationality Acts relating to renunciation, deprivation etc of citizenship. As to the availability of information necessary to establish the parentage of a person adopted under the serial number system, see the suggestion on p 128.

5   Proprietary Rights

From the legal practitioner's point of view, it is probably under this head that the most practically significant effects of adoption fall.

It was expressly provided by the Adoption of Children Act 1926 that an adoption order did not deprive the child of any right to or interest in property to which, but for the order, he would have been entitled under an intestacy or disposition, whether occurring or made before or after the making of the order, nor confer any such right or interest on him as a child of the adopter. He therefore had no title to a grant of representation to his adopter's estate, nor to share in an intestacy, nor did he take, unless a contrary intention appeared, under a gift expressed to be to a child or issue.

This position was virtually reversed as regards devolution on a death occurring on or after 1 January 1950, and dispositions made after the end of 1949, by AA 1949. The object was to secure that adopted persons should be treated as children of their adopters for the purposes of any future devolution or disposal of real or personal property.

Only adoption orders made in England, Scotland or Northern Ireland carried the full effect of this statutory reversal. As respects anything done or any event occurring on or after 16 July 1964, Isle of Man and Channel Islands orders, whenever made, were brought in by s 1 (1) of the 1964 Act; and overseas adoptions, as defined (see p 111), as regards events between 31 January 1973 and 1 January 1976, by AA 1968, s 4 (2). As to the force of other foreign adoptions in this context in the English conflict of laws, see p 138. It would seem that (apart from statute) a foreign adoption, if it were to qualify for full recognition as affecting the interpretation of words such as 'child' or 'issue' when used by an English testator or settlor, would have to be such that under the relevant law it conferred the same incidents of filial status *vis-à-vis* the adopter as would bring the adopted person within the words in question as contemplated by the testator or settlor.

The relevant sections of the Adoption Act 1958 are ss 16 and 17. They apply to full adoption orders whenever made but not to interim or provisional orders (see 1958 Act, ss 8 (5) and 53

F

(4)). They do not affect the devolution of any property on the intestacy of a person who died before 1 January 1950, or any disposition made before that date (Sched 5, para 4) and, though they are repealed by CA 1975, Sched 4, Pt I, as from 1 January 1976 (as are the provisions mentioned immediately above cf the 1964 and 1968 Acts), that repeal does not affect their application (or the application of references to s 16 or s 17 in any other repealed provision) in relation to an intestacy occurring before 1 January 1976, or to a disposition of property effected by an instrument made before that date (Sched 1, paras 1 (5), 5 (2), (3)). Nor does the new general principle (p 133) apply in such a case (para 5 (1), (3)).

Sections 16 and 17 were extensively set out and discussed in earlier editions of this book. While stressing again that these sections are by no means spent, as they affect past devolutions and dispositions, the author considers it now to be a better use of the available space to expound here simply the provisions of the new law.

(a)   Instruments, Enactments and Intestacies after 1975: *General Rules*

The rules of devolution on intestacy are now consolidated with those relating to express dispositions by a deeming device. By para 5 (3) of CA 1975, Sched 1, the provisions of the law of intestate succession are to be treated for the purpose as if contained in an instrument executed by the deceased immediately before his death but while he was of full capacity.

In the case of a will or codicil clearly we do not need any deeming provision in order to identify it as an instrument; as to the date at which it is to be regarded as made, para 1 (6) of Sched 1 fixes this as the date of the testator's death.

Subject as stated above, and to any contrary indication, the general proposition of Sched 1, as to treating an adopted person in law as having been born to the adopter in wedlock, or born as a child of the marriage of joint adopters (pp 133–134), applies for the construction of enactments or instruments (including the 'instrument' which the Act deems to be constituted by the law of intestacy) passed or made before or after the adoption, but only so far as passed or made after 31 December 1975 (paras 1 (5), 3 (5)).

(*b*) *Rules relating to Dispositions of Property Contained in Instruments Made after 1975*

(*i*) *Definitions*

References to dispositions of property include a disposition by the creation of an entailed interest (para 17). A disposition includes the conferring of a power of appointment and any other disposition of an interest in or right over property. In its turn, 'power of appointment' includes any discretionary power to transfer a beneficial interest in property without the furnishing of valuable consideration. An oral disposition of property is covered by Sched 1 as if contained in an instrument made when the disposition was made (para 2). An instrument here includes a private Act settling property, but not, in (*ii*), (*iii*) and (*iv*) below, any other enactment (para 6 (6)).

(*ii*) *Where date of birth material*

In applying the positive limb of the general principle ((*a*) on p 133) to a disposition which depends on the date of birth of a child or children of the adoptive parent or parents, the disposition is to be construed as if the adopted child had been born on the date of adoption, and two or more children adopted on the same date had been born on that date in the order of their actual births; but this does not affect any reference to the child's age (para 6 (2)). Parliament has followed a modern practice of enacting explanatory examples into the Act. Paragraph 6 (3) of Sched 1 thus gives the following instances of phrases in wills on which para 6 (2) can operate:

(*a*) Children [or grandchildren] of *A* 'living at my death or born afterwards'—with or without the addition of the words 'before any one of such children' [or 'grandchildren'] 'for the time being in existence attains a vested interest, and who attain twenty-one years.' The reference to age twenty-one will not be affected.

(*b*) *A* for life 'until he has a child', and then to his child or children.

Where a disposition depends on the date of birth of a child who was born illegitimate and who is adopted by one of his natural parents as sole adopter, the rule of construction in para 6 (2) above does not affect entitlement under Pt II of the Family

Law Reform Act 1969, which contains provisions about the property rights of illegitimate children (CA 1975, Sched 1, para 14 (1), as amended by the Legitimacy Act 1976). Where a disposition depends on the date of birth of an adopted child who is legitimated, or treated as such, CA 1975, Sched 1, para 6 (2) above continues to apply notwithstanding the new rule of construction generally applicable where the date of birth of the legitimated child is material, ie s 5 (4) of the Legitimacy Act 1976 (1976 Act, s 6 (2), replacing CA 1975, Sched 1, para 14 (2)). The statutory example given in para 14 (3) assumes that a testator dies in 1976 bequeathing a legacy to his eldest grand-child living at a specified time, that his daughter has an illegitimate child in 1977 and his married son a child in 1978. Subsequently the illegitimate child is adopted by his mother as sole adopter. The daughter's child remains the testator's eldest grandchild *throughout*.

(*iii*) *Interests already vested in possession or expectant thereon*

The negative part of the general principle ((*b*) on p 133), which in normal cases dissociates the child from his former family, does not prejudice any interest vested in possession in the adopted child before the adoption, or any interest expectant (whether immediately or not) upon an interest so vested (para 6 (4)). An interest is vested in possession (and not merely in interest) when there exists a right of present enjoyment as distinct from a firm right of future enjoyment (see 32 Halsbury, 3rd ed, para 474). The case of a pension presently payable to the child (head (*f*) below) is but a particular instance of para 6 (4).

(*iv*) *Child-bearing age applied to possibility of adopting*

Where it is necessary to determine for the purposes of a disposition of property effected by an instrument whether a woman can have a child, it is to be presumed that once a woman has attained age fifty-five she will not adopt a child after the instrument is executed. If she does so adopt, the child is not (despite the general principle) to be treated as her child or that of any spouse of hers for the purposes of the instrument (para 6 (5)).

(v) Contrary indication

Rules *(ii)*, *(iii)* and *(iv)* above are expressed to be subject to 'any contrary indication' (para 6 (1)). These words are perhaps narrower than those used in s 16 (2) of AA 1958—'unless the contrary intention appears', for it was held in *Re Jones' Will Trusts* [1965] Ch 1124 that this contrary intention need not appear on the face of the instrument. Buckley J admitted evidence that the testator had discussed his affairs on a certain footing. It is thought that the new context would require a contrary indication to be coupled with the disposition more closely since the rules themselves are more specific. On the other hand, a contrast with para 16 of Sched 1 (see head *(d)* below), where the words 'expressed in the instrument' are used, provokes some expectation that the *Jones* case would not be entirely irrelevant if the point arose.

(c) Adoption by Natural Parent

The negative part of the general principle (*(b)* on p 133) has no effect as respects entitlement to property depending on an adopted person's relationship to one of his natural parents if that parent is also his sole adoptive parent (Sched 1, para 9). It would in those circumstances contradict the positive principle.

(d) Peerages etc and Property Devolving therewith

By para 10 of the new Sched 1 it is declared that an adoption does not affect the descent of any peerage or dignity or title of honour. Nor, by para 16, does it affect the devolution of any property limited (expressly or not) to devolve, as nearly as the law permits, along with any peerage or dignity or title of honour; but para 16 applies only if and so far as a contrary intention is not expressed in the instrument, and has effect subject to the terms of the instrument.

(e) Protection of Trustees and Personal Representatives

Paragraph 15 of CA 1975, Sched 1, protects trustees and personal representatives who convey or distribute property to or among persons entitled thereto without enquiring whether any adoption has been effected or revoked which may affect entitlement. Section 7 of the Legitimacy Act 1976 extends a similar protection against the possibility of a person adopted by one of his natural parents becoming legitimated. Trustees or representatives are not liable to any person if they had no notice at the time of conveyance or distribution of such an adoption or possibility. The right of a person to follow the property into the hands of a person other than a purchaser is not prejudiced.

(f) Child's Pension

A reservation in part (b) of the general principle is made by para 8 of Sched 1, which enacts that the negativing in law of the child's relationship to any person other than the adopter or adopters does not affect entitlement to a pension which is payable to or for the benefit of a child and is in payment at the time of his adoption.

6   Marriage Laws

Section 13 (3) of AA 1958 deemed an adopter and the person whom he was authorised to adopt under an adoption order, whensoever made and including an order made in Scotland or Northern Ireland (s 13 (4) and Sched 5, para 1), to be within the prohibited degrees of consanguinity for the purpose of the law relating *to marriage.* (It was held in Scotland that it was not incest for a man to have intercourse with his adopted daughter: *HM Advocate* v *Mackenzie* [1970] SLT 82.) Adoption orders, whenever made, in the Isle of Man or any of the Channel Islands, had the like effect as respects events occurring on or after 16 July 1964 (1964 Act, s 1 (1) (a)), as had overseas adoptions, as defined (p 111), as respects events on or after 1 February 1973 (AA 1968, s 4 (1); SI 1973 No 18).

This statutory relationship continued notwithstanding that the adopted person was subsequently re-adopted by another person. It attached also in the case of provisional adoption (1958 Act, s 53 (4)). On the other hand, nothing in s 13 (3) invalidated a marriage solemnised before 1 January 1950 (Sched 5, para 1). The subsection did not bring any relatives of the adopter within the fiction of consanguinity with the adopted person.

Though s 13 (3) has been repealed as respects things done or events occurring after 31 December 1975 (CA 1975, Sched 4, Pt

I), the current position in law appears to be exactly as before, because of a precisely contemporaneous amendment of the Marriage Act 1949 (CA 1975, Sched 3, para 8) which inserts the relationships of adoptive or former adoptive mother, daughter, father and son into the catalogue of prohibited degrees; and because para 7 (1) of Sched 1 to the 1975 Act negates the application of the general principle of that Schedule (see p 133) to that table of kindred and affinity, or to the incest provisions (ss 10 and 11) of the Sexual Offences Act 1956 (thus apparently giving statutory recognition in England and Wales to the *Mackenzie* decision).

7 Matrimonial Proceedings by or against Adopter

(a) *Position of Adopted Child*

The general principle (p 133) applies after 1975. As respects things done or events occurring before 1 January 1976, a child adopted jointly by the parties to a marriage counted in the statutory provisions relating to custody and maintenance, as a child of the family by force of s 27 (1) of the Matrimonial Proceedings and Property Act 1970, and s 52 (1) of the Matrimonial Causes Act 1973, as did a child adopted by only one party who had been treated by *both* spouses as a child of their family; and adoption for this purpose might have been by order under the 1958 Act, an adoption recognised by the 1964 Act or an overseas adoption as defined (p 111).

The main branch of the decision of Davies J in *Crossley* v *Crossley* [1953] P 97 was that, once an adoption order has been made, it supersedes any *previous* custody order, and the child is no longer a child of the marriage of its natural divorced parents. With respect, this decision seems entirely sound, to be reinforced by the provisions of the 1975 Act as to the status of an adopted person (p 133 et seq), and not to be affected by the strictures passed by the Family Divisional Court on the remainder of the judgment in *Crossley* (see *Re B (Adoption by Parent)*, referred to at p 27).

(b) *Adoption as Bar to Nullity Decree*

In *W* v *W* [1952] P 152 it was held that, in the particular circumstances, the adoption of a child *jointly* by the parties to a marriage was an act approbating the marriage and so (with other factors) constituted a bar, as the law then stood, to a decree of nullity on the ground of incapacity to consummate. But the bar in question was re-formulated in 1971, and now requires (Matrimonial Causes Act 1973, s 13 (1)), if the grant of a decree is to be precluded on general grounds, both that the petitioner has so conducted himself *in relation to the respondent* as to lead her reasonably to believe that he would not seek to have the marriage avoided; and also that the grant of a decree would be unjust to the respondent. In *D* v *D* [1979] 3 WLR 185 it was held that on the facts the respondent was misled by the petitioner's agreeing (at a time when he knew he had grounds for petitioning for nullity) to the joint adoption of children, but that as the respondent was content to have the marriage annulled the second limb of the statutory bar was not satisfied.

8 Affiliation Orders and Agreements; Care Orders and Resolutions

Where an adoption order was made after 31 December 1949* but before 1 January 1976, in respect of an infant who was illegitimate any affiliation order in force with respect to him, and any agreement whereby his father had undertaken to make payments specifically for his benefit, ceased to have effect (except for recovery of arrears) *unless* the infant was adopted by his mother, being a single woman (s 15 (1) and Sched 5, para 3). See also, as to the marriage of a single woman adopter, AA 1950, s 12 (2) (before April 1959) and CA 1958, s 22 (4).

AA 1958, s 15 (4), provided for the cessation on adoption of certain local authority care orders and resolutions assuming

---

*This is the date after which the 1949 Act was in force. Section 11 of that Act produced the results stated under Head 8 as regards adoption orders made in England, Scotland or Northern Ireland between 31 December 1949 and 1 October 1950. Section 15 of the 1958 Act extended to Northern Ireland orders (s 15 (5)). Isle of Man and Channel Islands adoption orders had the same effect if made on or after 16 July 1964 (1964 Act, s 1 (2) (*b*)). Overseas adoptions, as defined (see p 111), had the same effect between 31 January 1973 and 1 January 1976 under s 4 (2) of the 1968 Act.

parental rights, and subs (5) extended s 15 to Northern Irish adoptions.

In future the general principle bars affiliation proceedings; s 15 (1) is repealed as respects post-1975 events, and s 15 (4) and (5) from 26 November 1976; to be replaced:

(a) as regards affiliation orders and agreements by CA 1975, s 8 (3) (b) (see p 139);

(b) as to care orders, by a new s 21A of CYPA 1969 (inserted by Sched 3, para 70, to the 1975 Act), providing for a care order to cease on the adoption or provisional adoption of the child to whom it relates; and

(c) for resolutions assuming parental rights and duties, by subs (8) (a) and (b) of the new s 2, substituted in CA 1948 by CA 1975, s 57, also providing for cessation of the resolution if the child is adopted.

Like AA 1958, s 15, the new enactments apply for the time being to provisional as well as to full orders (see the provisions cited, CA 1975, s 108 (7), and AA 1958, s 53 (4) as adapted by SI 1976 No 1744, Sched 3, para 10).

9 Industrial etc Insurance

Certain statutes regulate the business of friendly societies, collecting societies and industrial assurance companies, and in particular empower such societies to insure (notwithstanding that the member or insured person may have no insurable interest) the payment of money on the death of a parent, while they also authorise (to a limited extent) insurance for funeral expenses of the child of a member or assured and in some cases his parent. As regards registered friendly societies, insurance on endowment terms is still, in some circumstances, and was formerly more widely, available in respect of a member's parent.

For the purposes of all these enactments the adopter under an English or Scottish adoption order (full or provisional), whenever made, is regarded as the parent (AA 1958, s 14 (1) and Sched 5, para 2, for events before 1976: see now the general principle (p 133)). Further, where the insurance is for funeral expenses of a child and was effected by the natural parent before the making of an adoption order, the rights and liabilities under the policy are transferred to the adopter by virtue of the order, he being treated as the person who took out the policy (1975 Act, Sched 1, para 11, re-enacting s 14 (2) of AA 1958).

References in s 11 of the Married Women's Property Act 1882 to a person's children include, and are deemed always to have included, references to children legally adopted by that person. Section 11 of the 1882 Act is the section which creates a trust in favour of the spouse and children of the assured in the case of certain policies effected by a married person, and it had previously been held (*Re Clay's Policy* [1937] 2 All ER 548) not to extend to a case where the named beneficiary was an adopted child, but AA 1958, s 14 (3) and Sched 5, para 2, retrospectively reversed this decision. In 1975 the 1958 provisions were repealed·as tautologous with the general principle applicable thenceforth.

As to the extension of AA 1958, s 14, to Northern Irish, Isle of Man or Channel Island orders, see AA 1964, s 1 (*b*) and (2); and as to overseas adoptions, so far as concerns events of the period between 31 January 1973 and 1 January 1976, see AA 1968, s 4 (1) (as to s 14 (1) and (3)) and s 4 (2) (which specifically covered s 14 (2)).

10   Social Security

The general principle of CA 1975, Sched 1 (see p 133) seems generally adequate to constitute an adopted person as a member of the beneficiary's family (or, as the case may be, a child for whom the beneficiary is responsible) in both standard and supplementary benefit cases. There are express saving provisions in certain death grant and industrial death benefit cases (see below).

Before 1976 the inclusion in the regular statutory schemes of recognition of the adoptive relationship was secured by specific provisions (now repealed) in the relevant Acts. The legislation with regard to supplementary benefits never made express reference to adopted children, but statutory liabilities to maintain children probably fell to be interpreted in the light of AA 1958, s 13, so that they fell upon the adoptive parent.

Special provisions of the Children Act   Schedule 1, para 7 (3), preserves the right of a person to be treated as a 'near relative' of a deceased person for the payment of death grant under s 32 of the Social Security Act 1975 despite the general principle of the Schedule (see p 133) if apart from that principle he would be so treated. Nor does the principle apply for the purposes of s 70 (3) (*b*) or s 73 (2) of the Social Security Act, which provide for payment of industrial death benefit to or in respect of an illegitimate child of the deceased and the child's mother (para 7 (4)). Lastly, subject to regulations under s 72 of the Social Security Act, the principle is not to affect the entitlement to an industrial death benefit of a person who would otherwise be treated as a relative of the deceased (para 7 (5)).

11 The Child's Names

From at least 1950 it has been accepted that not only the surname but also the Christian name or forename of the child could be changed on adoption, and the surname almost invariably is so changed. It was provided in s 21 (2) of the 1958 Act that the names specified in the order should be those stated in the application, the child's original name and the surname of the applicant being used in default of specification.

Section 21 (2) has now been repealed and the matter appears to rest on the prescribed application forms. In all courts these require the child's first name and surname, corresponding with his birth certificate, to be stated (though the title of *High Court* proceedings uses the adoptive name: p 82), and then go on to propose in a later paragraph that if an adoption order is made 'the child is to be known by the following names', space being allowed for a surname and 'other names'. The position in practice appears therefore to be the same as before; though it may be surmised that, for proper reasons, a court would have a discretion to refuse to confer a surname that was not the applicant's or otherwise connected with the case; and could possibly reject an obviously unsuitable forename, eg one with scabrous associations. Giving first consideration to the child's welfare, the court would, in form, be inserting a condition into the adoption order, as CA 1975, s 8 (7), allows.

Chapter XVI

Adoption Societies and Local Authorities

As has been stated in the Introduction (p 13), the Act of 1958 at present governs the making of arrangements by adoption societies in connection with the adoption of children and ensures the supervision of adopted children by local authorities. When CA 1975, s 28 (see Appendix II, para 1) is implemented, adoption placements otherwise than through approved adoption societies or local authorities will be prohibited except where the adoption is proposed by a relative of the child, or where the arrangements are made pursuant to a High Court order.

In the meantime 'third-party' placements are allowed subject to the restrictions and conditions described in this chapter.

As to which councils are local authorities for the purposes of the Acts, see p 13. Every such authority has power to make and participate in arrangements for adoption (AA 1958, s 28 (2)), and its functions in that regard (and in regard to other matters relating to adoption) are among those which it must discharge through a social services committee established under the Local Authority Social Services Act 1970, preserved in this respect by the Local Government Act 1972. A director of social services (see s 6 of that Act of 1970) is appointed and among his duties are those relating to the care and protection of children, which include the authority's functions under the Adoption Acts.

Despite the delegation of adoption work to the social services committee, the authority itself remains the 'agency' (see p 14), so that a member of the authority may see confidential papers in the possession of the committee or its servants, though not himself a committee-member (*R* v *Birmingham City District Council, ex parte O* (1980) *The Times*, 26 March.

1 Restriction on Making Arrangements for the Adoption of Children

It is not lawful for any body of persons (corporate or unincorporate) to make arrangements for the adoption of a child, unless that body is a registered adoption society (as to which see p 13) or a local authority (1958 Act, ss 29 (1), 57 (1)).

A person is deemed to make arrangements for adoption if he enters into or makes any agreement or arrangement for, or for facilitating, the adoption of the child by another, whether the adoption is effected, or intended to be effected, by an adoption order or otherwise (s 57 (2)).

A registered adoption society or local authority may not place any child in the actual custody of a person who proposes to adopt the child if an adoption order in favour of that person in respect of the child could not lawfully be made (as to which, see pp 16–18: s 29 (2)).

For offences under s 29, see pp 171–172. In addition to imposing a sentence for contravention of the provisions of s 29 (2), the court by whom the offender is convicted may order any child in respect of whom the offence is committed to be returned to his parents or guardian or to the society or authority (s 29 (5)).

2 Arrangements to be Made by and with Adoption Agencies

(a) *Preliminary Matters*

In pursuance of ss 30 (1) and 32 (1) and (3) of the 1958 Act, the Secretary of State has made regulations (consolidated in SI 1976 No 1796), which are called the Adoption Agencies Regulations, for apart from the provisions as to the registration and control of adoption societies, they apply to local authorities making or participating in arrangements for the adoption of infants as well as to such societies (reg 9). Until CA 1975, ss 4–7 (see Appendix II, para 1) come into effect, both authorities and registered adoption societies come within the term 'adoption agency' as used in the 1958 Act (as amended) and the 1975 Act (1975 Act, s 108 (5)).

We use 'agency' in the remainder of this chapter in a similarly comprehensive way, even where the 1958 Act continues to refer to societies and authorities (when they function as agencies) seriatim. But in regard to their care and supervisory functions (see heads 3 and 4 below), local authorities must be referred to by that description, though they are also comprehended within the term 'agency' in their capacity as arrangers of adoptions.

Both societies and authorities consider adoption questions through 'case committees', and in relation to a local authority the expression means a committee set up by the Social Services Committee (p 156) (reg 2 (1)). Case committees must comprise not less than three persons (including so far as practicable at least one man and one woman) each of whom is competent to judge whether a proposed placing is likely to promote the child's welfare (reg 6) (cf s 3 of the 1975 Act: p 8).

(b) *Agency 'Placements'*

Under the regulations:
- (*a*) An agency proposing to make arrangements for a child's adoption must:
  - (i) secure that every parent or guardian* proposing so to place the infant is furnished with a memorandum in the prescribed form, and signs and returns to the agency a certificate that he has read and understood the memorandum;
  - (ii) if the parents or guardian so request, provide them with the names and addresses of any denominational agencies which might meet their wishes as to religious persuasion (cf CA 1975, s 13: p 39) but subject to the welfare principle in s 3 of the 1975 Act (reg 7).

  The forms of memorandum and certificate are reproduced at pp 220–221).
- (*b*) No child is to be placed by or on behalf of an agency in

---

*See the definition in the note on p 35.

the actual custody of a person proposing to adopt him until:

(i) the agency has, so far as is reasonably practicable, ascertained the particulars set out in Sched 4 to the Regulations (see pp 222–225);

(ii) the agency has obtained a report by a fully registered medical practitioner as to the health of the infant in a form set out in Sched 5 to the Regulations (this corresponds exactly with the form of certificate to be lodged on an adoption application);

(iii) the proposing adopter has been interviewed by or on behalf of the agency's case committee;

(iv) the agency has made an assessment of the proposing adopter's personality and of his attitude to matters which would bear on his suitability to bring up the child in question;

(v) the agency has endeavoured to ascertain, in the case of a married couple who propose to adopt, the state of the marriage and whether it has the stability which is likely to provide a sound basis for a secure parental relationship with an adopted child;

(vi) an inspection has been made, on the agency's behalf, of any premises in Great Britain in which the proposing adopter intends that the child shall have his home;

(vii) the agency has made enquiries to satisfy itself that there is no reason to believe that it would be detrimental to the child to be kept by that person in those premises (in the case of an adoption society it should enquire of the local authority for the area in which the premises are situated);

(viii) the agency's case committee, in reaching a decision, has ascertained as far as practicable the child's wishes and feelings regarding the decision and has given due consideration to them having regard to his age and understanding and after considering all the information obtained and having regard to all the circumstances (including, as far as is practicable, any wishes of the child's parents or guardian as to the religious upbringing of the child), first consideration being given to the need to safeguard and promote the child's welfare throughout his childhood, has approved of the child being placed for adoption (reg 8 (*a*) to (*h*)).

(*c*) Every adoption agency must make adequate arrangements for the supervision of every child placed by or on behalf of the agency in the actual custody of a proposing adopter until the latter gives notice under AA 1958, s 3 (2), of intention to adopt (see p 30). In particular every such child is to be visited by a representative of the agency within one month of being placed and thereafter as often as the case committee considers necessary; and after each visit the representative is to make a report as to the child's welfare (reg 9 (1), (2)). The agency must also arrange for certain blood and urine tests to be carried out unless it already has a report of the tests in question (reg 9 (3), (4)) and must furnish a copy of the report of them to the proposing adopter (reg 14 (2)).

Regulations 10 to 13 incorporate provisions as to the confidentiality of information and records, as to the preservation of records for a period of at least seventy-five years, and for their transfer if a society ceases to exist. Disclosure is allowed only:

(i) as necessary for proceedings under the Acts of 1958 or 1975, or for the proper execution of the duty of the person making the disclosure;

(ii) for research purposes, to a person authorised in writing by or on behalf of the Secretary of State;

(iii) for the purposes of counselling under AA 1958, s 20A (see p 130, 'New Provision for Access to Birth Records'), or the corresponding section as to counselling in Scotland; but authorisation of disclosure under this head is confined to information relating to the birth record of an adopted person aged at least eighteen in England or Wales or seventeen in Scotland, and to disclosure to the adopted person, the General Register Office, or the local authority in whose area the adopted person is or in whose area the court sat when making the adoption order;

(iv) to the proposing adopter or adopters to the extent laid down in reg 14. By reg 14 (1) the agency is to give her or them, when the child is placed for adoption:

(1) written information about the child's background, parentage, physical, mental and emotional development; and

(2) a memorandum (naturally, a different form from that given to parents under reg 7) advising the adopters of the need to tell the child about his adoption and origins, and of the child's right on reaching eighteen (seventeen in Scotland) to obtain a copy of his birth certificate, and of the counselling service. A counselling service on any problems relating to adoption is also to be offered in the memorandum to proposing adopters.

As to an agency applying to the court for directions about disclosure of any confidential information not covered by the Regulations, cf Practice Direction [1968] 1 WLR 373.

The regulations apply equally to provisional adoption cases (reg 2 (2)).

(c) Subsequent Proceedings

In the case of adoptions arranged by adoption agencies there is special provision for giving the agency a sort of reversion to the child. The general requirements in all cases of a trial period of three months' actual custody before application to the court is made (see p 29) applies to all adoptions. In addition the Act provides as follows:

(a) At any time after a child is delivered into the actual custody of a person in pursuance of arrangements made by an agency for the adoption of the child by that person, and before an adoption order has been made in favour of that person, the latter may notify the agency in writing of his intention not to retain the child's actual custody; or the agency may give written notice to the person concerned of its intention not to allow the child to remain in his actual custody (1958 Act, s 35 (1)). But after an application for adoption has been made the agency may give the notice only with the court's leave (s 35 (2)); the procedure for obtaining such leave is prescribed by H Ct R, r 23; Co Ct R, r 21; Mag Ct R, r 28, and corresponds, in all courts, with that on an application by a parent or guardian under s 34 or s 34A (see p 95 and Forms 15 and 16, pp 218–219). In all courts, if leave to give the notice is granted, the judge may treat the application as the hearing of the adoption application and refuse the adoption order accordingly.

(b) If a notice is given by or to an agency as described in (a) above or if an application for adoption by a person in whose actual custody the child has been placed by an agency is refused by the court or withdrawn, subss (3) and (5) of s 35 of AA 1958 fall to be observed. Under these provisions the intended adopter must, within seven days after the date on which the notice was given or the application refused or withdrawn, as the case may be, cause the child to be returned to the agency or to a suitable person nominated by it for that purpose. This requirement cannot be stayed pending an appeal against the court's refusal (*Re C S C (an Infant)* [1960] 1 WLR 304); but subs (5A), inserted by CA 1975, s 31, allows the court, if it thinks fit, at any time before the expiry of the seven-day period, to extend it to a specified duration of not more than six weeks, though only in a case where an adoption order has been refused.

The same obligation to return the child within seven days arises if an interim order (see p 53) expires (or if a permitted extension of it expires) without a full adoption order having been made (s 35 (4)).

For the offence of contravening s 35 of the Act, see p 173. The convicting court has power to order the return of the child to his parents or guardian or to the agency (s 35 (6)).

3 Children in Care of Local Authorities

In the case of children who, not being placed by an adoption agency for adoption, are nevertheless for the time being in the care of a local authority, the provisions of s 35 of the Act, set out immediately above, apply on notice being given to the local authority of intention to adopt (see p 30). This is subject to the qualification that, where the application for adoption is refused or withdrawn, the child need not be returned to the local authority unless that authority so requires (s 36 (1)).

In such cases, too, the following incidental consequences flow with the result of putting the child, during the trial period, into the effective possession of the intending adopter and in practice throwing into abeyance the care exercised by the authority (s 36 (2)):

(a) Any right of the authority to require the return of the child *otherwise* than pursuant to s 35 is suspended until the application for adoption has been made and disposed of.

(b) While the child remains in the actual custody of the person giving the notice of intention to adopt, no contributions are payable under CYPA 1933, s 86, without prejudice to the recovery of arrears.

But (b) above ceases to have effect when twelve weeks have elapsed since the notice of intention to adopt without the application being made or when the application has been refused or withdrawn.

The Child Benefit Act 1975 confers benefit on a person *responsible* for one or more children in any particular week. A proposing adopter may therefore number the child among his or her family for benefit purposes whilst it remains in his actual custody.

4 Supervision Pending Adoption

(a) General

The 1958 Act, as amended, embodies a system (parallel in some respects to that relating to foster children maintained for reward) under which local authorities exercise a protective supervision 'in relation to certain children awaiting adoption or placed with strangers', as the heading to Pt IV of the Act still says. But Pt IV has been amended by Pt II of CYPA 1969, and by CA 1975. Some of the 1975 amendments, namely those depending on the prospective need for notification to the local authority in *all* non-agency cases (s 18: see Appendix II, para 2) are not yet in force. The passages which follow attempt to describe the situation as it now exists, with particular reference to cases of proposed adoption.

For offences and penalties under Pt IV, see p 173.

(b) Protected Children

The children to whom the revised provisions apply are called protected children: and AA 1958, s 37 (amended in 1959, 1969 and 1975) is devoted to defining a protected child in terms which are quite extraordinarily obscure and puzzlingly tautologous. One might have hoped to find in AA 1976 (still comatose: see p 2) a kind of 'Keeling schedule' ironing out the obscurities and stitching in the cross-references. Alas, the draftsman has played safe and has had recourse residually to a reference back to s 37.

At any rate, and whatever other children may be within the conglomerate definition, a child is a protected child where he is:

(a) below the upper limit of compulsory school age (see p 30) and in the actual custody of a person (not his parent, guardian or relative) who proposes to adopt him, and another person (not being his parent or guardian) takes part in the arrangements for placing him; or

(b) (apparently overlapping with (a) in many cases) in the actual custody of a person who has given notice under s 3 (2) to the appropriate local authority (p 30)

unless some other code of protection, as specified in s 37 (2) or (3) of AA 1958, CA 1958, s 2, or s 19 of the Mental Health Act 1959, applies.

Protection, whether of a child placed with a stranger or of one awaiting adoption, ceases at the age of eighteen, or before then:

(a) on the appointment of a guardian for him under the Guardianship of Minors Act 1971;

(b) on the notification to the local authority where the child has his home that the adoption application has been withdrawn; or

(c) on the making of an adoption order, a care or supervision order on dismissal of an adoption application under CA 1975, s 17 (see p 92), a custodianship order (see Appendix II, para 9) when that becomes possible, or an order under s 42, 43 or 44 of the Matrimonial Causes Act 1973 (cf p 21) (AA 1958, s 37 (4), as substituted by Sched 3, para 31 (b), to the 1975 Act).

(c) *General Supervision*

Every local authority must secure that protected children within its area are visited from time to time by its officers, who are to satisfy themselves as to the well-being of the children and give such advice as to care and maintenance as appears needed (s 38). Such visiting officers may, on production, if requested, of due authority, inspect any premises in the area in which protected children are kept or are to be kept (s 39).

In cases where protection arises from placing arrangements, every person (other than a parent or the person with whom the child is placed) who takes part in the arrangements must give written notice to the local authority (s 40 (1), (2), (3)). Notice in other cases is implicit in the qualification for protection. But in all cases a person who has or proposes to have a protected child in his actual custody must at the request of the local authority give it such particulars as are known to him of the child's name, sex, date and place of birth, and the name and address of every person who is a parent or guardian, or who acts as guardian, or from whom the child has been or is to be received (s 40 (6)).

(d) *Change of Address*

Where a person having the actual custody of a protected child changes his permanent address, he must give the local authority written notice specifying the new address. The notice is to be given at least two weeks before the change, or, if the change is made in an emergency, not later than a week afterwards. If the new address is in the area of another authority, the notice is to the old authority, which furnishes relevant particulars to the new one (s 40 (4)).

(e) *Death of Child*

If a protected child dies, the person in whose actual custody he then was must give written notice of the death to the local authority within forty-eight hours (s 40 (5)).

(f) *Unsuitable Premises and Persons*

(a) Where placing arrangements, such that the subject of them would become a protected child, are made without the participation of an adoption agency, and it appears to the local authority that it would be detrimental to the child to be kept by the person with whom he is to be placed in the premises in which he proposes to keep him, the authority may by written notice prohibit that person from receiving the child in those premises (s 41).

A person aggrieved by such a prohibition may appeal to a *juvenile* court within fourteen days of being notified of the prohibition, and the notice to the person in question must inform him of this right of appeal (s 42 (1), (2)).

(*b*) On being satisfied that a protected child is being kept or is about to be received (i) by any person who is unfit to have his care; or (ii) in contravention of a prohibition as at (*a*) above; or (iii) in any premises or environment detrimental or likely to be detrimental to him, a juvenile court may, on the complaint of the local authority, make an order for the removal of the child to a place of safety until he can be restored to his parents or guardian or until other arrangements are made (s 43 (1)). A single justice may exercise a similar power on the application of a person authorised to visit protected children if it is proved that the health or well-being of the child is in imminent danger (ibid).

It is worthy of note that the juvenile court retains jurisdiction in proceedings under s 42 or s 43 cf AA 1958, for such proceedings are in terms excepted by s 65 (5) cf MCA 1980 from the otherwise universal definition of proceedings under the 1958 Act as 'domestic proceedings' (see p 60). Offences under the Adoption Acts (see p 171) are of course matters for the summary criminal courts, adult or juvenile according to circumstances.

(*g*) *Insurance*

A person who maintains a protected child is deemed to have no interest in the child's life for the purposes of the Life Assurance Act 1774 (AA 1958, s 46), and a policy on that life for the use or benefit of the person first mentioned is therefore void. Certain other policies (eg for personal accident) may also be affected by this provision (see 25 Halsbury, 4th ed, para 558). As to industrial insurance in cases where the adoption is completed, see pp 153–154.

(h)   *Appeals under Pt IV*

By AA 1958 s 48, and the Courts Act 1971, an appeal lies to the Crown Court from any order made under Pt IV (ss 37–49) of the 1958 Act by a juvenile court or any other magistrates' court. This would include the single justice empowered to make a removal order.

Chapter XVII

Miscellaneous

1 Restriction on Advertisements

It is not lawful to publish an advertisement indicating that the parent or guardian of a child wishes it to be adopted; or that a person wishes to adopt a child; or that any person, not being a registered adoption society or local authority, is willing to make arrangements for adoption (s 51 (1)).

Neither may any advertisement be published indicating that a person will undertake or arrange for the care and maintenance of a child unless the advertisement truly states that person's name and address (CA 1958, s 37 (1)). (There is provision in s 97 of CA 1975—not yet operative—for regulations to be made forbidding altogether advertisements seeking foster parents, and certain other advertisements by members of a specified class of persons.)

As to offences contravening these provisions, see pp 173–174.

2 Prohibition of Unauthorised Payments and Rewards

(1) By s 50 (1) of AA 1958 it is not lawful to make or give to any person any payment or reward for or in consideration of:

(*a*) the adoption by that person of a child;

(*b*) the grant by that person of any agreement or consent required in connection with an adoption;

(*c*) the transfer by that person of the actual custody of a child with a view to its adoption; or

(*d*) the making by that person of any arrangements for the adoption of a child.

(2) Payments may, however, be made *to* an adoption society or local authority by a parent or guardian or by an adopter or proposing adopter for expenses reasonably incurred by the

society or authority in connection with the adoption. And the court to which an adoption application is made may authorise a payment or reward (s 50 (3)).

(3) By s 50 (3A) (added by the Criminal Law Act 1977, Sched 12) the general prohibition in s 50 is excluded in the case of payments *by* adoption agencies for:

(a) legal or medical expenses incurred or to be incurred by an applicant or proposing applicant for an adoption order or provisional adoption order in connection with the adoption;

(b) placing (to another agency); or

(c) a contact fee to an approved voluntary organisation.

In cases (a) and (b) the exclusion is in effect deemed always to have applied.

(4) As to the approval of schemes for the payment by an adoption agency of allowances to adopters, see CA 1975, s 32, not yet in force (Appendix II, para 8).

(5) For the offence of contravening s 50, see p 173. The court may order any child in respect of whom an offence is committed to be removed to a place of safety until he can be restored to his parents or guardian, or until other arrangements can be made for him (s 50 (2)).

3 Restrictions on Sending Children for Adoption Abroad

Under earlier Acts restrictions were imposed on the transfer of the care of British children to persons who were strangers to them and were resident abroad, though a licence could be obtained from a magistrate if the person to whom care was to be transferred was a British subject.

This licensing system was abolished in 1959 and its place taken by a scheme of provisional adoptions covering a wider range of cases but on a condition that appears to be more stringent (see p 55). The prohibition of the unauthorised removal abroad of a British child, however, remains, and it will remain after CA 1975, s 25, has replaced provisional adoptions by the system of vesting parental rights, and obligations in corresponding circumstances (see Appendix II, para 7).

Section 52 (1) of AA 1958 provides that, except under the

authority of a provisional adoption order, it is not lawful for any person to take or send a child who is a British subject* out of Great Britain to any place outside the United Kingdom, the Channel Islands or the Isle of Man with a view to the adoption of the child by any person not being its parent, guardian or relative.† Section 52 does not apply to children emigrating under the authority of the Secretary of State under CA 1948, s 17 (CYPA 1963, s 55, as amended by CYPA 1969, Sched 6). It does, however, effectively prevent any part of the trial period in a provisional order case concerning a British child from being spent abroad (*Re M (a Minor)* [1973] Fam 66: see p 32).

As to the summary offence of contravening s 52 (1), see p 174. Section 52 (2) makes admissible in evidence, in proceedings under the section, a report by a British consular officer or a deposition made before such an officer if duly authenticated under his signature and on proof that the officer or deponent is not in the United Kingdom.

---

*Or a citizen of the Republic of Ireland. The 1958 Act (s 57 (3)) treats such citizens as if they were British subjects.

†'Relative' is defined on p 18*n* and 'guardian' on p 35*n*.

Chapter XVIII

Offences

The 1958 Act creates several offences consisting of the contravention of its provisions, and these and their penal sanctions (together with some offences constituted by CA 1958 and CYPA 1969) are tabulated below. It is provided by s 54 (1) of AA 1958 that, where any offence under the Act committed by a body corporate is proved to have been committed with the consent or connivance of, or to be attributable to any neglect on the part of, any director, manager, member of the committee, secretary or other officer of the book, he, as well as the body, shall be deemed to be guilty of that offence and shall be liable to be proceeded against and punished accordingly. All the offences are summary ones and therefore MCA 1980, s 127 (1), requiring the laying of the information within six months of the commission of the offence, applies. Proceedings for any of these offences may, in England or Wales, be taken by a local authority (AA 1958, s 54 (2); CA 1948, s 55 (1); CA 1958, s 37 (3)).

The penalties given below are as adjusted (usually by way of increase in the maximum fine, but in some cases also by reduction of the maximum terms of imprisonment) by various paragraphs of CA 1975, Sched 3, and by the Criminal Law Act 1977, s 31 (5), (6).

Statute	*Offence*	*Penalty*
AA 1958, s 29 (1), (3)	Body of persons making any arrangements for adoption of child unless it is a registered adoption society or local authority. Every person guilty of a contravention commits the offence.	Imprisonment not exceeding three months and/or fine not exceeding £400.

Statute	*Offence*	*Penalty*
s 29 (2), (3)	Registered adoption society or local authority placing any child, for the adoption of whom arrangements are made by the society or authority, in the care and possession of a proposing adopter in whose favour an adoption order in respect of the child cannot lawfully be made. Every person guilty of a contravention commits the offence.	Imprisonment not exceeding three months and/or fine not exceeding £400. As to the court's power to order the return of the infant, see p 157
AA 1958, s 29 (3)	Taking part in the management or control of a body of persons which exists wholly or in part for the purpose of making arrangements for the adoption of children, and which is not a registered adoption society or local authority. For a provision as to the evidence admissible in proceedings for this offence, see s 29 (4).	Imprisonment not exceeding three months and/or fine not exceeding £400.
s 32 (2)	Contravening or failing to comply with the provisions of a regulation made under s 32 (1A).	Fine not exceeding £400.
s 33 (3)	Failing to comply with the requirements of a notice given by the local authority to a registered adoption society or to an officer of such a society under s 33 (1), (2), requiring production of books and documents.	Imprisonment not exceeding three months and/or fine not exceeding £50.
s 34 (1), (3)	Parent or guardian who has agreed to the making of an adoption order removing the child, while the application for that order is pending, from the custody of the person with whom the child has his home against that person's will, without the court's leave.	Imprisonment not exceeding three months and/or fine not exceeding £400.
s 34 (2), (3)	Parent or guardian who did *not* consent to a freeing application (see Appendix II, para 3) removing the child from the custody of the person with whom the child has his home against that person's will, while the freeing application is pending and the child is in the care of the applicant-agency, without the court's leave.	
s 34A (1), (2), (6)	Any person removing a child from the custody of an applicant for its adoption, or of a prospective adopter who has given notice to the local authority, if the applicant or prospective adopter is the person with whom the child has had his home for the preceeding five years, against the applicant's or prospective adopter's will, except with the court's leave or under statutory authority or on the child's arrest.	

Statute	Offence	Penalty
AA 1958, s 35 (3), (6)	Proposing adopter failing to cause child to be returned to the registered adoption society or local authority which has made arrangements for its adoption, or to a suitable nominated person, within seven days of the date of (*a*) a notice by the adopter to the society or authority of his intention not to adopt the child, or (*b*) a notice by the society or authority of its intention not to allow the child to remain in his care and possession, or (*c*) the court's refusal of or the withdrawal of an application for an adoption order in respect of the child. [Note—The court can, however, extend within limits the time allowed following a *refusal* (see p 162).]	Imprisonment not exceeding three months and/or fine not exceeding £400. As to the convicting court's power to order the return of the infant, see p 162.
s 44 (1) (*a*)	Failure to give, within the time specified, a notice required under Pt IV of the Act, ie a notice required under s 40 (1) by a person taking part in placing arrangements (see p 165), under s 40 (4) on change of permanent address (see p 165) or under s 40 (5) on death of a child (see p 165).	
	Failure to give, within a reasonable time, any information required under Pt IV of the Act, ie under s 40 (6) (see p 165).	Imprisonment not exceeding three months and/or fine not exceeding £400. As to the court's power to order the removal of the child, see p 166.
	Knowingly making or causing or procuring another to make any false or misleading statement in any such notice or information.	
s 44 (1) (*b*)	Refusing to allow the visiting of a protected child by a duly authorised officer of a local authority or the inspection of any premises under s 39 (see p 165).	
s 44 (1) (*c*)	Keeping any child in any premises in contravention of a prohibition imposed under Pt IV of the Act, ie under s 41 (see p 166).	
s 44 (1) (*d*)	Refusing to comply with an order under Pt IV of the Act for removal of a child, ie under s 43 (see p 166)).	
	Obstructing any person in the execution of such an order.	
AA 1958, s 50 (2)	Making or giving, or agreeing or offering to make or give, receiving or agreeing to receive, or attempting to obtain any payment or reward prohibited by s 50 of the Act (see p 169).	Imprisonment not exceeding three months and/or fine not exceeding £400. As to the court's power to order removal of the child, see p 169.
s 51 (2)	Causing to be published or knowingly publishing an advertisement contravening s 51 (see p 168).	Fine not exceeding £400.

Statute	Offence	Penalty
CA 1958, s 37 (2)	Causing to be published or knowingly publishing an advertisement in contravention of s 37 or of regulations made under it (see p 168).	Imprisonment not exceeding six months and/or fine not exceeding £400.
AA 1958, s 52 (1)	Taking or sending a child who is a British subject* out of Great Britain to any place outside the United Kingdom, the Channel Islands and the Isle of Man in contravention of s 52 (1), or making or taking part in any arrangements for transferring the care and possession of a child to any person for that purpose (see p 170).	Imprisonment not exceeding three months and/or a fine not exceeding £400.
CYPA 1969, s 59 (2)	Obstructing the exercise by an inspector authorised under ibid, s 58(1), of the right of entry to premises at which a protected child within AA 1958, Pt IV, is being accommodated or maintained.	First offence: fine not exceeding £25; second and subsequent offences: £50. Refusal to allow entry is deemed reasonable cause for suspicion on which a search warrant may be issued.

* Or a citizen of the Republic of Ireland (s 57 (3)).

Appendix I

Forms

A—HIGH COURT FORMS

1 FORMS IN CASES OTHER THAN CONVENTION CASES
[Scheduled to the H Ct R]

Rule 4 (1)

FORM 1
*Originating summons for an adoption order or a provisional
adoption order*

In the High Court of Justice No.   of 19
  Family Division.

IN THE MATTER OF The Adoption Act 1958
                  and

IN THE MATTER OF The Children Act 1975
                  and

IN THE MATTER OF .... [1] a child.

Let .... of .... attend at the Royal
Courts of Justice, Strand, London, WC2A 2LL, on a date to be fixed
for the hearing of the application of.................................... of ....
for an order:

   [1. That a guardian *ad litem* be appointed for the purpose of safeguarding
the interests of the said ....][2]
   [2. That the applicant do adopt [*or* be granted a provisional adoption
order in respect of] the said ....]
   [3. That the costs of this application be provided for.]

  Dated the................................day of................................ 19......
  This summons was taken out by.. of
.... solicitor for
the above named ....

Notes
  1 Enter the name(s) and surname by which the child is to be known if adopted.
  2 Delete if the Official Solicitor has consented to act as the guardian *ad litem*.

Rule 6

FORM 2
[as amended by SI 1978 No 1519]

Affidavit in support of an application for an adoption order or a provisional adoption order[1]

[*Every paragraph must be completed or, if it is not applicable, deleted*]
[*Heading as in Form 1*]

I/We, ...
of..
wishing to adopt [*or* obtain a provisional adoption order in respect of]
.... [2] a child
under the Adoption Act 1958 and the Children Act 1975, hereby make
oath and say that the particulars set out in paragraphs 1 to .... of this
affidavit are true:—

PART I
Particulars of the applicant(s)

   1. Name of (first) applicant in full..
       Address[3] ....
       Occupation..
       Date of Birth..
       Relationship (if any) to the child..
       [Name of second applicant in full..
       ....
       Address[3] ....
       Occupation..
       Date of Birth..
       Relationship (if any) to the child..]
   2. I am/We are/One of us [namely..] is
domiciled in England and Wales/Scotland/Northern Ireland/The Channel
Islands/the Isle of Man [*or* I am/We are not domiciled in England and
Wales or Scotland].
   3. I am unmarried/a widow/widower/divorced [*or* We are married to
each other and our marriage certificate (or other evidence of marriage) is
exhibited to this affidavit [*or*] I am applying alone as a married person
and can satisfy the court that..][4].
   [4. I am applying alone for an adoption order/a provisional adoption
order in respect of my own child and can satisfy the court that the other
natural parent ....
....][5].
   [5. A certificate as to my/our health, signed by a fully registered medical
practitioner, is exhibited to this affidavit][6].

PART II
Particulars of the child

6. The child is of the.. sex and is not and has not been married. He/She was born on the .... day of.................................. 19...... and is the person to whom the birth/adoption certificate exhibited to this affidavit[7] relates [*or* was born on or about the.................................... day of .... 19......, in..............................][8].

[7. A report on the health of the child, made by a fully registered medical practitioner on the.................................... day of.. 19...... is exhibited to this affidavit][9] [10].

8. *Parentage, etc.* The child is the child[11] of...[12] whose last known address was..
....

[*or* deceased] and[13]...
....

[*or* deceased].

[9. The guardian(s) of the child (other than the mother or father of the child) is/are..
....
....

(and..
.... of..
....)][14].

[10. *Parental Agreement.* A document/documents signifying the agreement of the said:..[15]
[and..]
to the making of an adoption order/provisional adoption order in pursuance of my/our application is/are exhibited to this affidavit.]

[11. I/We request the judge to dispense with the agreement of:
....
on the ground/s that..[15] [16]
[and..]
and there are exhibited to this affidavit two copies of a statement of the facts on which I/we intend to rely.]

[12. *Care, etc.* The.................................... Council (or....................................)
of...
has/have the powers and duties of a parent or guardian of the child [or the parental rights and duties with respect to the child]][17] [17a].

[13. *Maintenance.* .... of.. is liable by virtue of an order made by the..court at...
on the.................day of.. 19......(or by an agreement dated the.................day of..19......)
to contribute to the maintenance of the child][18].

G

14. *Proposed names.* If an adoption order/a provisional adoption order is made in pursuance of this application, the child is [until adopted under the law or within the country of my/our domicile] to be known by the following names:—

Surname ....

Other names ....

PART III
General

15. The child was received into my/our actual custody on the.........................
day of...19......, and has been continuously in my/our actual custody since that date (*or as appropriate*)[19].

16. The child has/has not had his home with me/us for the five years preceding the date of this application.

[17. I/We/One of us (namely...)
notified the .... Council on the............
day of...19......, of my/our intention to apply for an adoption order/provisional adoption order in respect of the child][20].

18. No proceedings relating in whole or in part to the child have been completed or commenced in any court in England or Wales or elsewhere [except...
....
....
....][21 22 23].

19. I/We have not received or given any reward or payment for, or in consideration of, the adoption of the child or for any agreement to the making of the adoption order/provisional adoption order [except as follows:—

....
....][24].

20. As far as I/we know no person or body has taken part in the arrangements for placing the child in my/our actual custody [except
....][25].

[21. For the purpose of this application reference may be made to
....
....][26].

[22. I/We desire that my/our identity should be kept confidential, and the serial number of this application is..][27].

[23. I/We intend to adopt the child under the law of or within
...., which is the country of my/our domicile, and evidence as to the law of adoption in that country is filed with this affidavit][28].

[24. I/We desire to remove the child from Great Britain for the purpose of adoption].

I/We accordingly apply for an adoption order/a provisional adoption order in respect of the child.

Sworn, etc.

This affidavit is filed on behalf of the applicant(s).

Notes

General. The footnotes to this Form are for guidance only and need not appear as part of the affidavit.

1. Documents referred to in this affidavit should be separately exhibited.

2. State the first name(s) and surname as shown in any certificate referred to in paragraph 6. Otherwise state the first name and surname by which the child was known before being placed for adoption.

3. State the address where the applicant has his home and the place (if different) where documents may be served on him.

4. A married applicant can apply alone only if he or she can satisfy the court that his or her spouse cannot be found, or that they have separated and are living apart and that the separation is likely to be permanent, or that by reason of physical or mental ill health his or her spouse is incapable of making an application for an adoption order. Any documentary evidence (including death certificate where relevant) on which the applicant proposes to rely should be exhibited to the affidavit. The name and address (if known) of the other spouse should be supplied.

5. State the reason to be relied upon (that the other natural parent is dead, or cannot be found, or that there is some other reason, which should be specified, justifying his or her exclusion.) Documentary evidence, *e.g.*, a death certificate should be exhibited to the affidavit where appropriate.

6. A separate medical certificate is required in respect of each applicant. There is an official form (Form 4) which may be used for this purpose. No certificate, however, need be exhibited to the affidavit if the child is the child of the applicant or either of them, or has reached the upper limit of the compulsory school age.

7 If a child has previously been adopted, a certified copy of the entry in the Adopted Children Register should be exhibited to the affidavit and not a certified copy of the original entry in the Registers of Births.

8 Where a certificate is not exhibited to the affidavit, state the place including the country of birth if known.

9 There is an official form (Form 5) which may be used for this purpose. No certificate need be exhibited to the affidavit if the child is the child of the applicant or one of them, or has reached the upper limit of the compulsory school age.

10 If the child is less than one year old on the date of the originating summons the report should have been made during the month preceding that date. If the child is one year old or more on that date, the report should have been made during the period of six months before that date.

11 If the child has previously been adopted, state the names of his adoptive parents and not those of his natural parents.

12 State mother's name.

13 State name of father, if known.

14 State particulars of any person appointed by deed or will in accordance with the provisions of the Guardianship of Infants Acts 1886 and 1925 or the Guardianship of Minors Act 1971, or by a court of competent jurisdiction to be a guardian. Do not include any person who has custody of the child only: under section 57 (1) of the Act of 1958 (as amended by paragraph 39 (*d*) of Schedule 3 to the Act of 1975), a father of an illegitimate child who has custody of the child under section 9 of the Guardianship of Minors Act 1971 (or section 2 of the Illegitimate Children (Scotland) Act 1930) is a guardian, so that his agreement to the adoption is required unless dispensed with, but his identity should be given at paragraph 8 above.

180 *Adoption of Children*

15 State either in paragraph 10 or 11 the names of the persons mentioned in paragraphs 8 and 9 except that in the case of an illegitimate child the father of the child should be stated only if he has custody of the child by virtue of an order under section 9 of the Guardianship of Minors Act 1971, or under section 2 of the Illegitimate Children (Scotland) Act 1930.

16 State one or more of the grounds set out in section 12 (2) of the Act of 1975.

17 This paragraph should be completed where some person or body has the power and duties of a parent or guardian of the child by virtue of section 24 of the Children and Young Persons Act 1969 or has vested in it or them the parental rights and duties with respect to the child under section 2 of the Children Act 1948, or section 60 of the Act of 1975.

17a Where the child is in the care of a local authority or voluntary organisation, this paragraph may be modified so as to state that the body has the child in its care under section 1 of the Children Act 1948 (or, where appropriate, under or within the meaning of any other enactment). In the case of a voluntary organisation, care is defined by section 88 of the Act of 1975.

18 This paragraph should be completed where some person or body is liable to contribute to the maintenance of the child under a court order or an agreement.

19 Under section 3 (1) of the Act of 1958, an adoption order cannot be made unless the child has been continuously in the actual custody of the applicant during the three months before the order is made; this is modified to some extent by section 12 (3) in the case of a married couple where both are or one is living outside Great Britain (so that a continuous period of at least three months' actual custody with one applicant which includes a period of one month with the other will suffice). In this case the relevant facts should be stated. In the case of a provisional adoption order under section 53 of the Act of 1958, the relevant period of actual custody before an order can be made is six months.

20 Notice does not have to be given if the applicant or one of the applicants is a parent of the child or if at the time of the hearing the child will have reached the upper limit of the compulsory school age.

21 The court cannot proceed with the application if a previous adoption application made by the same person in relation to the child was refused, unless one of the conditions in section 22 (4) of the Act of 1975 is satisfied.

22 Where the application is made by a married couple of whom one is a parent and the other is a step-parent of the child, or by a step-parent of the child alone, the court must under section 10 (3) and section 11 (4) of the Act of 1975 dismiss the application if it considers that the matter would be better dealt with under section 42 (orders for custody etc. in matrimonial proceedings) of the Matrimonial Causes Act 1973.

23 State the nature of the proceedings and the date and effect of any orders or judgments.

24 Any such payment or reward is illegal except payment to an adoption society or local authority in respect of their expenses incurred in connection with the adoption.

25 State the name of the local authority, adoption society or individual who has taken part in the arrangements for placing the child in the actual custody of the applicant with a view to his adoption.

26 Where the applicant or one of the applicants is a parent of the child, or a relative as defined by section 57 (1) of the Act of 1958, no referee need be named.

27 If the applicant wishes his identity to be kept confidential the serial number obtained under rule 5 of the Adoption (High Court) Rules 1976 should be given.

28 Any accompanying affidavit must be sworn by a person who is suitably qualified on account of his knowledge or experience to give evidence as to the law concerned.

Rule 7 (1)

FORM 3

Agreement to an adoption order or a provisional adoption order
[*Heading as in Form* 1]

Whereas an application is to be/has been made by... /
and.. [*or* under the serial number...................],[1]
for an adoption order/a provisional adoption order in respect of
.... [2] a child:

[And whereas the child is the person to whom the birth certificate[3] now produced and shown to be marked "A" relates:][4]

And whereas the child is not less than six weeks old:

I, the undersigned...
of..
being a parent/guardian[5] of the child hereby state as follows:—

1. I understand that the effect of an adoption order/a provisional adoption order will be to deprive me permanently of the parental rights and duties relating to the child and to vest them in the applicant(s); and in particular I understand that, if an order is made, I shall have no right to see or get in touch with the child or to have him/her returned to me.

2. I further understand that the Court cannot make an adoption order/a provisional adoption order without the agreement of each parent or guardian of the child unless the Court dispenses with an agreement on the ground that the person concerned—

    (*a*) cannot be found or is incapable of giving agreement, or
    (*b*) is withholding agreement unreasonably, or
    (*c*) has persistently failed without reasonable cause to discharge the parental duties in relation to the child, or
    (*d*) has abandoned or neglected the child, or
    (*e*) has persistently ill-treated the child, or
    (*f*) has seriously ill-treated the child and the rehabilitation of the child within the household of the parent or guardian is unlikely.

3. I further understand that, when the application for an adoption order/provisional adoption order is heard, this document may be used as evidence of my agreement to the making of the order unles I inform the Court that I no longer agree[6].

4. I hereby freely, and with full understanding of what is involved, agree unconditionally to the making of an adoption order/a provisional adoption order in pursuance of the application.

5. As far as I know, no other person or body has taken part in the arrangements for placing the child in the actual custody of the applicant(s) [except..
....
of...][7].

(*Signature*) ....

This form, duly completed, was signed by the said...
before me[8] at ....
on the.................. day of..19......
(*Signature*) ....
(*Address*) ....
....
(*Description*) ....

WARNING: It is an offence to receive or give any reward or payment for, or in consideration of, the adoption of the child or for agreeing to the making of an adoption order or provisional adoption order, other than a payment to a local authority or adoption society for their expenses incurred in connection with the adoption.

Notes

1 Insert either the name(s) of the applicant(s) or the serial number assigned to the applicant(s) for the purpose of the application.

2 Insert the name(s) and surname as known to the person giving agreement.

3 If the child has previously been adopted, a certified copy of the entry in the Adopted Children Register should be attached and not a certified copy of the original entry in the Registers of Births.

4 Where two or more forms of agreement are supplied to the court at the same time they may both or all refer to a certificate attached to one of the forms of agreement.

5 The father of an illegitimate child is not a parent for this purpose, but is a guardian if he has custody of the child by virtue of an order under section 9 of the Guardianship of Minors Act 1971, or under section 2 of the Illegitimate Children (Scotland) Act 1930: 'guardian' also means a person appointed by deed or will in accordance with the provisions of the Guardianship of Infants Acts 1886 and 1925, or the Guardianship of Minors Act 1971, or by a court of competent jurisdiction, to be the guardian of the child.

6 Notice will be given of the making of the application and of the Court by which it is to be heard. After the making of the application the agreeing parent or guardian cannot remove the child from the custody of the applicant(s) except with the leave of the court.

7 Enter the name of any local authority, adoption society or person who is known to have arranged, or to have taken part in the arrangements, for the child to be placed in the actual custody of the applicant(s).

8 In England or Wales the document should be signed before a justice of the peace, a duly authorised county court officer or a justices' clerk and in Scotland before a justice of the peace or a sheriff. In Northern Ireland it should be signed before a justice of the peace. Outside the United Kingdom it should be signed before a person authorised by law in the place where the document is executed to administer an oath for any judicial or legal purpose, a British Consular officer, a notary public or, if the person executing the document is serving in the regular forces of the Crown an officer holding a commission in any of those forces.

Rule 9 (1) (*a*)

FORM 4
Medical certificate as to the health of applicant

I examined...
on...19......, and have formed the opinion that he is physically, mentally and emotionally suitable to adopt a child.

Signature.. *Date*.....................................
Qualifications..
Address...

Rule 9 (1) (*b*)

FORM 5
Medical report on health of child

This form is for a medical report on a child who may be adopted. The report is for the benefit of the adopters and the court. In order that the adopters may benefit fully from the report, it is important that the certifying doctor should explain to the adopters the nature and extent of any disability or abnormality disclosed by the examination which might affect their decision whether or not to adopt the child.

Child's name..Date of Birth.................
Sex.......................................Weight.......................................Height.......................

A. General condition.
   Skin.
   Eyes (including vision).
   Ears (including hearing).
   Nose and throat.
   Speech.
   Cardio-vascular system.
   Respiratory system.
   Alimentary system.
   Genito-urinary system (including examination of urine for sugar).
   Skeletal and articular system (including examination for congenital dislocation of hip).
   Nervous system (including fits).
   Lymphatic system.
   Any other comments.
   Is the child physically normal having regard to his age?
B. Are there any items in the child's history or examination which suggest that he may be mentally abnormal having regard to his age?
C. Particulars of any illnesses from which the child has suffered.
D. If known—
   Weight at birth (if child is under one year of age).
   Details of birth, including result of mother's serological tests for syphilis.
   Particulars, with dates, of vaccination or immunization against:—
      Tuberculosis (state result of Mantoux test or whether child has been successfully vaccinated with B.C.G. vaccine).
      Smallpox.
      Diphtheria.
      Whooping cough.
      Poliomyelitis.

Tetanus (active).

Any other disease.

E. (i) (*Result of serological test for syphilis of the child's blood or the mother's blood carried out six weeks or later after the child's birth; either test (a) or tests (b) (i) and (ii) may be carried out when the child is at least six weeks old. If test (b) (i) or (ii) is positive, test (a) must also be carried out*).

(*a*) Result of a suitable serological test of the child's blood for syphilis (please specify test).

(*b*) Result of suitable serological tests of the mother's blood for syphilis—

(i) Reagin (please specify test).

(ii) Verification (please specify test).

(ii) (*To be completed in the case of a child over six complete days (excluding the day of his birth) and under two years old at the time of the test*).

Result of test of the child's blood for the purpose of estimating the level of phenylalanine therein.

F. I examined the child on the.................day of...
19...... and I have informed the adopters of the state of health of the child disclosed by the examination.

Signature... *Date*.....................

Qualifications...

Address...

....

2 FORMS IN CONVENTION CASES

[Scheduled to the Convention Adoption Rules: see p 115]

Rule 4(2)(*b*)

*Affidavit in support of application for a
Convention adoption order*

Modification to Form in General Rules Form 2 shall contain the following additional paragraphs after paragraph 22:—

PART IV

Additional information required for a Convention adoption application

23. *The child*. The child—

(*a*) is a United Kingdom national [*or* a national of...
which is a Convention country][28 29 30], and

(*b*) habitually resides at...which is in
British territory[31] [*or* a Convention country].

24. *The applicants*. We are applying together, in reliance on section 24(4)(*a*) of the Act of 1975, and the first applicant is a United Kingdom national [*or* a national of...which is a Convention country][28 30] and the second applicant is a United Kingdom national [*or* a national of ....which is a Convention country][28 30] and we habitually reside at...which is in Great Britain.

[*or* 24. *The applicants.* We are applying together in reliance on section 24(4)(*b*) of the Act of 1975, and are both United Kingdom nationals[28], and we are habitually resident at.. which is in British territory[31] [*or* a Convention country].]

[*or* 24. *The applicant.* I am applying alone in reliance on section 24(5)(*a*) of the Act of 1975, and am a United Kingdom national [*or* a national of................. .... which is a Convention country][28] [30] and habitually reside at..which is in Great Britain.]

[*or* 24. *The applicant.* I am applying alone in reliance on section 24(5)(*b*) of the Act of 1975, and am a United Kingdom national[28] and habitually reside at.. which is in British territory[31] [*or* a Convention country].]

[25. *Specified Provisions*[32] [33]. We are both [*or* I am], accordingly, nationals of the same [*or* a national of a] Convention country, namely .... and there are no specified provisions in respect of that country [*or* there are no relevant specified provisions in respect of that country because ....].]'

Notes

28 Documentary evidence of nationality should be exhibited. Where the child or an applicant is a national of a Convention country, evidence as to the law of the country relating to nationality applicable to that person should be supplied.

29 Where the child is not a United Kingdom national, evidence as to the provisions relating to consents and consultations of the internal law relating to adoption of the Convention country of which the child is a national should be supplied.

30 Any accompanying affidavit on foreign law must be sworn by a person who is suitably qualified on account of his knowledge or experience to give evidence as to the law concerned.

31 British territory is defined in section 107(1) of the Act of 1975.

32 Specified provision is defined in section 24(8) of the Act of 1975.

33 Expert evidence as to specified provisions may be necessary: if so see note 30 above.

Rule 2(4)
Rule 13(1)

FORM 6

Originating summons for the annulment or revocation of an
adoption[1] [2] [3]

In the High Court   No.   of 19
     Family Division

IN THE MATTER OF ....
                                     and
IN THE MATTER OF the Adoption Act 1968

Let... of..
attend at the Royal Courts of Justice, Strand, London, WC2A 2LL on a date to be fixed for the hearing of the application of..
.... of..
for an order:—

1. That the adoption which was authorised on the..
day of................................19........at ....[5],
by which.. [and ....]
was [*or* were] authorised to adopt the said..
be annulled [*or* revoked].

[2. That the leave of the court be granted for the purpose of making this application out of time[3].]

3. That the costs of this application be provided for.

Dated this.. day of .... 19........
This summons was taken out by..of..
solicitor for the above-named ....

Notes

1 This Form is for use when the adoption is to be annulled or revoked under section 6(1) or (2) of the Adoption Act 1968.

2 An application may not be made unless either the adopter or both adopters, as the case may be, or the adopted person habitually resides in Great Britain immediately before the application is made.

3 Except with the leave of the court an application to annul an adoption may not be made later than two years after the date of the adoption to which it relates.

4 Enter the full names by which the adopted person has been known since the adoption.

5 Enter the description and address of the authority by which the adoption was authorised.

Rule 14

FORM 7

*Originating summons for an order that an overseas adoption
or a determination cease to be valid or that a determination
has been affected by a subsequent determination*[1]

In the High Court   No.   of 19
    Family Division

IN THE MATTER OF..

and

IN THE MATTER OF the Adoption Act 1968

Let.. of..
attend at the Royal Courts of Justice, Strand, London, WC2A 2LL on a date to be fixed for the hearing of the application of
.... of..for:

[1. An order that an overseas adoption which was authorised on the
.... day of .... 19........ at
.... by which..
[and..] was [*or* were] authorised to adopt the said..do cease to be valid in Great Britain;[2]]

[2. An order that a determination made by an authority of a Convention country [*or* a specified country] to authorise [*or* review the authorisation of] a convention adoption [*or* an adoption order made under any enactment in force in a specified country and corresponding to sections 8(1) and 24 of the Children Act 1975] do cease to be valid in Great Britain;[2] [3]]

[3. An order that a determination made by an authority of a Convention country [*or* a specified country] to give [*or* review] a decision revoking [*or* annulling] a convention adoption [*or* an adoption order made under any enactment in force in a specified country and corresponding to sections 8(1) and 24 of the Children Act 1975] [*or* an order made under section 8 of the Children Act 1975 as a convention adoption order] do cease to be valid in Great Britain;[2] [3]]

[4. A decision as to the extent, if any, to which a determination mentioned in paragraph 2 [*or* 3] above has been affected by a subsequent determination;]

5. An order that the costs of this application be provided for.

Dated this.. day of.. 19........
This summons was taken out by.................................... of....................................
solicitor for the above-named..

Notes

1 This Form is principally for use if the applicant claims that the adoption or determination is contrary to public policy or that the authority which purported to authorise the adoption or make the determination was not competent to entertain the case. The applicant should delete the paragraphs which are not relevant.

2 An overseas adoption is one specified in an order made under section 4(3) of the Adoption Act 1968: a convention adoption is an overseas adoption of a description designated in such an order as that of an adoption regulated by the Hague Convention on the Adoption of Children 1965.

3 A Convention country means a country designated by an order of the Secretary of State as a country in which the Hague Convention on the Adoption of Children 1965 is in force (section 107(1) of the Children Act 1975). A specified country means Northern Ireland, the Channel Islands, the Isle of Man, or a colony, unless this meaning is modified by an order of the Secretary of State (section 11(1) of the Adoption Act 1968). [But see p 114 of this book.]

———

Rule 15(1)

FORM 8
Affidavit in support of application under section 6
of Adoption Act 1968

In the High Court   No.   of 19
  Family Division

IN THE MATTER OF.. [1]

and

IN THE MATTER OF the Adoption Act 1968

I/We.. of..
hereby make oath and say that the particulars set out in this affidavit are true.

PART I

1. Name of [first] adopter in full..

Address..

   [2. Name of second adopter in full...

Address...]

3. Name of adopted person in full... [1]

   [4. The said... [2]/[and the said

.... [3]] habitually reside in Great

Britain.] [4]

5. The adopted person is of the.. sex, is a national

of.. and was born at..

on the.. day of.. 19........

   6. On the.. day of.. 19........

the said.. [and...]was

[*or* were] authorised to adopt the said..

by.. at.. [5]

and those persons are the persons to whom the certified copy of an entry in a
public register (or other evidence of adoption [6]) which is exhibited to this
affidavit relates.

   [7. At the time at which the adoption was authorised the said.........................

.... [7] was a national of.............................

and resided in.. [the said..................................... [8]

was a national of.. and resided

in..] and the adopted person was a

national of.. and resided in.............................

....] [9] *or*

   [7. *For other applications details of the marriage or, as appropriate, of the determination or determinations should be given and any necessary documentary evidence
relating thereto supplied.*]

   [8. *A statement of the facts is exhibited to this affidavit.*] [10] [11]

Sworn, etc.

This affidavit is filed on behalf of the applicant(s).

Notes

   1 Enter the name(s) by which the adopted person has been known since the
adoption.

   2 Enter the name(s) of either the adopter(s) or the adopted person. Where this
paragraph is required (see note 4 below), no application may be made to the court
unless the adopter or, as the case may be, both adopters or the adopted person
habitually reside in Great Britain immediately before the application is made.

   3 Delete unless both the adopter(s) and the adopted person habitually reside in
Great Britain.

   4 This paragraph is not required for applications made under section 6(3) of the
Adoption Act 1968.

   5 Enter the description and full address of the authority which authorised the
adoption.

   6 Evidence of the adoption may be given either by a certified copy of an entry in a
public register relating to adoptions or by a certificate that the adoption has been
effected signed by a person who is authorised by the law of the country concerned to
do so.

7 Enter the name of the first adopter.

8 Enter the name of the second adopter if applicable.

9 This paragraph should be completed where the application is made under section 6(1).

10 A statement of facts is not required for an application to revoke a convention adoption under section 6(2) of the Adoption Act 1968.

11 Expert evidence as to notified provisions may be necessary. In that or any other case where the applicant intends to rely on any provision of foreign law relating to adoption, any accompanying affidavit thereon must be sworn by a person who is suitably qualified on account of his knowledge or experience to give evidence as to the law concerned.

B—COUNTY COURT FORMS
[Scheduled to the Co Ct R]

Rule 4 (1)

Form 1

*Originating application for an adoption order**

In the .... County Court.

No. ....

In the Matter of The Adoption Act 1958

and

In the Matter of The Children Act 1975

and

In the Matter of[1] .... a child.

I/We, the undersigned, ...

[and] ....

wishing to adopt ....[1]

a child, who is within the district of this county court,[2] under the Adoption Act 1958 and the Children Act 1975, hereby give the following further particulars in support of my/our application.

[There follow Parts I, II and III of the form, containing 22 numbered paragraphs, corresponding with the first 22 paragraphs of Form 2 in the High Court Forms (pp 176–178, *ante*) and worded in the same way, except that—

(*a*) there are sub-headings in Parts I and II ('Name and address, etc', 'Domicile', 'Status', etc);

(*b*) documents are referred to as 'attached' where High Court Form 2 says 'exhibited to this affidavit';

(*c*) instead of the jurat the form concludes:—

I/We accordingly apply for an adoption order in respect of the child.

Dated this .... day of ...., 19........

Signature(s) ....

....

Note: This Form must be filed in duplicate, but duplicates of the attached documents need not be filed. Every paragraph must be completed or deleted, as the case may be.

---

*Copies of this form are obtainable from the publishers of this book.

The notes to the form are to the same effect as those to High Court Form 2 except as follows:—

Note (1) corresponds with Note (2) on p 179.

Note (2) is to the effect that the child must be within the district of the county court to which the application is made.

Note (28) is omitted.]

[Forms 2,* 3 and 4 correspond exactly with the High Court Forms 3, 4 and 5 (pp 181–184) and the notes to County Court Form 2 are also identical with those to High Court Form 3.]

Rule 12(2)

FORM 5

Notice of an application for an adoption order or a provisional adoption order

[*Heading as in Form 1*]

To..

of..

Whereas an application for an adoption order/a provisional adoption order in respect of...

....[1]

a child of the.. sex born on the......................................

19........, has been made [by ....

and ....]

[*or* under the serial number..][2]

And Whereas..

of..

was appointed guardian *ad litem* of the child;

Take notice:

A. [3] [That the said application will be heard before the judge at

....

on the............day of... 19........at............o'clock, and that you may then appear and be heard on the question whether an adoption order/a provisional adoption order should be made].

B. [3] [That if you wish to appear and be heard on the question whether an adoption order/a provisional adoption order should be made, you should give notice to the court on or before the.. day of

.... 19........, in order that a time may be fixed for your appearance].

C. That while the application is pending, a parent or guardian of the child who has agreed to the making of an order must not, except with the leave of the court, remove the child from the custody of the applicant.

[D. That the application states that the child has had his home with the applicant for the five years preceding the application and accordingly, if that

---

*Copies of this form are obtainable from the publishers of this book.

is correct, no person is entitled, against the will of the applicant, to remove the child from the applicant's custody except with the leave of the court or under authority conferred by any enactment or on the arrest of the child][4].

[E. That the court has been requested to dispense with your agreement to the making of an order on the ground(s) that...
and a statement of the facts on which the applicant intends to rely is attached][5].

It would assist the court if you would complete the attached form and return it to me.

Dated the..............day of...19........
.... Registrar.

To the Registrar of the.. County Court
.... No..
I answer the following questions as follows:

On what date did you receive notice of the hearing of the application for an adoption order/a provisional adoption order in respect of...........................
a child?.................................. 19........
Do you wish to oppose the application? (*Answer Yes or No*)...........................
Do you wish to appear and be heard on the question whether an adoption order/a provisional adoption order should be made? (*Answer Yes or No*)..................

....
(*Signature*)

....
(*Address*)

....
(*Date*)

General note

Where this form is used under rule 29(3) to give notice of a further hearing of an application it is to be amended so as to refer to a further hearing and so as to give particulars of the interim order.

Notes

1 Enter the name(s) and surname of the child as shown in the heading of the originating application.

2 The name of the applicant(s) must not be given where a serial number is specified in the originating application and the notice is addressed to an individual, other than the spouse of the applicant. In that case complete the second entry in square brackets.

3 Paragraph A should be completed and paragraph B struck out where the notice is addressed to a local authority, an adoption society, any other body of persons or the spouse of the applicant or where the applicant does not desire his identity to be kept confidential. Where a serial number is specified in the originating application and the notice is addressed to an individual respondent, other than the spouse of the applicant, paragraph A must be struck out and paragraph B completed.

4 Paragraph D should be deleted except where it appears from the originating application that the child has had his home with the applicant for five years.

5 Unless deleted, this paragraph should contain the grounds specified in the originating application.

———

Rule 14

FORM 6
Notice to the applicant that the child's presence is required at the hearing
[*Heading as in Form* 1]

To...
of...
Whereas an application has been made by you for an adoption order/a provisional adoption order in respect of the above-named child;

And Whereas the said application will be heard at..
County Court at ....19........, at..................o'clock:
Take notice that no adoption order/provisional adoption order can be made unless the child is present at the hearing,[1] and the court is satisfied that he has been informed of the nature of the order and that he has been given an opportunity of expressing his wishes and feelings regarding the decision.

And take notice that if the hearing is adjourned or an interim order is made no adoption order/provisional adoption order can be made at a subsequent hearing unless the child is present at the subsequent hearing[1] and the court is satisfied as aforesaid.

Dated...

....Registrar.

Note

1 The judge may be prepared to waive this requirement if there are special circumstances making the child's attendance unnecessary.

———

Rule 22 (1)

FORM 7
[as amended by SI 1978 No 1518]
Originating application for a provisional adoption order
[*Heading as in Form* 1]

I/We, the undersigned...
....
[and]...
wishing to obtain a provisional adoption order under section 53 of the Adoption Act 1958 in respect of... [1]
a child who is within the district of this county court,[2] hereby give the following particulars in support of my/our application.

PART I
[*Heading as in Form* 1]

1. [*As in Form* 1.]
2. *Domicile.* I am/We are not domiciled in England or Wales or Scotland.
3. [*As in Form* 1.]
[4. I am applying on my own for a provisional adoption order in respect of my own child, and can satisfy the court that the other natural parent

....

....].[5]

[5. (*As in Form* 1.]]

PART II
[*Heading as in Form* 1]

6. [*As in Form* 1.]
[7. [*As in Form* 1.]]
8. [*As in Form* 1.]
[9. [*As in Form* 1.]]
[10. *Parental agreement.* I/We attach a document/documents signifying the agreement of the said ....
[and...].[15]
to the making of a provisional adoption order in pursuance of my/our application.]
[11. [*As in Form* 1.]]
[12. [*As in Form* 1.]]
[13. [*As in Form* 1.]]
14. *Proposed names.* If a provisional adoption order is made in pursuance of this application, the child is, until adopted under the law of or within the country of my/our domicile, to be known by the following names:—

Surname..
Other names ....

PART III
[*Heading as in Form* 1]

15. The child was received into my/our actual custody on the
.... day of.. 19........,
and has been continuously in my/our actual custody since that date (*or as appropriate*)[19]
16. [*As in Form* 1.]
[17. I/We/One of us (namely..)
notified the...Council on the
..................day of... 19......., of my/our intention
to apply for a provisional adoption order in respect of the child].[20]
18. [*As in Form* 1.]

19. I/We have not received or given any reward or payment for, or in consideration of, the adoption of the child, or for any agreement to the making of the provisional adoption order [except as follows—

....

....].[24]

20. [*As in Form* 1]

[21. [*As in Form* 1]]

[22. [*As in Form* 1]]

23. I/We intend to adopt the child under the law of or within........................ which is the country of my/our domicile, and I/we attach an affidavit as to the law of adoption in that country.[28]

24. I/We desire to remove the child from Great Britain for the purpose of adoption.

I/We accordingly apply for a provisional adoption order in respect of the child.

Dated this.. day of.. 19........

Signature(s)..

....

Note: This form must be filed in duplicate, but duplicates of the attached documents need not be filed. Every paragraph must be completed or deleted, as the case may be.

Notes

1 Enter the first name(s) and surname as shown in any certificate referred to in entry No. 6; otherwise enter the first name(s) and surname by which the child was known before being placed for adoption.

2 The child must be within the district of the county court to which the application is made.

5 Enter the reason to be relied on (that the other natural parent is dead, or cannot be found, or that there is some other reason, which shall be specified, justifying his or her exclusion). Documentary evidence, e.g., a death certificate should be supplied where appropriate.

15 [As in footnote 15 in Form 1].

19 Under section 3(1) of the Act of 1958, as modified by section 53(5), a provisional adoption order cannot be made unless the child has been continuously in the actual custody of the applicant during the six months before the order is made.

20 Notice does not have to be given if the applicant or one of the applicants is a parent of the child, or if at the time of the hearing the child will have reached the upper limit of the compulsory school age.

24 Any such payment or reward is illegal except payment to an adoption society or local authority in respect of their expenses incurred in connection with the adoption.

28 The affidavit must be sworn by a person who is suitably qualified on account of his knowledge or experience to give evidence as to the law concerned.

Rule 25 (1)

FORM 8
Adoption order or provisional adoption order
[Heading as in Form 1]

Whereas an application has been made by ....
of..
whose occcupation is.. [and................................
.... his wife] (hereinafter called the applicant(s))......
for an adoption order/a provisional adoption order in respect of......................,[1]
a child of the .... sex, the child of..
[and..];

And whereas the court is satisfied that the applicant is/applicants are qualified in accordance with the provisions of the Adoption Act 1958 and the Children Act 1975, to be granted an adoption order/a provisional adoption order in respect of the child and that all conditions precedent to the making of such an order have been fulfilled:

It is ordered that [the applicant(s) do adopt the child;] [*or* that the applicant(s) be authorised to remove the child from Great Britain for the purpose of adopting him/her under the law of or within the country in which the applicant is/applicants are domiciled, and that the parental rights and duties relating to the child (including the legal custody of the child) be vested in the applicant(s), pending the adoption of the child as aforesaid;]

[And the following payment or reward is authorised..
....];

[And as regards costs it is ordered that ....
....
....];

[And it is recorded that the.. Council was notified of the applicant's/applicants' intention to apply for an adoption order/a provisional adoption order in respect of the child and that the.......................... [2] took part in the arrangements for placing the child in the actual custody of the applicants with a view to adoption;]

[And whereas the precise date of the child's birth has not been proved to the satisfaction of the court but the court has determined the probable date of his/her birth to be the.................................... day of....................................
19........;]

[And whereas the country of birth of the child has not been proved to the satisfaction of the court [but it appears probable that the child was born within the United Kingdom, the Channel Islands or the Isle of Man];]

[And whereas the child was born in England/Wales but the registration district and sub-district in which the birth took place have not been proved to the satisfaction of the court;]

[And whereas is has been proved to the satisfaction of the court that the child is identical with..

to whom the **entry numbered**...........................made on the...........................day of
....19........., in the Registers of Births for the registration
district of................................... and sub-district of..in
the county of...............................relates [*or* with...
to whom the entry numbered....and dated the...
day of................................. 19........., in the Adopted Children Register relates];]

[And whereas the name or names and surnames stated in the application
as those by which the child is to be known are..:]

It is directed that the Registrar General shall make in the Adopted
Children Register an entry in the form specified by regulations made by him
recording the particulars set out in the Schedule to this Order;

[And it is further directed that the aforesaid entry in the Register of
Births/Adopted Children Register be marked with the word 'Adopted'/'Re-
adopted'/'Provisionally adopted'/'Provisionally re-adopted']³.

Dated this..................day of... 19........

Registrar.

Notes

1 As in the heading to the form.

2 Enter the particulars of any local authority or adoption agency supplied at
paragraph 20 of Form 1.

3 This paragraph should be deleted where the child is not proved to be identical
with a child to whom an entry in the Registers of Births or Adopted Children Register
relates.

SCHEDULE

1. No. of entry
2. Date..   *Registration District* and .... *Sub-district* country... of birth of child ....
3. Name and surname of child
4. Sex of child
5. Name and surname. address and occupation of adopter or adopters
6. Date of adoption order and description of court by which made
7. Date of entry
8. Signature of officer deputed by Registrar General to attest the entry

Notes to Certain Paragraphs in the Schedule

1. *No. of entry.*
7. *Date of entry.*   } for completion by the Registrar General.
8. *Signature of officer.*

2. *Date and country of birth.* Where the precise date of the child's birth is not proved, enter the date determined by the court to be the probable date. The particulars of the country of birth may be omitted unless it appears probable that the child was born within the United Kingdom, the Channel Islands or the Isle of Man. In that event enter England or Wales, as the case may be, as the country of birth.

Where the child was born in England or Wales but the registration district and sub-district in which the birth took place are not proved, or where the child is treated as born in England or Wales, enter the district and sub-district in which the court sits.

3. *Name and Surname.* Enter the name or names and surname stated in the originating application as those by which the child is to be known or, if no name or surname is so stated, the original name or names of the child and the surname of the applicant.

5. *Name etc., of adopters.* Enter the place or places stated in the originating application where the applicant or each of them is living unless some later such address has come to the notice of the court.

6. *Date of order, etc.* In the case of a provisional adoption order enter the words 'Provisional Adoption Order' followed by the date of the order and the name of the court.

APPENDIX

This Appendix forms part of the adoption/provisional adoption order but shall not form part of any copy supplied to any person under Rule 31 (3) or (4) of the Adoption (County Court) Rules 1976.

1. The agreement of...
of... the parent/guardian of the child is dispensed with on the ground(s) that.. .¹
[2. The order is made on the application of one person who [is married] [*or* is the mother/father of the child] and the court is satisfied that...................
....].²

Notes

1 Enter the appropriate ground(s) in section 12 (2) of the Act of 1975.

2 Enter the appropriate ground(s) in section 11 (1) (*b*) or (3) of the Act of 1975, and specify where appropriate the matters of which the court is satisfied.

Rule 25 (2)

FORM 9

Abridged form of adoption order or provisional adoption order
[*Heading as in Form* 1]

Whereas an application has been made by..
....of..
.... [and..
his wife] for an adoption order/a provisional adoption order in respect of
.... ¹ a child:

It is ordered that the applicant(s) do adopt the child [*or* that the applicant(s) be authorised to remove the child from Great Britain for the purpose of adopting him/her under the law of or within the country in which the applicant is/applicants are domiciled and that the parental rights and duties relating to the child (including the legal custody of the child) be vested in the applicant(s) pending the adoption of the child as aforesaid] :

And it is recorded that the...Council was notified
of the applicant's/applicants' intention to apply for an adoption order/a
provisional adoption order in respect of the child and that the...........................[2]
took part in the arrangements for placing the child in the actual custody
of the applicant(s) with a view to adoption.

And it is directed that the Registrar General shall make in the Adopted
Children Register an entry recording the particulars set out in the Schedule
to this order.

Dated this...day of...19........

Registrar.

SCHEDULE
[*As in Form* 8]

Notes

1 As in the heading to the form.

2 Enter the particulars of any local authority or adoption society supplied at
paragraph 20 of Form 1.

Rule 26

FORM 10

Form of bilingual schedule for inclusion in adoption orders made by Welsh courts

1. No of entry   Rhif y cofnod

2. Date..............................   *Registration District Dosbarth Cofrestru*
    Dyddiad..
    and   *Sub-district   is-ddosbarth*
    a'r
    country of birth of child............................
    wlad lle ganwyd y plentyn........................   ....

3. Name and surname of child   Enw a chyfenw y plentyn
4. Sex of child   Rhyw y plentyn

5. Name and surname,
    Enw a chyfenw,
    address
    cyfeiriad
    and
    a
    occupation of adopter or adopters
    gwaith y mabwysiadwr neu'r mabwysiadwyr

6. Date of adoption order ....
    Dyddiad y gorchymyn mabwysiadu..
    and description of court by which made........................
    a disgrifiad o'r llys a'i gwnaeth ....

7. Date of entry   Dyddiad y cofnod

8. Signature of officer deputed by Registrar General to attest the entry
    Llofnod y swyddog a benodwyd gan y Cofretrydd Cyffredinol i
    ardystio'r cofnod

Notes to Paragraphs in the Schedule
Nodiadau Ar Y Paragraffau Yn Yr Atodlen

1. *No. of entry.*
7. *Date of entry.*   } For completion by the Registrar General.
8. *Signature of officer.*

1. *Rhif y cofnod.*
7. *Dyddiad y cofnod.*   } I'w llenwi gan y Cofrestrydd Cyffredinol.
8. *Llofnod y swyddog.*

2. *Date and country of birth.* Where the precise date of the child's birth is not

proved, enter the date determined by the court to be the probable date. The particulars of the country of birth may be omitted unless it appears probable that the child was born within the United Kingdom, the Channel Islands or the Isle of Man. In that event enter England or Wales, as the case may be, as the country of birth.

Where the child was born in England or Wales but the registration district and sub-district in which the birth took place are not proved, or where the child is treated as born in England or Wales, enter the district and sub-district in which the court sits.

2. *Dyddiad a'r wlad lle'i ganwyd.* Lle na phrofir yr union ddyddiad y ganwyd y baban, cynhwyswch y dyddiad a bendefrynwyd fel y dyddiad tebygol gan y llys. Gellir peidio â chynnwys manylion am y wlad lle'i ganwyd onid ymddengys yn debygol mai of ewn y Deyrnas Gyfunol, Ynysoedd y Sianel neu Ynys Manaw y ganwyd y baban. Osfelly cynhwyswch Gymru neu Loegr fel y bo'r achos fel y wlad lle'i ganwyd.

Lle bo'r baban wedi'i eni yng Nghymru neu yn Lloegr ond na phrofwyd ym mha ddosbarth neu is-ddosbarth cofrestru y bu hynny neu lle trinir y baban fel un a anwyd yng Nghymru neu yn Lloegr, cynhwyswch y dosbarth a'r is-ddosbarth lle bo'r ilys yn eistedd.

3. *Name and Surname.* Enter the name or names and surname stated in Form 1 or 7 as those by which the child is to be known or, if no name or surname is so stated, the original name or names of the child and the surname of the applicant.

3. *Enw a Chyfenw.* Cynhwyswch yr enw neu'r enwau a'r cyfenw a fynegwyd yn Ffurflen 1 neu 7 fel y rhai yr adnabyddir y baban wrthynt neu, os na fynegir yr enw neu'r cyfenw felly, enw neu enwau gwreiddiol y baban a chyfenw'r sawl sy'n gwneud y cais.

5. *Name etc., of adopters.* Enter the place or places stated in the originating application where the applicant or each of the applicants is living unless some later such address has come to the notice of the court.

5. *Enw etc., y rhai sy'n mabwysiadu.* Rhowch yr enw neu'r enwau a nodwyd yn y cais gwreiddiol lle y mae'r ymgeisydd neu bob un o'r ymgeiswyr yn byw, oni fydd rhyw gyfeiriad diweddarach o'r fath wedi dod i sylw'r llys.

6. *Date of Order, etc.* In the case of a provisional adoption order enter the words 'Provisional Adoption Order' followed by the date of the order and the name of the court.

6. *Dyddiad y Gorchymyn, etc.* Mewn achos gorchymyn mabwysiadu tros dro rhowch y geiriau 'Gorchymyn Mabwysiadu Tros Dro' ac yna ddyddiad y gorchymyn ac enw'r llys.

Rule 27

Form 11
Interim order
[*Heading as in Form 1*]
[*First two recitals as in Form 8*]

It is ordered that the determination of the application be postponed and that the applicant(s) do have the custody of the child until the

..................day of..19........, by way of a probationary
period [*or* that the determination of the application be postponed to the
..................day of..19........, and that the applicant(s)
do have the custody of the child until that day by way of a probationary
period] [upon the following terms, namely..

....];

   [And as regards costs it is ordered that ....

....];

   [And it is ordered that the application be further heard before the
judge at ....

....

on the.................day of... 19........, at.............o'clock].
   Dated this.................day of...19........

Registrar.

APPENDIX

   This Appendix forms part of the interim order but shall not [*continue as in
Form* 8]

Rule 27

FORM 12
Abridged form of interim order
[*Heading as in Form* 1]
[*Recital as in Form* 9]

   It is ordered that the determination of the application be postponed
and that the applicant(s) do have the custody of the child until the
..................day of..19........, by way of a probationary period [*or* that the determination of the application be postponed
to the.................day of...19........, and that the
applicant(s) do have the custody of the child until that day by way of a
probationary period] [upon the following terms, namely

....

....].

   [And as regards costs it is ordered that ....

....];

   [And it is ordered that the application be further heard before the
judge at ....

....

on the.................day of...19........, at.............
o'clock].
   Dated this.................day of...19........

Registrar.

C—DOMESTIC COURT FORMS
[Scheduled to the Mag Ct R, including amendments introduced by SI 1979 No 1222]

Rule 4

FORM 1
Application for adoption order

This Form must be lodged in duplicate, but duplicates of the attached documents need not be lodged. Every paragraph must be completed or deleted, as the case may be.

To the   Domestic Court

PART I

Particulars of applicant(s)

1. Name of (first) applicant in full..
   Address...
   Occupation..
   Date of Birth...
   Relationship (if any) to child...
   [Name of second applicant in full...
   Address...
   Occupation..
   Date of Birth...
   Relationship (if any) to child...]
2. I am/We are/One of us (namely...)is
   domiciled in England or Wales/Scotland/Northern Ireland/Channel Islands/Isle of Man.
3. I am a widow/widower/not married/divorced/I am married to
   .... of..........................
   ..../We
   are married to each other and our marriage certificate (or other evidence of marriage) is attached.
4. A. I am married and I require the court to dispense with an application from my husband/wife on the ground that:
   i. he/she cannot be found; or
   ii. we have separated and are living apart, and the separation is likely to be permanent; or
   iii. my husband/wife is incapable of joining in the application because of mental or physical ill health.

   B. Particulars of Husband/Wife:
   Name...
   Address (if known) ....
   ....
5. I/We attach a certificate as to my health/the health of each of us signed by a fully registered medical practitioner[1].

PART II

To be completed only by a single parent applying for an adoption order in respect of his/her own child.

6. I am applying on my own for an adoption order because:
    (i) the other natural parent is dead and I attach a copy of the death certificate; or
    (ii) the other natural parent cannot be found (see statement attached)[2]; or
    (iii) the circumstances are...
    ....
    ....

PART III

Particulars of child

7. Name in full[3] ....

8. The child is of the..sex and is not and has not been married.

9. The child is the person to whom the attached birth or adoption certificate relates/the child was born in...
on..or about..........................[4].

10. I/We attach a report as to the health of the child made by a fully registered medical practitioner[5 & 6].

11. The child is the child[7] of
Name of mother ....
Address..
and Name of father[8] ....
Address..

12. The guardian(s)[9], if any, of the child is/are
Name..
Address..

13. I/We attach a document/documents signifying the agreement of the child's mother/father/guardian to the making of an adoption order authorising me/us to adopt the child.

14. I/We request the court to dispense with the agreement of the child's mother/father/guardian on the ground that the parent or guardian[10]
    (a) cannot be found or is incapable of giving agreement; ☐
    (b) is withholding his agreement unreasonably; ☐
    (c) has persistently failed without reasonable cause to discharge the parental duties in relation to the child; ☐
    (d) has abandoned or neglected the child; ☐
    (e) has persistently ill-treated the child; ☐
    (f) has seriously ill-treated the child and (because of the ill-treatment or for other reasons) the rehabilitation of the child within the household of the parent or guardian is unlikely; ☐
    and I/we attach a statement of the facts on which I/we intend to rely in support of this request.

15. The following body or person has the rights and duties of a parent of the child or is the body into whose care the child was received[11]:
Name...
Address...

16. The following person is liable by virtue of an order of a court or an agreement to contribute to the maintenance of the child[12].
Name...
Address...
Particulars of court order or agreement:
Name of court...
Date of order..
or Date of agreement..

17. If an adoption order is made in pursuance of this application, the child is to be known by the following names:
Surname..
Other Names...

Part IV

General

18. The child was received into my/our actual custody on the...........................
day of................................... 19......., and has been continuously in my/our actual custody since that date[13].

19. The child has/has not had his home with me/us for the five years preceding the date of this application.

20. The child was placed with me/us by:
(i) a local authority, adoption society or voluntary organization
Name...
Address...
(ii) the child's parent or guardian
Name...
Address...
(iii) any other person
Name...
Address...

21. I/We/One of us (namely..) notified the
....Council on the...............day of...................
19.............., of my/our intention to apply for an adoption order in respect of the child[14].

22. I have not made/Neither of us has made a previous application for an adoption order in respect of the child; *or* (name of applicant)
....made an application No...
to the...court on the.......................................
day of...19......., which was dealt with as follows[15]:

23. No proceedings have been completed or commenced (other than for an adoption order) in any court in England or Wales or elsewhere relating in whole or in part to the child *except* application No......................
to the.. court on the ....day
of... 19........, which was dealt with as follows:[16]

24. I/We have not received or given any reward or payment for, or in consideration of, the adoption of the child or for giving agreement to the making of the adoption order except as follows[17]:

25. As far as I/we know, no person or body other than the one shown in paragraph 20 above has taken part in the arrangements for placing the child in my/our custody except:
Name...
Address..

26. For the purposes of this application reference may be made to ....[18] of (Address)...
....

27. I/We desire that my/our identity should be kept confidential. The serial number of this application is..[19].
I/We accordingly apply for an adoption order in respect of the child.

(Signature(s)) ....
Dated the......................day of........................19......

Notes

1 A separate medical certificate is required in respect of each applicant. There is an official form (Form 3) which may be used for this purpose. No certificate, however, need be supplied if the child is the child of the applicant or either of them, or has reached the upper limit of the compulsory school age.

2 The statement should include details of the last known whereabouts of the child's father/mother and any attempts that have been made to trace him/her.

3 Enter the surname and other names shown in the child's birth certificate or, if the child has been previously adopted, in the adoption certificate. If the child has no birth or adoption certificate enter the surname and other names by which the child was known before being placed for adoption.

4 If a child has previously been adopted, a certified copy of the entry in the Adopted Children Register should be attached and not a certified copy of the original entry in the Register of Births. Where a certificate is not attached, enter the place including the country of birth if known.

5 There is an official form (Form 4) which may be used for this purpose. No certificate need be supplied if the child is the child of the applicant or one of them, or has reached the upper limit of the compulsory school age.

6 If the child is less than one year old on the date of the application, the report should have been made during the month preceding that date. If the child is one year old or more on that date, the report should have been made during the period of six months before that date.

7 If the child has previously been adopted, give the names of his adoptive parents and not those of his natural parents.

8 Enter name of father if known.

9 Guardian means: (*a*) a person appointed by deed or will in accordance with the provisions of the Guardianship of Infants Acts 1886 and 1925 or the Guardianship of

Minors Act 1971 or by a court of competent jurisdiction to be the guardian of the child, and (*b*) includes the father of an illegitimate child who has custody of the child by virtue of an order under section 9 of the Guardianship of Minors Act 1971, or under section 2 of the Illegitimate Children (Scotland) Act 1930.

10 Put a tick in the box against the grounds on which you are asking for the parent's or guardian's agreement to be dispensed with.

11 This entry should be deleted except (*a*) where any local authority has the parental rights and duties with respect to the child by virtue of section 24 (2) of the Children and Young Persons Act 1969, or under section 2 (11) of the Children Act 1948, (*b*) in the case of an application made after the coming into force of section 60 of the Children Act 1975 any voluntary organization in whom the parental rights and duties with respect to the child are vested, (*c*) where the child was received into care under section 1 of the Children Act 1948, or (*d*) is in the care of a voluntary organization within the meaning of section 88 of the Children Act 1975.

12 The making of an adoption order operates to extinguish any order of a court to make payments in respect of the child's maintenance in any period after the making of the adoption order (section 8 (3) of the Children Act 1975).

13 Where the applicants are domiciled in Great Britain but one or both normally live abroad, the child must have had his or her home with one of them in Great Britain for three months before the date of the adoption order, and with both applicants together for at least one of those months.

14 Notice does not have to be given if the applicant or one of the applicants is a parent of the child or if at the time of the hearing the child will have reached the upper limit of the compulsory school age.

15 The court cannot proceed with the application if a previous application made by the same person in relation to the child was refused unless one of the conditions in section 22 (4) of the Children Act 1975 is satisfied.

16 Delete this entry unless the application is made by (*a*) a married couple, one of whom is a parent and the other is a step-parent, or (*b*) a single person who is a step-parent. The court must dismiss such applications under sections 10 (3) and 11 (4) of the Children Act 1975 if it considers the matter would be better dealt with under section 42 (order for custody etc. in matrimonial proceedings) of the Matrimonial Causes Act 1973.

17 Any such payment or reward is illegal except payment to an adoption society or local authority in respect of their expenses incurred in connection with the adoption.

18 Where the applicant or one of the applicants is a parent of the child, or a relative as defined by section 57 (1) of the Adoption Act 1958 no referee need be named.

19 If the applicant wishes his identity to be kept confidential the serial number obtained under rule 5 should be given.

Rule 6

FORM 2
Agreement to adoption order

1. I understand that an application for an adoption order has been or is to be made in respect of.. [to whom the birth/ adoption certificate now produced and shown to me marked "A" relates][1] (hereinafter called the child) by.. and .... *or* by a person or persons identified in the petty sessions area of.. under the serial number (hereinafter called the applicant)[2]...

2. I am the mother[3] father[4] guardian[5] of the child. I understand that the effect of an adoption order will be to deprive me permanently of my rights and duties as a parent or guardian and to transfer them to the applicant: in particular I understand that, if an order is made, I shall have no right to see or get in touch with the child or to have the child returned to me.

3. I understand that the court cannot make an adoption order without the agreement of each parent or guardian of the child unless the court dispenses with an agreement on the ground that the person concerned:

   (*a*) cannot be found or is incapable of giving agreement;

   (*b*) is withholding his or her agreement unreasonably;

   (*c*) has persistently failed without reasonable cause to discharge the parental duties in relation to the child;

   (*d*) has abandoned or neglected the child;

   (*e*) has persistently ill-treated the child;

   (*f*) has seriously ill-treated the child and (because of the ill-treatment or for other reasons) the rehabilitation of the child within the household of the parent or guardian is unlikely.

4. I further understand that, when the application for an adoption order is heard, this document may be used as evidence of my agreement to the making of the order unless I inform the court that I no longer agree[6].

5. I hereby unconditionally agree to the making of an adoption order authorising the adoption of the child by the applicant.

6. As far as I know, no person or body has taken part in arranging for the child to be placed in the actual custody of the applicant except—[7]
Full name ....
Address ....

....

Signature ....
Address ....

....

Paragraphs 1, 2 and 6 of this Form having been duly completed, this Form was signed by the above-mentioned person before me at .... on the .... day of .... 19 ....
Signature ....
Full name ....
Description[8] ....

Warning. It is an offence to receive or give any reward or payment for or in consideration of, the adoption of the child or for giving agreement to the making of an adoption order, other than a payment to a local authority or adoption society for their expenses incurred in connection with the adoption.

Notes

1 Insert the surname and other names of the child as shown in the child's birth certificate, or, if the child has previously been adopted, his adoption certificate. If the child has no birth or adoption certificate, enter the surname and other names by

which the child was known before being placed for adoption. The words in square brackets should be deleted except where the person agreeing to the child's adoption is the mother or father of the child and the child's birth or adoption certificate has not already been identified by the other parent.

2 Insert either the name(s) of the applicant(s) or the serial number assigned to the applicant(s) for the purpose of the application.

3 The agreement of the mother cannot be given before the child is six weeks old.

4 'Father', in this context, does not include the natural father of an illegitimate child; he may however be the guardian, as defined in Note 5 below.

5 'Guardian' means (*a*) a person appointed by deed or will in accordance with the provisions of the Guardianship of Infants Acts 1886 and 1925 or the Guardianship of Minors Act 1971 or by a court of competent jurisdiction to be the guardian of the child, and (*b*) in relation to the adoption of an illegitimate child, includes the father where he has custody of the child by virtue of an order under section 9 of the Guardianship of Minors Act 1971, or under section 2 of the Illegitimate Children (Scotland) Act 1930.

6 Notice of the making of the application and of the court by which it is to be heard will be given. After the making of the application a parent or guardian who has agreed to the adoption cannot remove the child from the applicant except with the leave of the court.

7 Enter the name of any local authority, adoption society or person who is known to have arranged, or to have taken part in the arrangements, for the child to be placed in the actual custody of the applicant.

8 In England or Wales the agreement should be signed before a justice of the peace, or a justices' clerk or a duly authorised county court officer. In Scotland, it should be signed before a justice of the peace or a sheriff. In Northern Ireland it should be signed before a justice of the peace. Outside the United Kingdom, it should be signed before a person authorised to administer an oath for any judicial or legal purpose, a British consular officer, a notary public or, if the person signing it is serving in the regular armed forces, a commissioned officer.

[Forms 3 and 4 correspond exactly with High Court Forms 4 and 5: see pp 182–184, *ante.*]

Rule 11 (1)

FORM 5
Notice to applicant of time of hearing

In the [county of............................ Petty Sessional Division of ....].

To...of..

I hereby give notice that your application for an adoption order to be made in respect of (name of child) will be heard before the Domestic Court sitting at...

on the.................day of.., 19........ at..............o'clock in the [county] aforesaid and that your attendance [and that of (name of child)] is required.

[Take note that no adoption order can be made unless the child is present at the hearing and the court is satisfied that he has been informed of the nature of the order and that he has been given an opportunity of expressing his wishes and feelings regarding the decision.]

Dated the...................................... day of......................................, 19........

(Signature)
Justice of the Peace for the [county]
first above-mentioned or Clerk of the Court.

H

Rule 11 (2)

FORM 6
Notice to respondent of application for adoption order
[*Heading as in Form* 5]

I hereby give notice that—

1. An application has been made by (name and address of applicant) or under the serial number.. for an adoption order to be made in respect of (identify the child);

2.. of............................ has been appointed guardian *ad litem*;

*3. The application will be heard before the Domestic Court sitting at .... on the.............................. day of.................................., 19........., at............o'clock in [the county] aforesaid and you may then appear to be heard on the question whether an adoption order should be made.
OR

*3. The application will be heard before the Domestic Court sitting at ....
You may appear before the court and be heard on the question whether an adoption order should be made.

If you wish to appear, write to the Clerk of the Court at.................................. .... on or before the .... day of...................................... , 19........, in order that a time may be fixed for your appearance.

4. While the application is pending you are not entitled,
  †(*a*) if you have signified your agreement to the making of an adoption order in pursuance of the application, or
  (*b*) if the child has had his home with the applicant for the five years preceding the application,
to remove the child from the actual custody of the applicant except with the leave of the court or in a case to which paragraph (*b*) above relates under authority conferred by any enactment or on the arrest of the child.

**5. The court has been requested to dispense with your agreement on the ground that .... and a statement of the facts on which the applicant(s) intend(s) to rely is attached.

Dated the .... day of...................................... , 19........

(Signature)
Justice of the Peace for [the county]
first above-mentioned or Clerk of the Court

It would assist the court, if you would complete and return the attached reply form.

---

* The second alternative should be struck out except where the applicant desires that his identity should not be disclosed *to the person to whom the notice is given* in which case the first alternative should be struck out.

† Delete except where notice is addressed to a parent or guardian.

** Delete if inapplicable.

Reply Form

To the Clerk of the.. Domestic Court

(Address)..

....

[*The text of the reply corresponds with that on p 191 except that there is no reference to a provisional order.*]

Rule 21 (2) (*a*)

FORM 7
*Notice to applicant of time of further hearing after
interim order made*

In the [county of............................ Petty Sessional Division of ....].

To...

of...

I hereby give notice that your application for an adoption order to be made in respect of..

(name of child) will be further heard before the Domestic Court sitting at

....

on the.. day of.., 19......., at............

o'clock in [the county] aforesaid and that your attendance [and that

of..

(name of child)] is required.

[Take note that no adoption order can be made unless the child is present at the hearing and the court is satisfied that he has been informed of the nature of the order and that he has been given an opportunity of expressing his wishes and feelings regarding the decision.]

[And] [Take note that if the hearing is adjourned or an interim order is made, no adoption order can be made at a subsequent hearing unless the child is present at the subsequent hearing and the court is satisfied as aforesaid.]

Dated the ....day of.., 19........

(Signature)
Justice of the Peace for the [county]
first above-mentioned or Clerk of the Court

Rule 21 (2) (*b*)

FORM 8

*Notice to respondent of time of further hearing after
interim order made*

[*Heading as in Form* 7]

I hereby give notice that the application by (state name and address of applicant) *or* under the serial number..that an adoption order should be made in respect of (*identify the child*) will be further heard before the Domestic Court sitting at.. *
on the.. day of.. , 19........, at............
o'clock in the [county] aforesaid; and you may then appear and be heard on the question whether an adoption order should be made.
OR
*and you may appear before the court and be heard on the question whether an adoption order should be made. If you wish to appear, write to the Clerk of the Court at..
on or before the.. day of.. , 19........, in order that a time may be fixed for your appearance.

Dated the.. day of.. , 19........

(Signature)

Justice of the Peace for [the county]

first above-mentioned or Clerk of the Court

It would assist the court, if you would complete and return the attached reply form.

---

* The second alternative should be struck out except where the applicant desires that his identity should not be disclosed to the person to whom the notice is given, in which case the first alternative should be struck out.

Reply Form

[*As on p 211.*]

Rule 22 (1)

FORM 9

Adoption order

Domestic Court

No............................

In the [county of.. Petty Sessional Division of.........
....]
Before the Domestic Court sitting at..
Whereas an application has been made by..
[and..his wife] (more particularly described in the

Schedule hereto and hereinafter called the applicant[s]) for an adoption order in respect of[1] ....
a child of the .... sex the [adopted] child of ....
(hereinafter called the child);

And whereas arrangements for the adoption of the child have been made by[2].................................*or* notice has been received under Section 3 (2) of the Adoption Act 1958 by[3]... .

And whereas the name or names and surname by which the child is to be known are ....

And whereas the court is satisfied that the applicant(s) is/are qualified in accordance with the provisions of the Children Act 1975 to adopt the child and that all conditions precedent to the making of an adoption order by the court have been fulfilled;

It is ordered that the applicant[s] adopt the child;

[And as regards costs, it is ordered that.. :]

[And the court not being satisfied as to the precise date of the child's birth, it is determined that the probable date thereof was that specified in the Schedule hereto:]

[And the Court not being satisfied as to the country of the child's birth and it [not] appearing probable that the child was born within the United Kingdom, the Channel Islands or the Isle of Man the child's country of birth is [not] specified in the Schedule hereto [as [England] [Wales]]]

[And the country of the child's birth being specified in the Schedule hereto as [England] [Wales] but the court not being satisfied as to the registration district and sub-district in which the child was born, the district and sub-district in which the court sits are specified in the Schedule hereto as those in which the child was born;]

And it is directed that the Registrar General shall, in accordance with the Adoption Act 1958, enter in the Adopted Children Register the particulars specified in Regulation 3 of and Schedule 1, or as the case may be Schedule 2, to the Forms of Adoption Entry Regulations 1975 (S.I. 1975/1959).

[And the court being satisfied that the child is identical with ....
.... to whom the entry numbered .... made on the............................day of..................................., 19........., in [the Register of Births for the registration district of.................................... and sub-district of... in the county of..]
[the Adopted Children Register] relates, it is directed that the said entry be marked with the word ["Adopted"] ["Re-adopted"].]

[The following payment or reward is sanctioned...]

Dated the .... day of..................................., 19........

> (Signature)
> Justice of the Peace for the
> [county] first above-mentioned

[or By order of the Court,

> (Signature)
> Clerk of the Court]

Notes

1 Enter names and surname as shown in birth certificate or Adopted Children Register or, if not so shown, by which known before being placed for adoption.

2 Enter name and address of adoption agency/local authority.

3 Enter name and address of local authority.

SCHEDULE

[*The Schedule is the same as that on p* 197 *and the notes to similar effect, except that the following notes—*

3 *Name and surname of child.* Enter the name or names and surname by which the child is to be known.

4 *Sex of child.* Enter 'male' or 'female' as the case may be.

5 *Address of adopter or adopters.* If the applicant does not have his home in Great Britain, enter the place abroad where he lives.

are substituted for those from the second paragraph of 2 onwards.]

APPENDIX

This Appendix forms part of the adoption order but shall not form part of any copy supplied to any person under Rule 22 (2), 23, 25 (1) (*b*) or 25 (1) (*c*) of the Magistrates' Courts (Adoption) Rules 1976.

1. The agreement of...
of...
the parent/guardian of the child is dispensed with on the ground(s) that...
.... (enter the appropriate ground(s) in section 12 (2) of the Act of 1975).

2. The order is made on the application of one person who [is married] [is the mother/father of the child] and the court is satisfied that
....
(enter the appropriate ground(s) in section II (1) (*b*) or (3) of the Children Act 1975, and specify where appropriate the matters on which the court is satisfied).

———

Rule 22 (2)

FORM 10
Abridged form of adoption order
[*Heading as in Form* 9]

Whereas an application has been made by...[and
....his wife] (more particularly described in the Schedule hereto and hereinafter called the applicant[s] for an adoption order in respect of...(*enter names and surname as shown in birth certificate or Adopted Children Register or, if not so shown, by which child was known before being placed for adoption*) (hereinafter called the child); And whereas arrangements for the adoption of the child have been made by ....

(enter name and address of adoption agency/local authority); *or* notice has been received under section 3 (2) of the Adoption Act 1958 by

....

(enter name and address of local authority); it is ordered that the applicant[s] adopt the child.
     Dated the .... day of .... 19.........

                              (Signature)
                              Justice of the Peace for the
                              [county] aforesaid.
[or By Order of the Court,

                              (Signature)
                              Clerk of the Court]

                              SCHEDULE
[*As in Form 9, without the entries there numbered 1, 7 and 8.*]

FORM 11
Form of bilingual schedule for inclusion in adoption orders made by
Welsh courts (Magistrates' Courts (Adoption) Rules 1976 r 23)
[*Corresponds with County Court Form 10, the notes being to similar effect.*]

FORM 12
*Form of bilingual schedule for inclusion in abridged adoption orders made by
Welsh courts (Magistrates' Courts (Adoption) Rules* 1976 *r* 23)

SCHEDULE

Date..	*Registration District* *Dosbarth Cofrestru*
Dyddiad.. and a'r country of birth of child.. wlad lle canwyd y plentyn..	.... *Sub-district Is-ddosbarth*
Name and surname of child Enw a chyfenw y plentyn	....
Sex of child	Rhyw y plentyn
Name and surname, Enw a chyfenw, address, cyfeiriad and a occupation of adopter or adopters gwaith y mabwysiadwr neu'r mabwysiadwyr	
Date of adoption order Dyddiad y gorchymyn mabwysiadu and description of court by which made a disgrifiad o'r llys a'i gwnaeth	....

Rule 24

FORM 13
Interim order

In the [county of.. Petty Sessional Division
of..]. Whereas an application has been made by
.... of.. (hereinafter called the
applicant) for an adoption order in respect of..
(*enter names and surname of child as shown in birth certificate or Adopted Children
Register or, if not so shown, by which child was known before being placed for
adoption*), a child of the.. sex (hereinafter called the child);
And whereas arrangements for the adoption of the child have been made by

(enter name and address of adoption agency/local authority); And whereas the court is satisfied that the applicant is qualified in accordance with the provisions of the Children Act 1975 to adopt the child and that all conditions precedent to the making of an interim order by the court have been fulfilled;

It is ordered that the determination of the application be postponed and that the applicant do have the custody of the child until the ....
day of.. 19........, by way of a probationary period;
   [On the following terms, namely:.. ,*]
   [And as regards costs, it is ordered that.. :]
   [And that the application shall be further heard on ....].
   Dated the...................................... day of..., 19.........

(Signature)
Justice of the Peace for the
[county] first above-mentioned.

---

* Provision may be made for the maintenance, education and supervision of the welfare of the child and otherwise.

APPENDIX

[*As Appendix to Form 9 on p* 214.]

Rule 27 (1)

FORM 14
Application to amend or revoke adoption order

To the.. Domestic Court.
   1. Identification of adoption order to be amended or revoked—
Name of adopters...
Date of adoption order..
Name of child adopted...
   2. Particulars of person making this application
      Name...
      Address...
         ....
      State relationship to adopted person or, if no such relationship, state reason for application ....
   3. If application is made under section 24 of the Adoption Act 1958, state the amendments desired, and the facts relied on in support of the application.
      ....
      ....
   4. If application is made under section 26 of the Adoption Act 1958 or section 1 (1) of the Adoption Act 1960, state the facts relied on in support of the application.
      ....
      ....

I apply for the adoption order to be amended or revoked in accordance with this application.

Dated the..day of... , 19........

(Signature)

Rule 28 (1)

FORM 15

Notice asking for leave of court to remove child from applicant for an adoption order

In the [county of.......................... .] [Petty Sessional Division of..........................].
    Whereas an application has been made by [..
(enter name and address of applicant for an adoption order)] [under the serial number................................] (hereinafter called the applicant) for an adoption order to be made in respect of...
(identify the child)... (hereinafter called the child);
    I hereby give notice that—
    *(a) I..the parent/guardian of the child seek leave of the court to remove the child from the custody of the applicant;
    *(b) The.. *(insert name of local authority or adoption society)* seek the leave of the court to give notice of their intention not to allow the child to remain in the custody of the applicant:
    The grounds on which the leave of the court is sought are as follows:

Date... Signature...
Address...
        ....

*Delete either (a) or (b) (see notes below).
Notes
    1 A notice can be given by a parent or guardian of the child (a) who has agreed to the making of an adoption order; or (b) where the child has had his home with the applicants for the preceding five years.
    2 Where the child has had his home with the applicants for the preceding five years, a notice can be given by a registered adoption society, voluntary organization or, if the child was in the care of a local authority before he began to have his home with the applicants, by that local authority, or by any other person.

Rule 28 (2)

FORM 16

Notice asking for leave of court to remove child from prospective adopters

In the [county of..........................] [Petty Sessional Division of..........................].
    Whereas ....
(enter name and address or serial number of prospective adopters) have given

notice in writing to.. (*enter name of local authority*) that they intend to apply for an adoption order in respect of... (*identify the child*) (hereinafter called the child) who for the preceding five years had his/her home with the prospective adopter;

I hereby give notice that—

*(a) I..the parent/guardian of the child seek the leave of the court to remove the child from the actual custody of the prospective adopter;

*(b) The...
(*enter name of local authority or adoption society*) seek the leave of the court to give notice of their intention not to allow the child to remain in the actual custody of the prospective adopter:

The grounds on which the leave of the court is sought are as follows:

Date...Signature...

Address..

....

---

* Delete either (*a*) or (*b*) (see note below).

Notes

1 A notice can be given by a parent or guardian of the child where the child has had his home with the applicants for the preceding five years.

2 Where the child has had his home with the applicants for the preceding five years, a notice can be given by a registered adoption society, voluntary organisation or, if the child was in the care of a local authority before he began to have his home with the applicants, by that local authority, or by any other person.

Rule 31

FORM 17
Register of Adoptions

In the [county of.. Petty Sessional Division of
....].

No.	Date of decision	Name and address of applicant	Names of infant prior to adoption	Sex of infant	Age of infant	Names of infant after adoption	Minute of decision	Signature of justice adjudicating

D—SCHEDULES 3 and 4 TO THE ADOPTION AGENCIES
REGULATIONS 1976 (*see* pp 14, 157)
Regulation 7 (*a*)
SCHEDULE 3
ADOPTION OF CHILDREN
Explanatory memorandum

This Memorandum must be given to the parent or guardian of a child who is about to be adopted. This includes the natural father of an illegitimate child if he has an order for custody under section 9 of the Guardianship of Minors Act 1971 or section 2 of the Illegitimate Children (Scotland) Act 1930.

What does adoption mean?

When a court makes an adoption order, your rights as a parent or guardian will be transferred to the adopters and they will become in law the child's parents. This means that you will have no further right to see the child or to have the child returned to you.

If you wish your child to be brought up in a particular religious faith, you should tell your social worker who must take your wishes into account as far as is practicable. If you ask him, he will be able to tell you if there are any adoption societies which specialize in arranging adoptions with families of a particular faith.

Your agreement to the adoption

Before a court can make an adoption order, it has to be satisfied that you agree freely to the order being made, so you will be asked to sign a form of agreement to adoption which will be shown to the court. The proposed adopters will either be referred to on this form by a number or they may be named. If they are referred to by a number it will not be possible to tell you who they are but your social worker will be able to tell you something about them. You are not allowed by law to receive any money for giving your agreement. You will have the opportunity of making your views known to the court on the adoption application if you so wish, but where the proposed adopters are referred to by a number on the form of agreement, arrangements will be made for you to attend the court at a different time from them. The court will appoint a person called the guardian *ad litem* who will need to see you before the court makes the adoption order to make sure that you understand what the effect will be. The guardian *ad litem* has a duty to ensure that an adoption order will be in the interests of the child and the court must give first consideration to the welfare of the child. If you sign the form of agreement and then, before the adoption order is made, you wish to withdraw your agreement, you must inform your social worker and the court. If you have signed your agreement and the proposed adopters have already sent the application papers to the court, the law does not allow you to remove the child unless you obtain the permission of the court. The court cannot make an order without your agreement unless it dispenses with your agreement on certain grounds. The grounds on which a court can dispense with a parent's agreement are that he or she:—

(a) cannot be found or is incapable of giving agreement;

(b) is withholding his or her agreement unreasonably;

(c) has persistently failed without reasonable cause to discharge the parental duties in relation to the child;

(d) has abandoned or neglected the child;

(e) has persistently ill-treated the child;

(f) has seriously ill-treated the child and rehabilitation in his or her home is unlikely.

Birth records

When an adoption order is made, the Registrar General makes an entry in the Adopted Children Register showing the adopters as the parents of the child. A certificate is issued from that register which takes the place of the child's birth certificate but when the child reaches the age of 18 he will be entitled to obtain a certificate of the original birth entry if he so wishes. This means that when he is 18 he will be able to find out his original name as well as your name and the address you were living at when you registered his birth.

Your social worker is...

Address...

....

....

Telephone...

CERTIFICATE

To...
          (name of agency)

I certify that I have received from you a memorandum called 'Adoption of Children' from which I have detached this certificate of acknowledgment and that I have read the memorandum and understood it.

Signature...

Address...

....

....

.... Date.......................

Regulation 8 (*a*)

SCHEDULE 4

PARTICULARS TO BE ASCERTAINED

PART I

Particulars relating to the child

1. Name..
2. Date and place of birth..
3. If baptised, date and place of baptism and denomination.................

4. If not baptised, religious persuasion of the child's father and mother
....
....

5. Have the parents any wishes regarding the child's religious upbringing? If so, what are they?...
....

6. Name, address and age of the child's father and mother. If either is dead, date of death...
....

7. If the child is legitimate, whether there have been any matrimonial proceedings (separation, divorce or annulment) and if so whether any orders in respect of the child have been made.......................................
....

8. If either the father or mother has any other children, the age and sex of each child...
....

9. Whether there is any history of tuberculosis, epilepsy, mental illness or other disease in either the father's or mother's family.......................
....

10. Why adoption is being sought for the child and whether adoption has previously been sought for him...
....

11. Having regard to his age and understanding, what are the wishes and feelings of the child about being adopted...
....
....

12. Whether the mother agrees to the child being adopted, and, if not, her reasons for not agreeing...
....

13. If the child is legitimate, whether the father agrees to the child being adopted, and, if not, his reasons for not agreeing.........................
....
....

14. If the child is illegitimate and the father has legal custody under section 9 of the Guardianship of Minors Act 1971 or section 2 of the

Illegitimate Children (Scotland) Act 1930, whether the father agrees to the child being adopted and, if not, his reasons for not agreeing........................

....

....

15. If the child is illegitimate, whether the father (if known) has any objection to the child being adopted and whether he intends to apply for custody of the child..

....

16. The names and addresses of the child's guardians (other than the putative father, if any), how and by whom they were appointed, and whether they agree to the child being adopted, and, if not, their reasons for not agreeing..

....

17. Whether any other body or person has the rights and duties of a parent of the child, the length of time the child has been in the actual custody of that body or person and whether that body or person has any objections to the child being adopted..

....

18. Whether the child has any right to or interest in any property

....

19. Whether an insurance policy for the payment on the death of the child of money for funeral expenses has been effected..

....

....

PART II

Particulars relating to the proposed adopters

1. Names..

....

2. Address..

....

....

3. Dates of birth..

....

4. Religious persuasion..

5. Occupation..

6. Where the proposed adopters have not their home (or one of them has not his home) in Great Britain, their (or his) address, if different from 2 above.

....

....

7. Whether the proposed adopters are domiciled in the United Kingdom (ie England . and Wales, Scotland, Northern Ireland), the Channel

Islands or the Isle of Man, and, if not, the country in which they are domiciled..
....

8. If the proposed adopters intend to apply for a provisional adoption order, whether they intend to adopt the child in law or in fact in the country in which they are domiciled...
....

9. If there are two proposed adopters, the date and place of the proposed adopters' marriage, and whether either proposed adopter has previously been married and, if so, whether that marriage was dissolved or annulled, the grounds for the divorce or annulment and whether there are any commitments in respect of a former spouse and/or children of a previous marriage...
....
....

10. If there is only one proposed adopter, whether that person is married, and, if so, why the spouse does not join in the application. Is the spouse:—
    (*a*) unable to be found;
    (*b*) separated and living apart and the separation likely to be permanent; or
    (*c*) by reason of ill-health, physical or mental, incapable of joining in the application?

....
....

11. Particulars of all members of the proposed adopters' household and their relationship (if any) to the proposed adopters.......................................
....
....

12. The accommodation in the proposed adopters' home and the condition of the home...
....
....

13. The means of the proposed adopters...
....

14. The names and addresses of two persons selected by the proposed adopters to whom reference can be made as to character...................................
....
....

15. Whether either of the proposed adopters has previously:—
    (*a*) notified a local authority of his intention to adopt a child;
    (*b*) applied to an adoption society or local authority with a view to adopting a child;
    (*c*) had in his actual custody a foster child within the meaning of section 2 of the Children Act 1958, who has been removed under section 7 of that Act;

(*d*) been prohibited from keeping a foster child under section 4 of that Act;

(*e*) had in his actual custody a protected child who has been removed under section 43 of the Adoption Act 1958;

(*f*) been prohibited from keeping a protected child;

(*g*) been a member of a household where a child has been the subject of an order arising from care proceedings under section 1 of the Children and Young Persons Act 1969, or has been found by a children's hearing to be in need of compulsory measure of care under Part III of the Social Work (Scotland) Act 1968;

(*h*) been convicted of an offence under Schedule 1 to the Children and Young Persons Act 1933, or an offence under Schedule 1 to the Criminal Procedure (Scotland) Act 1975;

(*i*) had parental rights in respect of their own children assumed by a local authority under section 2 of the Children Act 1948 or under section 16 of the Social Work (Scotland) Act 1968;

(*j*) been refused registration under the Nurseries and Child-Minders Regulation Act 1948 (as amended).

....

....

....

....

I

Children Act 1975—Provisions Not Yet in Force

The following is a summary of adoption provisions of the Children Act 1975 not in operation on 16 October 1980.

1 *Adoption Services*

Sections 1 and 2 and 4 to 7 specify the essentials of a service which it will be the duty of every local authority (see p 13) to establish and maintain within their area. The service must be designed to meet the needs in relation to adoption of children who have been or may be adopted, their parents and guardians, and adopters and prospective adopters. The authority must provide requisite facilities or secure that approved adoption societies provide them. By s 1 (2) the facilities to be provided include arrangements for assessing children and prospective adopters, placing children for adoption and counselling those with adoption problems. The facilities are to be provided in conjunction with the local authority's other social services and with adoption societies in their area which obtain the approval of the Secretary of State (renewable every three years) under s 4. Approval may be withdrawn (s 5) and directions given for completing the placement of children in the care of inactive or defunct societies (s 7).

The placement restrictions and conditions set out in Chapter XVI of the book will continue to exist subject to some modification, the most important being an amendment of AA 1958, s 29 (p 157), so as to provide that a person other than an adoption agency shall not make arrangements for the adoption of a child, or place the child for adoption, unless the proposed adopter is a relative of the child, or he is acting pursuant to a High Court order (see 1975 Act, s 28). On conviction of the offence of contravening AA 1958, s 29, in its new form, s 17 of the 1975 Act (see p 92) authorising the making of a supervision or a care order will apply as if an adoption order had been refused.

2 *Trial Period*

Section 3 of AA 1958 has already been reworded (p 29*n*), but this is only the first stage of a complete overhaul of the requirement for a trial period and for notification to the local authority.

It will be a condition precedent to an adoption order, when CA 1975, s 9, is brought into force, that the child shall have *had his home with* the adopters or one of them for one of two alternative periods. These apply (*a*) where the applicant or one of the applicants is a parent, step-parent or relative of the child, or the child was placed with the applicant by an adoption agency or in pursuance of a High Court order, and (*b*) in all other cases. Under (*a*) the condition is that the child shall be at least nineteen weeks old at the time of the order and at all times during the preceding thirteen weeks have had his home with the applicants or one of them; under (*b*) the child must be at least twelve months old, and at all times within the twelve months preceding the order have had his home with the applicants or one of them.

In addition, by a new requirement aimed at securing adequate mutual acquaintance between the child and the adopter, the court must be satisfied that sufficient opportunities to see the child with the applicant (or both married applicants in the home environment) have been afforded to the agency, in the case of an agency placement, or in other cases to the local authority in whose area the home is (s 9 (3)).

Section 18 restates the requirement about notification of the local authority (see p 30). The notice will need to be given in respect of *any* child who was not placed by an adoption agency. It must go to the authority within whose area the proposing adopter has his home at least three months before the date of the order. On receipt of the notice that authority must investigate the matter, in particular the suitability of the applicant and any other matters relevant to the operation of the welfare principle (s 3: p 8) in relation to the application, and whether the child was placed contrary to s 29 of AA 1958 (p 157 and para 1 above), and must submit a report to the court.

3 'Freeing' for Adoption

Sections 14 to 16 and 23 will introduce a new system of obtaining the acquiescence of parents or guardians in adoption agency cases. This will be alternative to the system of consent or agreement hitherto in force. The aim is to reduce, both for natural parents and for proposing adopters, the period of anxiety and uncertainty which may now occur between the original placement and the completion of the adoption process.

The method adopted is to provide for an application to the court for an order declaring a particular child 'free for adoption' (s 14). The application can be made only by an agency, and at least one of the child's parents or guardians must consent to the freeing, unless the child is in the agency's care and the agency is applying for the court's dispensation with the agreement of *each* parent or guardian (s 14 (2)). Subject to this the court must be satisfied either that each parent or guardian agrees generally and unconditionally to an adoption, or that his agreement should be dispensed with on one of the grounds stated in s 12 (2) (see pp 42–49). But there is to be no dispensation unless the child is already placed for adoption or the court is satisfied that it is likely that he will be so placed (s 14 (3)). As under s 12, the mother's agreement will be ineffective if given less than six weeks after the child's birth (s 14 (4)), but there appears to be nothing to prevent a freeing application being made straight away and put down for hearing after the child is six weeks old, the mother's consent being given at the hearing, for no trial period is prescribed. Rules may provide for the appointment of a guardian *ad litem* and a reporting officer on the basis described in para 5 below. Where a parent or guardian did *not* consent to a s 14 application, he will be within the terms of the new s 34 (2) of AA 1958 (see p 95) and must therefore not remove the child. On the other hand a consenting parent or guardian can apparently change his mind, and in a s 14 case, will not be affected by s 34 (2).

On the making of an order under s 14, the parental rights and duties relating to the child will vest in the agency, and the parents' or guardian's rights and duties and any arising under agreements or orders will be extinguished except those relating to past periods (s 14 (6), applying s 8 (2) and (3)). The parental rights and duties may be transferred by the court, if it thinks fit, from one adoption agency to another, on a joint application by the agencies (s 23).

Before the court makes a s 14 order, it must satisfy itself—

(1) that each parent or guardian who can be found has been given an opportunity of making, if he so wishes, a declaration of non-interest, ie that he prefers not to be involved in future questions concerning the child's adoption; and any such declaration is to be recorded by the court (s 14 (7));

(2) in the case of an illegitimate child whose father is not its guardian, either that any person claiming to be the father has no intention of applying for its custody under s 9 of the Guardianship of Minors Act 1971, or that if he did so his application would be likely to be refused (s 14 (8)).

If any person (referred to as 'the former parent') was required to be given an opportunity of declaring his non-interest, but did not do so, the agency must make to him the progress reports referred to in s 15, beginning a fortnight after the expiration of twelve months after the s 14 order was made. By s 16, the former parent may, after the twelve months, apply to the court to revoke the s 14 order (s 16 (1)), thus reversing its effect as described above (s 16 (3)), on the ground that he wishes to resume parental rights and duties. He can do this only where, at the time of his application, no adoption order has been made and the child does not have his home with a person with whom he has been placed for adoption; and while any such revocation application is pending, the adoption agency having the parental rights may not place the child without the court's leave (s 16 (2)).

If a revocation application is dismissed on what appears to be the only possible ground if the formal conditions are satisfied (namely the application of the welfare principle of s 3: see p 8), the former parent who made it is not entitled to apply again under s 16 unless the court which dismissed his application gives him leave, which it cannot do in the absence of a change in circumstances or other proper reason (s 16 (4), (5)). After dismissal, the adoption agency need not report to the unsuccessful former parent.

4 *Interim Orders*

Section 19, when in force, will adapt to the new law and terminology the provision, now in AA 1958, s 8, about interim orders (p 53) without significant practical change. The new possibility of custodianship (see para 9 below) may present the court with an alternative to an interim adoption order in some cases.

5 *Guardians ad litem and Reporting Officers*

Section 20 revises the wording of the rule-making power (in a manner which may or may not turn out to be significant) as to the appointment of guardians ad litem, and also brings on to the scene another auxiliary personage, to be known as the reporting officer. The appointment of a guardian may be required (as rules shall prescribe) in adoption applications, or those under s 14 or s 16 (above) or s 25 (below). Rules may also provide for the appointment on the like applications of a person to act as reporting officer for the purpose of witnessing agreements to adoption (thus superseding the arrangements in that regard contained in the present rules: p 41) and of performing such other duties as the contemplated rules may prescribe. Admissibility of witnessed agreements and consents will be secured by s 102. An administrative provision allowing the Secretary of State to form a panel of persons from whom guardians ad litem and reporting officers may be drawn is already in force (s 103). The same person may be both guardian and reporting officer, but s 20 (2) excludes from appointment in either capacity a person employed by the adoption agency concerned.

6 *Notification of Proceedings*

Another enabling provision, but one of a mandatory nature, comprises s 22 (1) and (2), under which rules must (when the provisions are brought into effect) provide for notifications to every person who can be found and whose agreement or consent would be required to the making of an adoption order or a freeing order (para 3 above) or a s 25 order (para 7 below). Possibly the reporting officer (para 5) will prove to be the appropriate communicant of the necessary details to the persons concerned in so far as it cannot be shown that notices from the court have reached the addresses.

By s 22 (3) adoption agencies will have to submit reports to the court in matters relative to the welfare principle (pp 159–160), and to assist the court as directed.

7 *Orders with a View to Adoption Abroad*

Section 25 will in due course replace the system of provisional adoptions now obtaining under s 53 of AA 1958 (see p 55). The categories of person who can apply and the conditions of application will be broadly the same, but instead of the order resulting from a successful application authorising an adoption (albeit a provisional one), it is to be an order vesting in the applicant the parental rights and duties relating to the child, leaving the actual adoption to be effected under the law of the applicant's domicile. As with provisional adoptions, only the High Court and the appropriate county court will be able to make a s 25 order.

The statutory provisions relating to placement and arrangements for adoption will apply, and references in Pts IV and V of AA 1958 (see pp 163–170) and in CA 1975 to an adoption order include references to a vesting order under s 25 (s 25 (4)). Conditions for a s 25 order are the same as for adoption, except those relating to domicile; and the trial period for CA 1975, s 9 (1) (para 2) is adapted in agency and relative cases to make the minimum age of the child read thirty-two weeks instead of nineteen, and the period of trial twenty-six weeks instead of thirteen (s 25 (2)).

The consequences in English law set out in Sched 1 to the 1975 Act (pp 133 et seq) will not of course apply, but the order will extinguish the parental rights and duties in parents or guardians under orders or agreements (p 139) as for an adoption order. There can be no interim order in a s 25 case, nor will the system of freeing for adoption be applicable. Instead of the 'provisional' markings against entries in the Registers of Birth etc (p 125), the marking in a s 25 case is to consist of the words 'Proposed Foreign Adoption' and the noting of the Adopted Children Register modified accordingly in the case of a re-adoption (s 25 (3)).

The provisions restricting the sending of children for adoption abroad (p 169) will be adjusted consequentially so as to except, not a provisional order, but one under s 25 (1975 Act, Sched 3, para 36 (*a*)).

8 *Payment of Allowances to Adopters*

A notable *general* departure from the rule prohibiting adoption for reward (except under the court's control) is enacted in CA 1975, s 32—additional to the special cases already effective as noted at p 169. When s 32 comes into force, yet further subsections will be added to AA 1958, s 50, in effect enabling payment of allowances by adoption agencies to adopters or intending adopters. Payment must accord with a scheme submitted by an agency to the Secretary of State and approved by him. The subsections contemplate an experimental period of seven years for the new facility, but the additions to s 50 may be made permanent by the Secretary's order after he has published a report on their operation and after Parliament has approved a draft of his perpetuation order.

9 *Custodianship*

By Pt II of CA 1975 provision is made for the introduction of this new kind of statutory relationship, as to which see p 11. The court may make a custodianship order (and subsequently revoke or vary it) whereby the legal custody of a child is vested in the applicants (suspending the rights of other persons), with consequential provisions for maintenance and for access by the parents. Apart from the right to custody, none of the other effects of an adoption order flow from custodianship.

A provision which will directly affect some adoption applications is that in s 37 of the 1975 Act, whereby in one of two sets of circumstances such an application (including a Convention application) may result in an order, not for adoption, but for custodianship. The two events are—

- (*a*) Where the adoption application is by a relative of the child (except a sole parent) or the spouse of the child's mother or father (whether alone or jointly with the mother or father), provided that the applicant is not disqualified for custodianship by the child having been named in a divorce order pursuant to s 41 of the Matrimonial Causes Act 1973 (s 37 (6)). In this case the court *must* treat the application as one for custodianship (dropping the father or mother out of a joint case) if, though the consent or dispensation conditions are met, the court is satisfied that the child's welfare would *not* be better safeguarded and promoted by adoption by the applicant, and that it would be appropriate to order custodianship in the applicant's favour (s 37 (1)).
- (*b*) Where the applicant is not (or neither of two joint applicants is) a relative of the child or its mother's or father's spouse and is not a sole parent-applicant. Here the test is a positive one, and the court's power discretionary. It *may* direct the application to be treated as one for custodianship if the agreement or dispensation conditions are met but it is of opinion that it would be more appropriate to make a custodianship order in the applicant's favour (s 37 (2)).

Index

233